Steve Parish

Field
Guide
to
Australian Mammals

PASCAL
PRESS

Steve Parish

Field Guide
to
Australian Mammals

PHOTOGRAPHY ACKNOWLEDGEMENTS

While the majority of the photographs in this book were taken in the
wild, it was necessary to photograph rare or very shy species in several
of Australia's zoos and fauna parks. A special thanks to the staff and
management of Healesville Sanctuary, Victoria; Territory Wildlife Park,
Northern Territory; Australian Wildlife Conservancy, Western Australia
and New South Wales; Monarto Zoo, South Australia; Currumbin Wildlife
Sanctuary, Queensland; Australian Bat Clinic & Wildlife Trauma Centre,
Queensland. A special thanks to all those who supplied images and
especially to Jiri Lochman for his generous support.

Field Guide to Australian Mammals

Published by Pascal Press
PO Box 250, Glebe, NSW 2037 Australia

© Pascal Press 2016

National Library of Australia
Cataloguing-in-Publication data:

Hall, Leslie S., author.

The Field Guide to Australian Mammals
Les Hall, Renee Chamberlin; author and editor:
Lee Curtis, author and photographer: Steve Parish,
illustrator: Maria Mason.

ISBN 978 1 92222 531 3 (paperback)
Includes index.

Subjects: Mammals - Australia - Identification.
Mammals - Australia - Handbooks, manuals, etc.

Other Creators/Contributors:
Chamberlin, Renee, author.
Curtis, Lee, 1957- author, editor.
Parish, Steve, 1945- author, photographer.
Mason, Maria, illustrator.

599.0994

Text: Renee Chamberlin, Les Hall, Lee Curtis, Steve Parish
Principal photographer: Steve Parish
Publisher: Lynn Dickinson
Editorial: Lee Curtis, Marie Theodore, Les Hall
Design: Leanne Nobilio
Illustrations: Stephen Lee, Maria Mason, Marlo Webber
Consultants: Clancy Hall, Terry Reardon, Dr Tom Grant
Additional photography: As credited on images.
p. 267: The Black Rat – Rattus Rattus, CSIRO/CC BY 3.0,
http://www.scienceimage.csiro.au/image/10564/the-black-rat-rattus-rattus/.
Licence at http://creativecommons.org/licenses/by/3.0/.

First edition published 2016

CONTENTS

RENEE CHAMBERLIN
BSc. (Zoology) GradCertEnvtMngt.

Renee is an accomplished Zoologist, Educator, Writer, and Conservationist. She spent her early career as a Zookeeper and Wildlife Education Officer. For the last 13 years, Renee has been training the next generation of Environmental Professionals; she is passionate about helping others and leaving a better earth for future generations.

STEVE PARISH OAM

Steve Parish is a passionate promoter of the natural world. He is thrilled that we have so much wildlife in Australia to appreciate and protect, while also having so many secrets left to discover about it. Steve has been photographing nature and the Australian lifestyle for more than 40 years. His company, Steve Parish Publishing, is known throughout the world for its colourful images, striking designs and innovative content.

LESLIE S. HALL BSc, PhD

Les retired to Maleny in 2001 after 26 years at the University of Queensland where he lectured in human and veterinary anatomy. Previous to that he worked for the CSIRO Division of Wildlife Research. He has had a long time interest in birds, bats and wildlife in general which has led him to conduct field work over many parts of Australia.

LEE K CURTIS MA

Lee is a freelance writer passionate about Australia's wildlife, has written several books and numerous articles about Australian wildlife. Her work with threatened species projects in Queensland inspired her to compile — with the help of 200+ volunteer contributors — a resource guide, *Queensland's Threatened Animals*, published by CSIRO Publishing in 2012.

INTRODUCTION

The mammals of Australia include some of the world's most amazing creatures, such as the Platypus, Kangaroos, the Koala and the Tasmanian Devil. These animals are iconic representations of Australia. There are approximately 380 terrestrial and a further 50 or so marine mammal species found on and around the island continent. Mammalian fauna is dominated by marsupials but there are also a large number of rodents, bats and other placental mammals, like the Dingo, seals, whales, dolphins and introduced feral species. The majority of the terrestrial species (87%) are found nowhere else in the world, but most of the marine mammals have an offshore or global distribution.

The reason for this unique collection of mammals lies in Australia's ancient history. The continent was once part of a large landmass called Gondwana. About 40 million years ago, the Australian continent drifted free, carrying with it the ancestors of the current Australian fauna. Over time, the continent drifted close to islands to the north, which allowed additional species, such as rodents, to enter Australia.

The Australian continent can be a harsh place. Floods, wildfires, droughts and cyclones present numerous challenges to Australian animals. Few mammals have had the ability or luck to not be affected by man-made changes to the environment, including mining, land clearing, changes in fire regimes, urban spread, introduced feral animals, and land degradation. To add to these woes, mammals now have the looming challenges presented by climate change.

Australia has one of the worst mammal extinction rates in the world. Thirty native mammals have disappeared since European settlement. Today, 70 species are threatened. No other country has recorded such a high extinction rate in modern times.

Many Australian mammal species are difficult to find because they are cryptic, nocturnal or tree-dwelling, and it usually requires patience, luck, and a spotlight to observe them. On the other hand, some species, like possums and flying-foxes, have adapted well to urban development.

When using this book, most people will know the broad group of mammal they are looking at — possum, kangaroo, bat, seal, etc. — so readers can go directly to those sections and they will find a dichotomous key to the genera of that group. After identifying the genus, it is helpful to look at the distribution maps and check the photos to further identify the animal to species level. Species identification within a genus can be very difficult, particularly among the rats, bats, and some groups of marsupials, especially the small dasyurids and wallabies. There are few problems in identifying feral species.

The order in which the mammals appear in the book follows the standard arrangement according to their scientific classification, and the common names used are those most widely accepted. Body measurement data, a distribution map, general biological information, and a photo are provided in each mammal profile.

The aim of this book is to serve as a quick guide to Australian mammals. There are keys to identify large groups to the level of genus. Not all species are described in the book. Very rare species have been omitted as well as some marine mammals that are generally found offshore in deep water.

The book is meant to be a good home reference and mammal identification guide and will make an excellent companion for identifying mammals when travelling around Australia.

Les Hall

EVOLUTION OF MAMMALS

Mammals began to evolve from tetrapod (four-legged) reptiles some 250 million years ago, at a time when all of the continents were joined together in a supercontinent known as Pangaea. 'Protomammals' originated from the 'mammal-like reptiles' therapsids, the most advanced of which diverged as the cynodonts of the Triassic and early Jurassic and eventually evolved into mammaliaforms. Mammals' evolutionary rise from the cynodonts, is well documented in the vertebrate fossil record. However, conjecture about just where mammals stopped being reptilian and started being mammalian, remains.

The Oldest True Mammal

The oldest mammaliaform fossil to date is *Adelobasileus cromptoni*, discovered in Texas in the USA. It appears to be a 225-million-year-old transitional form between cynodonts and mammals and may be the common ancestor of all living mammals. Around 200 million years ago, during the peak of dinosaur domination, mammals were mostly small, nocturnal animals that later developed warm-bloodedness, such as in the mammal *Megazostrodon*.

Monotremes

Of living Australian mammal fauna, the anatomy and physiology of monotremes points to a close lineage to extinct therapsids and suggests that monotremes radiated from the early mammalian tree of life some 190 million years ago to be the surviving Australasian 'branches' of their kind. Outside of Australasia only one extinct species, *Monotrematum sudamerica*, has been found (in Argentina).

Marsupials

The oldest marsupial fossil, *Sinodelphys,* at 125 million years old, was found in China — evidence that despite Australia's proliferation of marsupials, they most likely arrived in Australia by a circuitous route, having arisen in Asia and radiated around the globe, reaching Australia when it and Antarctica were still joined to South America in the supercontinent Gondwana. However, Australia's oldest-known marsupial fossil, *Djarthia murgonensis* from 55 mya in the Early Eocene, has cast some doubt on whether marsupials radiated from South America to Australia or the other way around.

Placentals

Of the placental mammals, bats have the most antiquated fossil record in Australia, with the first Australian fossils dating to at least 55 million years, making *Australonycteris clarkae* — an Eocene fossil found at the Tingamurra fossil site near Murgon, Queensland — among the oldest bat fossils in the world. The Flat Rocks, Victoria, site has also yielded interesting small mammals such as *Ausktribosphenos nyktos*, but evolutionary biologists and palaeontologist's are yet to establish these ausktribosphenids' position in the evolutionary tree.

QUEENSLAND MUSEUM/GARY CRANITCH

Significant palaeontological mammal finds have been discovered at the World Heritage-listed Fossil Mammal Site at Riversleigh in central Queensland and Naracoorte Caves in South Australia. Finds include marsupial lions and giant flesh-eating kangaroos, as well as more familiar 'modern' mammals such as possums and bandicoots.

Changes Over Time

By the early Miocene Epoch (23.3 mya–5 mya) most of the ancestors of modern-day mammals, such as kangaroos, possums and the Koala, were in existence. This time of diversity also saw marsupial lions and carnivorous kangaroos roam Australia. Perhaps even more bizarre is the order Yalkaparidontia (or 'thingodonts' as they are colloquially known), which defies classification because the two species described within it exhibit a confusing blend of features.

By the mid–late Miocene (around 15 million years ago), changing climate caused by continental drift and a drying continent made many early mammal families extinct, including most of the thingodonts described from Riversleigh Fossil Mammal Site (such as miralinids, ilariids and yalkaparidontids).

From the late Miocene to early Pliocene, 15–5 million years ago, the world's climate was in a state of flux with polar ice caps growing and decreasing temperature and rainfall. Australia began its long, slow dehydration. The dry conditions may have created a corridor from some of the archipelagos of South-East Asia, from which rodents arrived in northern Australia around eight million years ago.

By the early Pliocene, marsupials began to flourish, overtaking the large browsing herbivores that had reigned in earlier times. Many of the genera we recognise today were in existence by the early Pliocene. As the continent became more arid, by around two million years ago, some marsupials became more arid-adapted. The first fossils of Red Kangaroo ancestors are from this time.

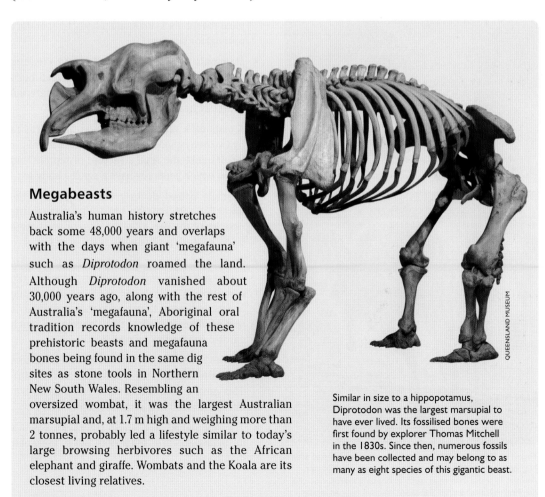

QUEENSLAND MUSEUM

Megabeasts

Australia's human history stretches back some 48,000 years and overlaps with the days when giant 'megafauna' such as *Diprotodon* roamed the land. Although *Diprotodon* vanished about 30,000 years ago, along with the rest of Australia's 'megafauna', Aboriginal oral tradition records knowledge of these prehistoric beasts and megafauna bones being found in the same dig sites as stone tools in Northern New South Wales. Resembling an oversized wombat, it was the largest Australian marsupial and, at 1.7 m high and weighing more than 2 tonnes, probably led a lifestyle similar to today's large browsing herbivores such as the African elephant and giraffe. Wombats and the Koala are its closest living relatives.

Similar in size to a hippopotamus, Diprotodon was the largest marsupial to have ever lived. Its fossilised bones were first found by explorer Thomas Mitchell in the 1830s. Since then, numerous fossils have been collected and may belong to as many as eight species of this gigantic beast.

AN INTRODUCTION TO AUSTRALIAN MAMMALS

More than any other continent, Australia can be considered a hotbed for mammal diversity. Amazing representatives from all three mammalian subclasses — Monotremata, Marsupialia and Eutheria — exist in Australia (the only continent to contain all three). Many species are unique and survive nowhere else.

Prolonged geographical isolation from other continents, coupled with numerous changes in climate, encouraged diversity and evolution on a grand scale on this continent, particularly among marsupials, which reach their zenith in Australia with more than 145 living species. Monotremes are represented by just two extant species — the Platypus and the Short-beaked Echidna. Placentals, the most diverse worldwide, also flourish in Australia, especially native rodent and bat species.

Top: The Short-beaked Echidna belongs to the unusual order Monotremata, now unique to Australia and New Guinea.
Above: In some mammals, such as hopping macropods, the diaphragm is responsible for more efficient oxygen intake during motion.

What makes a Mammal?

Before any involved discussion of mammalian orders can begin, it is helpful to clarify what distinguishes mammals from others in the kingdom Animalia. Apart from mammary glands and the fact that they nourish their young on milk — which is peculiar to mammals and gives them their class name, from the Latin *mammae* (breast) — seven characteristics typify mammals.

- Of all vertebrates, they alone are covered in hair. Hair is an extraordinary structure composed of keratin (a type of inert protein) and below the skin, at the hair's root, it is wrapped with nerve fibres that alert the owner to the hair's movement. Even animals seemingly devoid of hair, such as whales, have small vibrissae around their mouths, eyes or bodily crevices. Without hair, it would be extremely difficult for most mammals to maintain a body temperature optimal for survival.

- Mammals are warm-blooded (a feature shared only with birds) and able to keep body temperature constant without an external source of heat.

- A mammal's skull is joined to its first vertebra by two bony knobs (condyles) on the back of the head, unlike the skull structure of reptiles and birds, which generally have a single condyle.

- A single paired dentary bone comprises the lower jaw, with separate bones that make up the ossicles of the ear. All other vertebrates have a lower dentary made up of a number of bones.

- Mammals have four-chambered hearts — as do birds and crocodiles, although the composition of arteries in bird and reptile hearts indicates that convergent evolution is responsible, meaning they developed such cardiac similarities independently.

- Toothed whales aside, mammals are heterodonts (from the Greek, *hetero* = different, *dont* = teeth). This means their cheek teeth are not uniform but are divided into premolars and molars.

- The abdominal and chest (thoracic) cavities in mammals are separated by a muscular diaphragm.

Lactation is a mammalian trait that evolved long before modern mammals such as seals and sea-lions.

The Origins of Hair, Milk and Warm Blood

Although 'Mammalia' is Latin for breast, not all mammals have them; rather, lactation is the defining feature of the class. Tracing the evolution of hair and milk proves difficult because both are proteins that decompose over time and are rarely fossilised. However, the origins of warm blood and hair may stretch as far back as dinosaur days. Pterosaur fossils discovered in Russia and Germany appear to have been surrounded by furry remains. It is thought that this may have helped these flying contemporaries of dinosaurs stay warm in the air, compensating for the enormous amount of energy required to fly.

Pterosaurs may have been the first furred animals.

Scientific research indicates that somewhere around 310 million years ago, nutritional milk evolved in a common mammalian ancestor. Egg-laying mammals at the time laid thin, parchment-shelled eggs in which offspring were nourished on egg yolk — similar to those the Platypus lays today (Platypus eggs have retained a small yolk, unique among mammals). It was predicated that milk was developed as an egg-wetting substance that allowed the mother to roll the eggs in milk to prevent them from dehydrating. Genetic analysis of Platypus milk, undertaken by Henrik Kaessman at the University of Lausanne in Switzerland in 2008, confirmed that despite the Platypus being an egg layer, its milk contained casein-like proteins, which still help nourish mammalian babies today. Further genetic analysis revealed that lactation became a method of nourishment for mammalian offspring long before yolky eggs became redundant in mammals.

Warm bloodedness also appears to have a long history. Two hundred million years ago, a small, very active animal began to be able to moderate its body heat. As it scuttled and scurried, the body of *Megazostrodon* began to heat up. The faster it ran, the more heat its muscles produced. The heat it generated allowed it to have more young, run faster and may have eventually enabled it to hunt at night, when other animals were constrained by being cold-blooded. It was only when the dinosaurs succumbed to extinction that *Megazostrodon* and its relatives began to fully come into their own.

CLASSIFYING AND NAMING MAMMALS

All living things are described according to a system of taxonomy devised in the 18th century. The classification into a hierarchical system of groups helps scientists describe and identify them and determine their evolutionary relationships. Classification levels go from general to specific and each level describes the characteristic features of a group of organisms. Animals' diagnostic features are based on body structures, DNA, blood proteins and functional processes.

A mammal's **scientific name** is used worldwide and does not change unless it is reclassified. It consists of two or three latinised words and is written in reverse order to English names. The first, or genus, name describes the group of similar animals to which it belongs. The second, or species, name usually describes a distinctive feature of that specific mammal. A third, or subspecies, name is used to distinguish a race or subpopulation within a species. For example, *Macropus robustus* is the scientific name of the Common Wallaroo, and it means 'robust long-foot'.

A mammal's **common name** can vary from place to place: *Macropus robustus* is also known as the Euro, Hill Kangaroo, Eastern Grey Wallaroo, Red Wallaroo and Biggada.

The Common Wallaroo *Macropus* robustus is classified as follows:

Kingdom	Animalia	Multi-celled organism that is not a plant, bacterium or fungus
Phylum	Chordata	Animal with nerve chord along back
Subphylum	Vertebrata	Chordate with jointed backbones
Class	Mammalia	Vertebrate with mammary glands
Subclass	Marsupialia	Mammal whose young are born partially developed and may be protected by a pouch
Order	Diprotodontia	Marsupial with one pair of lower incisors
Family	Macropodidae	Diprotodont with long hind feet
Genus	Macropus	Macropod with typical features
Species	*robustus*	Robust

Class: Mammalia

All mammals belong to the class **Mammalia** and are classified into three subclasses according to the way they reproduce. The following gives the taxonomic breakdown to family; some families are further divided into subfamilies.

Eastern Quoll family

MONOTREMES – Prototherian Mammals

Female monotremes lay soft-shelled eggs. The baby hatches after a brief incubation, blind, furless and with hind legs incompletely formed. It feeds on milk that oozes from mammary ducts on its mother's belly. An echidna carries her eggs and developing young in a pouch, while a Platypus incubates her eggs and nurses her young in a nesting burrow.

Subclass: Prototheria

Order: Monotremata
Family: Ornithorhynchidae (Platypus)
Family: Tachyglossidae (Short-beaked Echidna)

Short-beaked Echidna

MARSUPIALS – Metatherian Mammals

Female marsupial mammals bear partially developed young after a brief gestation period. A newborn marsupial is blind, furless and its tail and hindlimbs are incomplete. Using its strong forelimbs, the tiny baby drags itself from the cloaca and continues development attached to a teat on its mother's belly which may be protected by a pouch or temporary folds of skin.

Subclass: Marsupialia (Metatheria)

Order: Dasyuromorphia
Superfamily: Dasyuroidea
Family: Dasyuridae (quolls, dibblers, pseudantechinuses, parantechinuses, Kowari, Mulgara, Ampurta, Kaluta, Tasmanian Devil, phascogales, antechinuses, planigales, ningauis, dunnarts, Kultarr)
Family: Myrmecobiidae (Numbat)
Family: Thylacinidae (Thylacine)

Order: Peramelemorphia
Superfamily: Perameloidea
Family: Peramelidae (bandicoots, Rufous Spiny Bandicoot)
Family: Thylacomyidae (bilbies)

Numbat

Koala

Order: Diprotodontia
Suborder: Vombatiformes
Family: Phascolarctidae (Koala)
Family: Vombatidae (wombats)

Suborder: Phalangerida
Superfamily: Burramyoidea
Family: Burramyidae (pygmy-possums)

Superfamily: Petauroidea
Family: Petauridae (Striped Possum, Leadbeater's Possum, wrist-winged gliders)
Family: Pseudocheiridae (ringtail possums, Greater Glider)
Family: Tarsipedidae (Honey Possum)
Family: Acrobatidae (Feathertail Glider)

Superfamily: Phalangeroidea
Family: Phalangeridae (brushtail possums, cuscuses, Scaly-tailed Possum)

Superfamily: Macropodoidea
Family: Hypsiprymnodontidae (Musky Rat-kangaroo)
Family: Potoroidae (potoroos, bettongs)
Family: Macropodidae (tree-kangaroos, hare-wallabies, wallabies, wallaroos, kangaroos, nailtail wallabies, rock-wallabies, pademelons, Quokka, Swamp Wallaby)

Order: Notoryctemorphia
Family: Notoryctidae (marsupial moles)

Tasmanian Pademelon

PLACENTALS – Eutherian Mammals

Subclass: Eutheria

Placental, or Eutherian, mammals give birth to fully formed young that develop inside the mother's body with the aid of a placenta. This mass of tissue allows nutrients and wastes to pass between the mother and foetus, and is expelled following birth (the afterbirth). Newborns are sparsely covered with hair, and eyes and limbs are well developed. Young suckle milk from the female's teats until they reach independence.

Australian Sea-lion mother with pup suckling

Order: Chiroptera

Suborder: Yinpterochiroptera

Family: Pteropodidae (blossom bats, tube-nosed bats, fruit-bats, flying-foxes)
Family: Megadermatidae (Ghost bat)
Family: Rhinolophidae (horseshoe bats)
Family: Hipposideridae (leaf-nosed bats)
Family: Rhinonycteridae (orange leaf-nosed bats)

Suborder: Yangochiroptera

Family: Emballonuridae (sheath-tailed bats)
Family: Miniopteridae (bent-winged bats)
Family: Vespertilionidae (Golden-tipped bats, Tube-nosed Insectivorous bat, long-eared bats, large-eared bats, forest bats, cave bats, pipistrelles, large-footed Myotis and broad-nosed bats)
Family: Molossidae (Free-tailed bats)

Grey-headed Flying-fox

Order: Rodentia

Family: Muridae (rats, mice, melomys)

Order: Sirenia

Family: Dugongidae (Dugong)

Order: Cetacea

Suborder: Mysticeti (baleen whales)

Family: Balaenidae (Southern Right Whale)
Family: Neobalaenidae (Pygmy Right Whale)
Family: Balaenopteridae (minke, Sei, Bryde's, Blue, Fin, Humpback Whales)

Suborder: Odontoceti (toothed whales)

Family: Physeteridae (sperm whales)
Family: Kogiidae (Pygmy & dwarf sperm whales)
Family: Ziphiidae (beaked whales)
Family: Delphinidae (dolphins, killer whales, pilot whales, Melon-headed Whale)
Family: Phocoenidae (Spectacled Porpoise)

Spinifex Hopping-mouse

Order: Carnivora

Family: Otariidae (sea-lions, fur-seals)
Family: Phocidae (earless seals)
Family: Canidae (Dingo, Red Fox)
Family: Felidae (Feral Cat)

Order: Lagomorpha

Family: Leporidae (Rabbit, Hare)

Order: Perissodactyla

Family: Equidae (Brumby, Donkey)

Order: Artiodactyla

Family: Suidae (Feral Pig)
Family: Camelidae (One-humped Camel)
Family: Bovidae (cattle, Swamp Buffalo, Feral Goat)
Family: Cervidae (deer)

Dingo

IDENTIFYING MAMMALS

Although it is easy to believe that superficially alike animals must be similar, that is not the case. Linnaeus himself at first grouped animals such as the pig and Armadillo in the same group, based on their physical similarities, but they are now recognised as belonging to different orders. Looking beyond the obvious to study skull and teeth anatomy, reproductive traits, and even hair samples, blood samples and DNA, can be important in mammal identification, particularly for some species, such as the Queensland rock-wallabies (which are superficially impossible to tell apart).

Several orders are unmistakeable in the wild, particularly the monotremes and cetaceans, while others exhibit visual similarities that could confuse a novice (especially dasyurids and rodents, and bandicoots and bettongs). William de Vlamingh also famously mistook the Quokka for a large rat, leading to the name Rottnest (rat's nest) Island, although he can be forgiven because, at the time,

macropods were new to science. Such a mistake should prove difficult for any avid mammal watcher to make today provided they have a small amount of knowledge about Australian marsupial orders.

Field identification of mammals relies on several factors, depending on whether identifying living or dead specimens. To identify living mammals, good research skills and keen observations are a must, as is some understanding of the distribution of certain mammal species. While remembering that distribution maps are only ever approximate — vagrants may from time to time venture out of the 'accepted' range — maps will provide some guide as to the likelihood of a sighting in a particular area.

Distinguishing features, such as a difference in teeth or the presence of a pouch, might require a closer inspection. Feet, especially the number, length and positioning of digits, can also help and may be visible from tracks left around waterholes, food sources or shelter.

Skulls and Teeth — Useful Identifiers

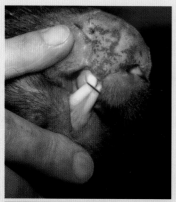

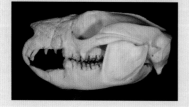

A mammal skull has two depressions (known as occipital condyles) at the place where vertebrae join the back of the skull; reptiles have just one of these. Once the skull has been identified as a mammal, it should be apparent whether it is the skull of a monotreme because it will have either no teeth in the upper and lower jaw (echidna) or very rudimentary cheek teeth (Platypus). Bandicoots and carnivorous marsupials are polyprotodonts with four or five incisors in their upper jaw. Three or fewer upper incisors with prominent, large incisors on the lower jaw mean it is a diprotodont, like macropods, possums, and the Koala and wombat.

For animals that have 'baby teeth' and lose their molars, or that have constant eruptions of teeth throughout their life, molar progression and eruption can also be used to 'age' specimens, either living or from fossil teeth. However, arboreal leaf-eating mammals acquire all of their teeth while still young, making molar eruption unhelpful in age determination. Instead, their teeth wear down as they age, so the extent of the wearing can help provide an indication of age.

Left, top to bottom: Wombats' two enlarged front teeth grow continuously (like a rodent's) and must be worn down; A dingo's skull will exhibit typical carnivore teeth, with enlarged canine teeth; Possum teeth are typically diprotodont, with gaps between the wedge-shaped incisors and the molars.

Kangaroo tracks on sand near Shark Bay, WA. While tracks and scats can help identify the group of animals a creature belongs to, they may not always help identify species unless they are very clear and show the length of limbs and the number of toes.

Scats and Tracks

Tracks and droppings (scats), coupled with sightings, might also help identify a particular group of animals. The presence of termite head casings in long, smooth, cylindrical echidna faeces or droppings carefully placed on top of rocks (peculiar to wombats) are signs of their presence in the area. Tracks may be the best way to identify terrestrial animals once they have passed by, but for arboreal animals (such as possums and Koalas) the best indication of their presence is scratches and worn patches on tree trunks and branches.

Locomotion

For some macropod species, many of which are typically fleeting in the wild, locomotion may aid in identification. How the animal holds its body and its arms as it hops bipedally, the length of its stride, and the positioning of its tail as it moves can give some indication of the species.

Larger, longer-legged macropods, such as the Red Kangaroo and Whiptail Wallaby, have a characteristic arch and a long stride — often with the tail nearly extended fully when in leap. The Agile Wallaby and Eastern Grey Kangaroo have a shorter stride with a more upright hop that is less bouncy than that of the rock-wallabies, smaller pademelons and the Quokka. The Swamp Wallaby and pademelons hold the tail straight out behind as they leap, rather than being slightly curved up like other macropods.

'Galloping' or scurrying on all fours typifies the Musky Rat-kangaroo, while the nailtail wallaby's arms rotate somewhat as it hops, giving rise to the colloquial name 'Organ grinders'.

Right, top to bottom: The height of a macropod's hop and its arched or upright posture can help identify kangaroo and wallaby species — Whiptail Wallaby; Agile Wallaby; Eastern Grey Kangaroo; Red Kangaroo; Western Brush Wallaby.

HOW TO USE KEYS

Instructions for how to use a dichotomous key

The following series of statements consist of two choices that describe characteristics of the unidentified mammal.

Start with number 1 and choose which of the two statements best describes the unknown mammal. The number on the right will either direct you to the next set of statements or list the animal's genus, family or species.

▶ SEE GLOSSARY p292 FOR DEFINITIONS

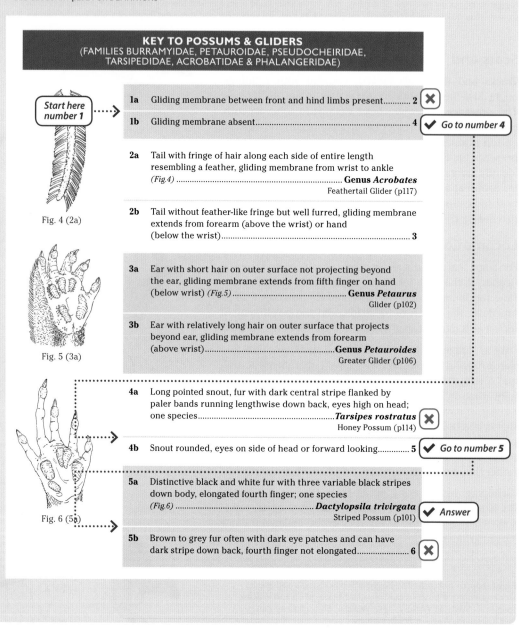

KEY TO POSSUMS & GLIDERS
(FAMILIES BURRAMYIDAE, PETAUROIDEA, PSEUDOCHEIRIDAE, TARSIPEDIDAE, ACROBATIDAE & PHALANGERIDAE)

Start here number 1

1a Gliding membrane between front and hind limbs present............ 2 ✖

1b Gliding membrane absent.. 4 ✔ *Go to number 4*

2a Tail with fringe of hair along each side of entire length resembling a feather, gliding membrane from wrist to ankle *(Fig.4)* .... **Genus *Acrobates***
Feathertail Glider (p117)

Fig. 4 (2a)

2b Tail without feather-like fringe but well furred, gliding membrane extends from forearm (above the wrist) or hand (below the wrist)... **3**

3a Ear with short hair on outer surface not projecting beyond the ear, gliding membrane extends from fifth finger on hand (below wrist) *(Fig.5)* .... **Genus *Petaurus***
Glider (p102)

3b Ear with relatively long hair on outer surface that projects beyond ear, gliding membrane extends from forearm (above wrist)... **Genus *Petauroides***
Greater Glider (p106)

Fig. 5 (3a)

4a Long pointed snout, fur with dark central stripe flanked by paler bands running lengthwise down back, eyes high on head; one species.. ***Tarsipes rostratus*** ✖
Honey Possum (p114)

4b Snout rounded, eyes on side of head or forward looking.............. 5 ✔ *Go to number 5*

5a Distinctive black and white fur with three variable black stripes down body, elongated fourth finger; one species *(Fig.6)* .... ***Dactylopsila trivirgata*** ✔ *Answer*
Striped Possum (p101)

Fig. 6 (5a)

5b Brown to grey fur often with dark eye patches and can have dark stripe down back, fourth finger not elongated....................... 6 ✖

KEY TO TASMANIAN DEVIL, QUOLLS, MULGARAS, KOWARIS, DUNNARTS, KULTARRS, PHASCOGALES, PLANIGALES, DIBBLERS, PSEUDANTECHINUSES & ANTECHINUSES (FAMILY DASYURIDAE)

1a Body weight >2 kg; fur black with variable white patches; one species .... ***Sarcophilus harrisii***
Tasmanian Devil (p43)

1b Body weight <2 kg; fur colour variable **2**

2a Fur with distinct white spots; weight >100 gm
.... **Genus *Dasyurus***
Quoll (p38)

2b Fur not spotted; if so, body weight <30 gm **3**

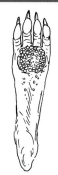

Fig. 1.1 (3a)

3a Four separate toes on hind foot; first toe absent *(Fig.1.1)*............... **4**

3b Five separate toes on hind foot; first toe can be reduced
(Fig.1.2) **5**

4a Limbs long and delicate; tail about 150% of head–body length
.... **Genus *Antechinomys***
Kultarr (p56)

4b Limbs robust; tail shorter than head–body length; one species only
.... ***Dasyuroides byrnei***
Kowari (p51)

Fig. 1.2 (3b)

5a Tail with distinct dense dark brush for outer half to last
two thirds **6**

5b Tail not as above, slight terminal crest may be present **7**

6a Tail with long black brush all round................... **Genus *Phascogale***
Phascogale (p54)

6b Tail with long black fur on dorsal surface only
.... **Genus *Dasycercus***
Mulgara (p50)

Fig. 2.1 (7a)

7a Hind feet relatively long and narrow <3 mm; no post interdigital
pads and usually no enlarged granules on outer half of sole;
may have dark midline or patch on forehead and crown;
tail may have slight crest or tuft *(Fig.2.1)* .... **Genus *Sminthopsis***
Dunnart (p56)

7b Hind feet relatively broad >3 mm; postdigital pads present on
outer half of sole; tail without brush or crest *(Fig.2.2)* **8**

Fig. 2.2 (7b)

| **8a** | Very small; adult weight usually <12 g; if >12 g then head flattened and triangular in shape; pads on forefeet without clearly defined striations .... **9** |

| **8b** | Adult weight >12 g .... **10** |

Fig. 3.1 (9a)

| **9a** | Straight and flat posterior to supratragus of ear *(Fig.3.1)* ....**Genus *Planigale*** |
| | Planigale (p54) |

| **9b** | Posterior edge of supratragus curled *(Fig.3.2)*......... **Genus *Ningaui*** |
| | Wongai & Southern Ningaui (p55) |

Fig. 3.2 (9b)

| **10a** | Tail clearly shorter than head–body, thick at base and tapering evenly to point at tip; dorsal fur uniformly coloured.................... **11** |

| **10b** | Tail thin, or if thick, reddish orange fur patches behind and below ears .... **12** |

| **11a** | Dorsal fur rich brown heavily grizzled with cream; strong contrast with light creamy belly fur; distinct pale eye ring; one species only .... ***Parantechinus apicalis*** |
| | Dibbler (p51) |

| **11b** | Fur uniformly russet or copper coloured above and below; very pale eye ring; one species only .... ***Dasykaluta rosamondae*** |
| | (Kaluta Little Red Antechinus. Not featured. Found in Pilbara, WA) |

| **12a** | Reddish or orange patches behind and below very large ears; tail may be thickened at base.................. **Genus *Pseudantechinus*** |
| | Pseudantechinus (p52) |

| **12b** | No obvious orange patches behind ears; tail never thickened .... **Genus *Antechinus*** |
| | Antechinus (p53) |

KEY TO BILBIES, BANDICOOTS & ECHYMIPERAS
(FAMILIES PERAMELIDAE & THYLACOMYIDAE)

1a   Long tail with whitish crest; long silky fur; only one species
.... ***Macrotis lagotis***
Bilby (p71)

1b   Tail with uniformly short hair 2

2a   Ears clearly longer than wide, and pointed .... **Genus *Perameles***
Bandicoot (p64)

2b   Ears not longer than wide and not pointed....................................... 3

3a   Four pairs of upper incisors; fur highly spiny; only one species
.... ***Echymipera rufescens***
Echymipera (p70)

3b   Five pairs of upper incisors; fur coarse.................. **Genus *Isoodon***
Bandicoot (p64)

KEY TO POSSUMS & GLIDERS
(FAMILIES BURRAMYIDAE, PETAUROIDAE, PSEUDOCHEIRIDAE, TARSIPEDIDAE, ACROBATIDAE & PHALANGERIDAE)

Fig. 4 (2a)

Fig. 5 (3a)

Fig. 6 (5a)

Fig. 7 (6a)

1a	Gliding membrane between front and hind limbs present	**2**
1b	Gliding membrane absent	**4**

2a	Tail with fringe of hair along each side of entire length resembling a feather, gliding membrane from wrist to ankle *(Fig.4)* ...... **Genus *Acrobates*** Feathertail Glider (p117)	
2b	Tail without feather-like fringe but well furred, gliding membrane extends from forearm (above the wrist) or hand (below the wrist)	**3**

3a	Ear with short hair on outer surface not projecting beyond the ear, gliding membrane extends from fifth finger on hand (below wrist) *(Fig.5)* ...... **Genus *Petaurus*** Glider (p102)	
3b	Ear with relatively long hair on outer surface that projects beyond ear, gliding membrane extends from forearm (above wrist) ...... **Genus *Petauroides*** Greater Glider (p106)	

4a	Long pointed snout, fur with dark central stripe flanked by paler bands running lengthwise down back, eyes high on head; one species ...... ***Tarsipes rostratus*** Honey Possum (p114)	
4b	Snout rounded, eyes on side of head or forward looking	**5**

5a	Distinctive black and white fur with three variable black stripes down body, elongated fourth finger; one species *(Fig.6)* ...... ***Dactylopsila trivirgata*** Striped Possum (p101)	
5b	Brown to grey fur often with dark eye patches and can have dark stripe down back, fourth finger not elongated	**6**

6a	Fingers with small claws and large tip pads, claws end slightly before or just beyond tips of fingers, tail length >180 mm *(Fig.7)*	**7**
6b	Claws large and extend well beyond fingertips	**8**

7a Tail fully furred **8**

7b Tail not fully furred **9**

8a Tail length <200 mm, tail bushy, narrowest at base
.... ***Gymnobelideus leadbeateri***
Leadbeater's Possum (p101)

8b Tail length >200 mm, tail evenly bushy, short naked tip
.... ***Hemibelideus lemuroides***
Lemuroid Ringtail Possum (p106)

9a Tail totally naked over full length.................................... **10**

9b Tail only naked for part of its length................................ **11**

10a Tail naked <130 mm long, teeth are broad, flattened and serrated, blade-like upper and lower premolars, premolars obviously larger than molars, found in high country of Australian Alps; one species... ***Burramys parvus***
Mountain Pygmy-possum (p97)

10b Tail length >110 mm, upper and lower premolars either peg-like and smaller or similar size to molars............... **Genus *Cercartetus***
Pygmy-possum (p96)

11a Tail thickly furred at base but then naked to tip **12**

11b Tail not thickly furred at base and naked area covered with smooth scales **13**

12a Naked area of tail skin covered with thick rough scales; one species only .... ***Wyulda squamicaudata***
Scaly-tailed Possum (p113)

12b Naked area of tail skin covered with smooth scales, tail tip blunt and carried downwards; one species only......***Petropseudes dahli***
Rock Ringtail Possum (p107)

13a Body fur almost black above or light brown with a dark longitudinal stripe from between eyes to lower back
.... **Genus *Pseudochirulus***
Daintree & Herbert River Ringtail Possum (p108)

13b Not as above.. **14**

14a Tail furred to upper tip; white fur below eye and ear;
greenish fur; two silvery stripes running down back;
one species only .... *Pseudochirops archeri*
Green Ringtail Possum (p107)

14b Not as above **15**

15a Fur short, variable colour from rufous-red to brown or greyish;
prehensile tail with white tip .... **Genus** *Pseudocheirus*
Western & Common Ringtail Possum (p109)

15b Not as above **16**

16a Ears short or almost invisible; tail fur not bush **17**

16b Ears prominent and large; tail bushy and dark, naked
underneath and tip .... **Genus** *Trichosurus*
Brushtail Possum (p112)

17a Skin yellowish-pink; no stripe along middle of back,
ears almost invisible under head fur; one species only
.... *Spilocuscus maculatus*
Common Spotted Cuscus (p111)

17b Skin greyish-brown, brownish stripe along middle of back
from ears to rump, ears obvious; one species only
.... *Phalanger mimicus*
Southern Common Cuscus (p111)

KEY TO RAT-KANGAROOS, BETTONGS & POTOROOS
(FAMILIES POTOROIDAE & HYPSIPRYMNODONTIDAE)

1a All claws on fore feet approximately equal in length; tail used to support body at rest and during slow locomotion *(Fig.8.1)* .... **Family Macropodidae**
Kangaroo, Wallaroo & Wallabies (p139)

1b Claw in middle digit of fore foot longer than claws on outer digits; tail partly prehensile, used to carry nesting material and not used to support body *(Fig.8.2)* **2**

Fig. 8.1 (1a)

2a Hind foot with five toes, second and third toes syndactylous, bounds on all four legs; only one species *(Fig.9.1)* .... ***Hypsiprymnodon moschatus***
Musky Rat-kangaroo (p128)

2b Hind foot with four toes; second and third toes syndactylous *(Fig.9.2)* **3**

Fig. 8.2 (1b)

3a Central part of rhinarium sparsely furred; only one species *(Fig.10.1)* .... ***Aepyprymnus rufescens***
Rufous Bettong (p130)

3b Rhinarium totally naked *(Fig.10.2)* **4**

4a Tail clearly longer than head–body length; hind foot 10–12 cm .... ***Caloprymnus campestris***
(Desert Rat-kangaroo. Extinct)

4b Tail shorter or not obviously longer than head–body length **5**

5a Head broad; muzzle short; eyes large; tail similar to head–body length; dorsal fur varying in colour on head, flanks and base of tail .... **Genus *Bettongia***
Bettong (p130)

Fig. 9.1 (2a)

5b Head tapering to narrow muzzle and flat on top; eyes small; tail 75% of head–body length; dorsal fur uniformly dark brown/grey colour... **Genus *Potorous***
Potoroo (p132)

Fig. 10.1 (3a)

Fig. 10.2 (3b)

Fig. 9.2 (2b)

KEY TO KANGAROOS & WALLABIES (FAMILY MACROPODIDAE)

1a Foot very broad; foot length roughly three to four times width; mainly tree-dwelling but agile over flat ground .... **Genus _Dendrolagus_**
Tree-kangaroo (p134)

1b Foot narrower, foot length more than four times width, occasionally found in trees... **2**

2a Tail with small horny tip (nail) on upper surface .... **Genus _Onychogalea_**
Nailtail Wallaby (p149)

2b Tail without nail on tip... **3**

3a Toes four and five with relatively short nails not extending far past tip of toe; underside of foot has thick grainy pads; mostly located on rocky outcrops .... **Genus _Petrogale_**
Rock-wallaby (p151)

3b Toes four and five with long nails, extending well beyond tip of toe.. **4**

4a Distinct bright orange to rufous fur eye ring; ears short, not reaching back edge of eye ring when folded forwards; only one species .... **_Lagorchestes conspicillatus_**
Spectacled Hare-wallaby (p137)

4b No distinct ring around eye; ears longer, with tip extending beyond back edge of eye when folded forwards **5**

5a Distinct transverse dark bands on lower back fur; restricted to Bernier and Dorre Islands WA; only one species .... **_Lagostrophus fasciatus_**
Banded Hare-wallaby (p138)

5a Lower back fur without transverse dark stripes............................. **6**

6a Small size; head and body length <630 mm; no dark fur stripe; can have rufous/red fur on parts of body... **7**

6a Large size; head–body length mostly >630 mm; if less, has dark fur stripe along midline of back or fur predominantly grey or sandy brown.. **8**

7a   Ears short, furred and rounded; tail short, broad and
slightly furred...***Setonix brachyurus***
Quokka (p162)

7b   Ears longer and almost naked on inside surface, can have reddish
fur areas; found in dense forest or rainforest...... **Genus *Thylogale***
Pademelon (p160)

8a   Distinctive fur colour; rufous to yellow cheek stripe; dorsal fur
dark; blackish hands, feet, tail, armpits and upper half of muzzle;
belly fur varies from light yellow/brown to golden/rufous;
tail often white-tipped; no dark stripe down midline of back;
upper premolar longer than largest molar;
only one species .... ***Wallabia bicolor***
Swamp Wallaby (p163)

8b   Fur colours not as above; upper premolar shorter than
largest molar ....**Genus *Macropus***
Kangaroo, Wallaroo & Wallabies (p139)

KEY TO BATS

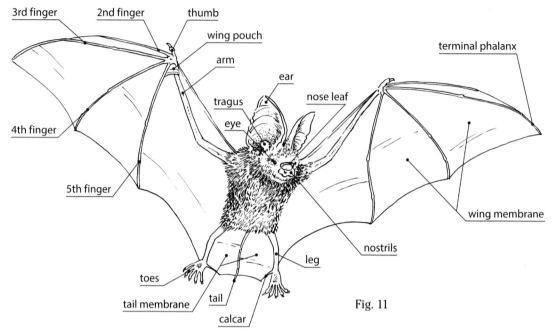

Fig. 11

Fig. 12 (1a)

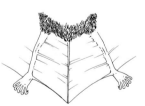

Fig. 13.1 (2a)

Fig. 13.2 (2b & 4a)

1a   Claws on thumb and second finger (except Dobsonia); tail membrane missing or not joined between the legs *(Fig.12)* ....Family **Pteropodidae** Megabats (p170)

1b   Claw absent on second finger; tail membrane joined between legs.. **2**

2a   Tail fully enclosed in tail membrane; or no tail but with full tail membrane *(Fig.13.1)* **3**

2b   Tail extends beyond tail membrane; or tail extends free above tail membrane and is enclosed within a membrane sheath *(Fig.13.2)* **4**

3a   Large complex noseleaf; tragus absent or, if present, forked **5**

3b   Noseleaf absent; tragus present.. **7**

4a   Tail clearly extends beyond tail membrane; blunt nose;
lips wrinkled; no wing pouch present
(Fig.13.2) .... Family **Molossidae**
Free-tailed Bat (p184)

4b   End of tail extends above tail membrane and enclosed in
membrane sheath *(Fig.14.1)*; pointy bare nose; lips smooth; wing
pouch present in some *(Fig.14.2)*................. Family **Emballonuridae**
Sheath-tailed Bat (p181)

Fig. 14.1 (4b)

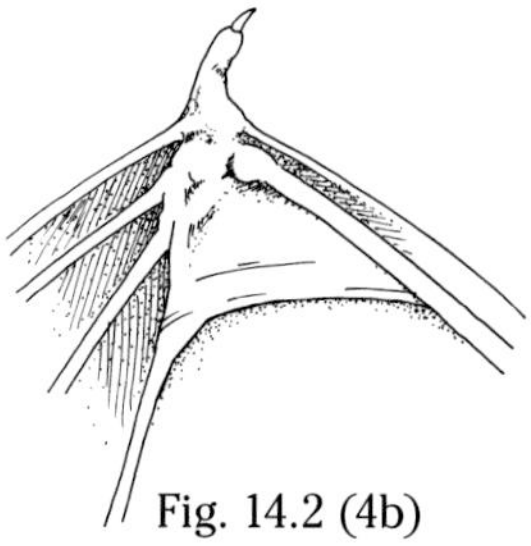

5a   Tail absent but complete tail membrane present;
forked tragus; large eyes .... Family **Megadermatidae**
Ghost Bat (p176)

5b   Tail present and fully enclosed by tail membrane **6**

Fig. 14.2 (4b)

6a   Noseleaf present; tragus absent... **7**

6b   Noseleaf absent; tragus present.. **9**

7a   Noseleaf large, complex, elongate and lower section horseshoe-
shaped and covers upper lip, central section projects forward
(Fig.15.1)... Family **Rhinolophidae**
Horseshoe Bat (p177)

7b   Noseleaf low, round or squarish without central protrubance;
nostrils obvious in centre of noseleaf *(Fig.15.2)* **8**

Fig. 15.1 (7a)

8a   Noseleaf round or squarish with projecting upper section
(Fig.20.1 p16)... Family **Hipposideridae**
Leaf-nosed Bat (p178)

8b   Noseleaf round and flat, lower portion notched at front, small
second leaflet behind main leaf; no projecting upper section
(Fig.20.2 p16).. Family **Rhinonycteridae**
Orange Leaf-nosed Bat (p178)

Fig. 15.2 (7b)

9a   Terminal phalanx of third finger about 3 times longer than
terminal phalanx *(Fig.16.1 p14)*......................... Family **Miniopteridae**
Bent-winged Bat (p186)

9b   Terminal phalanx of third finger about equal in length to
subterminal phalanx *(Fig.16.2 p14)* .... Family **Vespertilionidae**
Evening bats (p175)

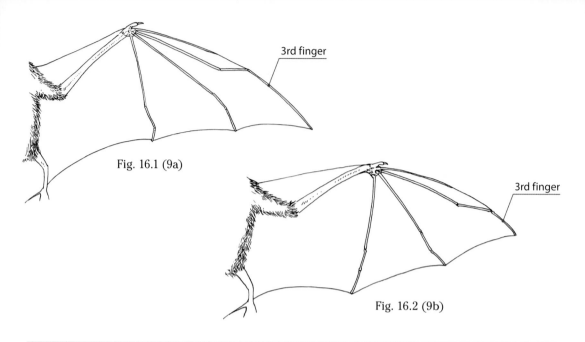

Fig. 16.1 (9a)

3rd finger

Fig. 16.2 (9b)

3rd finger

KEY TO FRUIT & BLOSSOM BATS (FAMILY PTEROPODIDAE)

1a   Large body size; forearm >100mm.. **2**

1b   Small body size; forearm <70mm.. **3**

2a   Wing membranes joined at midline of back, no claw on second finger; short tail; one species only .... ***Dobsonia moluccensis***
(Bare-backed Fruit-bat. Not featured.)

2b   Wing membrane attached along side of body; claw on second finger; no tail membrane .... **Genus *Pteropus***
Flying-fox (p173)

3a   Forearm >55mm, obvious tubular nostrils; yellowish to green spots on bare skin on wings, ears and nostrils *(Fig.17)* .... **Genus *Nyctimene***
Tube-nosed Bat (p172)

3b   Forearm <45 mm; small with long snout, no tubular nostrils **4**

Fig. 17 (3a)

4a   No tail or tail membrane, fringe of hair along inside of leg; one species only .... ***Syconycteris australis***
Eastern Blossom Bat (p172)

4b   No tail but tail membrane reduced to narrow flap along inside of legs; one species only............................ ***Macroglossus minimus***
Northern Blossom Bat (p171)

KEY TO FREE-TAILED BATS (FAMILY MOLOSSIDAE)

1a   Forearm >45 mm.. **2**

1b   Forearm <45mm.. **Genus *Mormopterus***
Free-tailed Bat (p184)

2a   Ears joined by a band of skin across the forehead; no throat
pouch present; one species only .... ***Chaerephon jobensis***
Great Northern Free-tailed Bat (p184)

2b   Throat pouch present, ears not joined along forehead; white fur
strip along junction of belly fur and wing; one species only
(Fig.18) .... ***Austronomus australis***
White-striped Free-tailed Bat (p184)

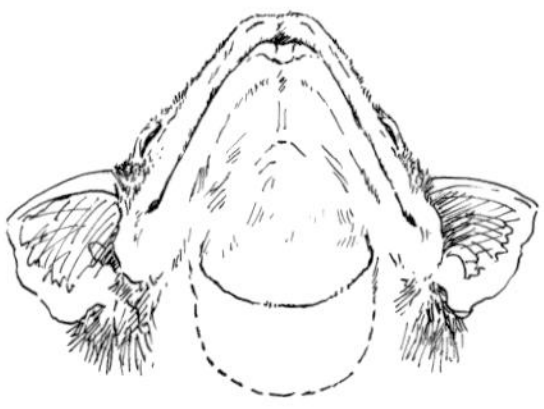

Fig. 18 (2b)

KEY TO SHEATH-TAILED BATS (FAMILY EMBALLONURIDAE)

1a   Tragus broad, flat and uniform in thickness; no wing pouch or,
if present, filled with white fur
(Fig.19.1).. **Genus *Saccolaimus***
Yellow-bellied Sheath-tailed Bat (p181)

1b   Tragus broad, flat and thicker toward top; wing pouch on
underside of wrist present in both sexes
(Fig.19.2) .... **Genus *Taphozous***
Sheath-tailed Bat (p182)

Fig. 19.1 (1a)

Fig. 19.2 (1b)

KEY TO GHOST BATS (FAMILY MEGADERMATIDAE)

There is only one genus and species in this family
.... ***Macroderma gigas***
Ghost Bat (p176)

KEY TO HORSESHOE BATS (FAMILY RHINOLOPHIDAE)

There is only one genus in this family .... **Genus *Rhinolophus***
Horseshoe Bat (p177)

KEY TO LEAF-NOSED BATS (FAMILY HIPPOSIDERIDAE)

Fig. 20.1

There is only one genus in this family
(Fig.20.1) .... **Genus *Hipposideros***
Leaf-nosed Bat (p178)

KEY TO NEW LEAF-NOSED BATS (FAMILY RHINONYCTERIDAE)

Fig. 20.2

There is only one genus in this family
(Fig.20.2) .... ***Rhinonicteris aurantia***
Orange Leaf-nosed Bat (p178)

KEY TO BENT-WINGED BATS (FAMILY MINIOPTERIDAE)

There is only one genus in this family ....**Genus *Miniopterus***
Bent-winged Bat (p186)

KEY TO EVENING BATS (FAMILY VESPERTILIONIDAE)

Fig. 21 (1a)

Fig. 22 (2a)

1a   Ears long and joined across forehead by flap of skin; simple
noseleaf in form of a post-nasal ridge and nasal exfoliations
(Fig.21) .... **Genus *Nyctophilus***
Long-eared Bat (p192)

1b   Ears not joined, no nasal exfoliations 2

2a   Nostrils tubular and point sideways; tail membrane heavily furred;
one species only *(Fig.22)* ....***Murina florium***
Flute-nosed Bat (p188)

2b   Not as above.. 3

3a   Fur curly, dark brown with golden tips, fur extends onto forearm, legs and tail; long narrow pointed tragus; one species only .... ***Phoniscus papuensis***
Golden-tipped Bat (p188)

3b   Not as above... **4**

4a   Fleshy lobes at base of ear and on lower lip near corner of mouth, high forehead and short roundish ears
(Fig.23).. **Genus *Chalinolobus***
Microbats (p175)

4b   No lobe on lower lip or near mouth; ear longer, often pointed **5**

Fig. 23 (4a)

5a   Forearm >45 mm.. **6**

5b   Forearm <45 mm.. **7**

6a   Two pairs of upper incisors; outer pair minute; gap between upper incisors and canines; ears long and overlap when folded together over head .... **Genus *Falsistrellus***
False Pipistrelle (p190)

6b   One pair of upper incisors; no gap between upper incisors and canines; ears barely touch when folded over head
.... **Genus *Scoteanax***
Greater Broad-nosed Bat (p196)

7a   Calcar long extending ¾ distance from ankle to tail tip; tragus long and slender; large feet (8–11 mm); one species only .... ***Myotis macropus***
Large-footed Myotis (p189)

7b   Not as above... **8**

8a   One pair of upper incisors; muzzle broad, naked and has swollen and secreting glandular areas........................... **Genus *Scotorepens***
Little & Eastern Broad-nosed Bat (p196 & p198)

8b   Two pairs of upper incisors (close together); muzzle not broad and lacks swollen glandular areas... **9**

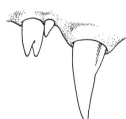

Fig. 24.1 (9a)

9a   Inner upper incisors have distinct cleft forming two lobes; outer upper incisors minute; only one pair of upper premolars *(Fig.24.1)* .... **Genus *Vespadelus***
Forest & Cave Bat (p199)

9b   Inner upper incisors cleft, but one lobe hidden behind the other when viewed from front; outer upper incisor obvious, but only slightly smaller than inner pair; two pairs of upper premolars, forward one only half the height of rear one
(Fig.24.2) .... **Genus *Pipistrellus***
Pipistrelle (p189)

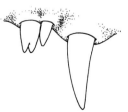

Fig. 24.2 (9b)

KEY TO SMALL TERRESTRIAL & ARBORIAL MAMMALS

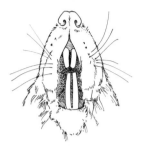

Fig. 25.1 (1a)

1a One pair of large upper incisors and one pair of lower incisors *(Fig.25.1)*; females with paired teats in rows on lower abdomen, sometimes extending onto chest area *(Fig.26.1)*, male scrotum located between penis and tail *(Fig.26.2)*

Rodents, Family **Muridae**: see Rodent Key (p19)

Fig. 25.2 (1b)

1b Four or occasionally five pairs of small incisors in upper jaw and three pairs in lower jaw *(Fig.25.2)*; females with teats in semicircle in lower abdomen with or without pouch covering *(Fig.26.3)*; males with scrotum anterior to penis on lower belly *(Fig.26.4)*

Polyprotodont marsupials, see keys for Families **Dasyuridae** (p3) or **Peramelidae** and **Thylacomyidae** (p5)

Fig. 25.3 (1c)

1c Only one pair of lower incisors which are large and elongate and pointing forwards; three or less pairs of upper incisors *(Fig.25.3)*; females with pouch covering four teats *(Fig.26.3)*; males with scrotum anterior to penis on lower belly *(Fig.26.4)*

Diprotodont marsupials, see keys for Families **Burramyidae, Petauridae, Tarsipedidae** and **Acrobatidae** (p6) or **Potoroidae** and **Hypsiprymnodontidae** (p9)

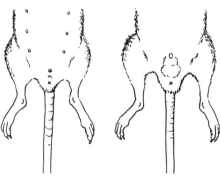

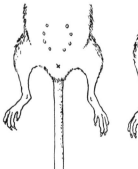

Fig. 26.1 ♀ (1a)   Fig. 26.2 ♂ (1a)   Fig. 26.3 ♀ (1b & 1c)   Fig. 26.4 ♂ (1b & 1c)

KEY TO RATS & MICE (FAMILY MURIDAE)

1a   Toes on hind foot partly webbed; claws as broad as tips of toes;
tail completely covered by short dense fur; one species only
(Fig.27.1).. ***Hydromys chrysogaster***
Water Rat (p205)

1b   Not as above *(Fig.27.2)* **2**

2a   Tail clearly greater than head–body length, prehensile, upper side
of tip flattened and lacking scales .... **Genus *Pogonomys***
Tree Mouse (p223)

2b   Not as above.. **3**

3a   Only two obvious interdigital pads on sole of hind foot; may have
two smaller outer digital pads; hind foot long and narrow;
fifth toe very short; tail long and tufted
(Fig.28.1) .... **Genus *Notomys***
Hopping-mouse (p214)

3b   Six pads on sole of hind foot; fifth toe extends past base of
fourth toe *(Fig.28.2)* **4**

4a   Upperparts uniformly mid-grey; underparts white with sharp
demarcation along throat and flanks; ears short <15 mm;
one species only ....***Xeromys myoides***
Water Mouse (p205)

4b   Upper parts not uniformly grey; if hairs on belly are white
they are grey at base **5**

5a   Tail swollen at base with terminal tuft or crest of terminal hair;
convex muzzle; large bulbous eyes .... **Genus *Zyzomys***
Rock-rat (p207)

5b   Tail not obviously swollen at base.................................... **6**

6a   Tail with obvious tuft of longer hairs towards tip........................... **7**

6b   Tail without obvious tuft of long hairs................................. **8**

Fig. 27.1 (1a)

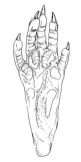

Fig. 27.2 (1b)

Fig. 28.1 (3a)

Fig. 28.2 (3b)

Fig. 29.1 (8a)

Fig. 29.2 (8b)

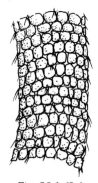

Fig. 30.1 (9a)

Fig. 30.2 (9b)

7a Tail distinctly bicoloured, brown above and white below; hind foot <46 mm; tail roughly same as head–body length; one species only .... ***Conilurus penicillatus***
Rabbit-rat (p208)

7b Hind foot >48 mm; tail clearly greater than head–body length
.... **Genus *Mesembryomys***
Tree-rat (p210)

8a Back of upper incisors with occlusal notch; tail roughly equal to head–body length *(Fig.29.1)* .... **Genus *Mus musculus***
House Mouse (p266)

8b Back of upper incisors smoothly curved *(Fig.29.2)*........................... **9**

9a Tail scales not overlapping or in distinct rings; tail naked with only minute hairs *(Fig.30.1)* **10**

9b Tail scales slightly overlapping and in clear rings; often hairy *(Fig.30.2)* **11**

10a Large rats; hind foot >35 mm; tail usually partly pinkish white often near tip.. **Genus *Uromys***
Giant White-tailed Rat (p213)

10b Hind foot <30 mm; tail brown................................... **Genus *Melomys***
Melomys (p208)

11a Hind foot <20 mm **12**

11b Hind foot >20 mm **13**

12a Hind foot broad, length roughly four times width at base of first digit; tail uniformly coloured... **13**

12b Hind foot narrow, length roughly five times width at base of first digit; tail often darker on upper side **14**

13a   Hind foot with elongate post hallucal pad; tail length variable *(Fig.31.1)*.. **Genus *Rattus***
Brown & Black Rat (p266)

13b   Hind foot with almost round post hallucal pad; tail about ¾ of head–body length; compact hunched posture; one species only *(Fig.31.2)*.................................. ***Mastacomys fuscus***
Broad-toothed Rat (p207)

Fig. 31.1 (13a)

14a   Tail clearly less than head–body length, thick with little taper; muzzle broad and blunt.. **Genus *Leggadina***
Short-tailed Mouse (p206)

14b   Tail usually less than head–body length, tapers to fine tip **15**

15a   Hind foot >40 mm; ears >27 mm .... **Genus *Leporillus***
(Greater Stick-nest Rat. Not featured. Uncommon)

15b   Hind foot <38 mm; ears <27 mm .... **Genus *Pseudomys***
Native Mouse (p216)

Fig. 31.2 (13b)

GUIDE TO QUICK REFERENCE

QUICK REFERENCE	
Average lifespan	18 years
Diet	Herbivore
Reproduction period	Sept–Feb
Number of offspring	1
Offspring maturity	2 years
Length ♂	750–820 mm
Length ♀	680–730 mm
Weight ♂	9.5–15 kg
Weight ♀	7–11 kg
Status	Vulnerable

SEE GLOSSARY p292 FOR DEFINITION

SEE GLOSSARY p292 FOR DEFINITION

QUICK REFERENCE	
Average lifespan	Unknown
Diet	Mostly fish
Reproduction period	Unknown
Number of offspring	1
Offspring maturity	Unknown
Length HT ♂	7.1 m
Length HT ♀	6.6 m
Weight	2–3 t
Status	Data Deficient

CURRENT DISTRIBUTION

TRANSLOCATION SITES

CURRENT DISTRIBUTION

Abbreviations & Symbols

♂	male
♀	female
l	litre/s
t	tonne
kg	kilogram/s
g	gram/s
mg	milligram/s
km	kilometre/s
m	metre/s
cm	centimetre/s
mm	millimetre/s
kHz	kilohertz
Hz	hertz
°C	degrees Celsius
HB	head to base of tail
T	length from base to tip of tail
HT	head to tail
CP	Conservation Park
NP	National Park
ACT	Australian Capital Territory
NT	Northern Territory
NSW	New South Wales
Qld	Queensland
SA	South Australia
Tas.	Tasmania
Vic.	Victoria
WA	Western Australia

MONOTREMES

PLATYPUS & ECHIDNA

ORDER: MONOTREMA

The order Monotremata is characterised by several features. The most amazing is that monotremes are egg-layers, a feature more often associated with birds and reptiles. Yet, like all other mammals, they are covered in hair and secrete milk, which in monotremes oozes from pores on the belly rather than from teats. The proteins responsible for milk production in the Platypus are the same in cows and humans, suggesting lactation evolved in a common mammalian ancestor that provides us with a direct, if very ancient, link to these fascinating mammals. However, that aside, how did these bizarre creatures with their conglomeration of curious traits and adaptations arise, and from where?

Egg-laying mammals have been around in some form since the Jurassic period when dinosaurs ruled the Earth, around 200 million years ago. Fossil evidence suggests monotremes originated in the land mass that became Australia and moved northwards before the final break-up of Gondwana. They have never been as diverse or numerous as marsupial and placental mammals, and there are now only five species of monotremes in the world. The Platypus is only found in Australia whereas the short and long-beaked echidnas reside in Papua New Guinea.

The word 'monotreme' means one hole and refers to the single opening, called a cloaca, where urine, faeces and eggs leave the body. This feature, along with egg-laying and the arrangement of the shoulder and collar bones, is a legacy of their reptilian ancestry. Platypus and Echidnas also lay soft, leathery-shelled eggs, a characteristic they share with reptiles, along with similar skeletal features.

Unlike other mammals, monotremes do not have whiskers or teats. Like marsupials, their considerably lower body temperature (32°C) and metabolic rate make them more energy efficient.

Platypus and Echidna numbers are considered to be reasonably secure when it comes to their conservation status, but this does not mean they are exempt from the threats posed to them by pollution, habitat degradation, vehicle accidents or introduced predators. Both species have also been historically hunted by Aborigines and European settlers but are now protected in all of Australia's states.

Opposite top: The Platypus swims with its eyes and ears closed, relying on the extremely sensitive bill to navigate and find food.
Opposite bottom: An Echidna moves about the landscape searching for ants and termites using its sensitive snout.

FACTS

- Monotremes first evolved during the Jurassic period.

- They share features with reptiles.

- There are only five species of monotremes in the world.

- All of the world's monotremes live in Australia or Papua New Guinea.

- Monotremes are the only mammals that lay eggs.

- The word monotreme means 'one hole'.

- Monotremes do not have teats; they secrete milk from an area of specialised pores on the belly.

- Platypus and echidnas lack external ears.

PLATYPUS

FAMILY: ORNITHORHYNCHIDAE

The first time European scientists saw a preserved specimen of a Platypus in 1798, they thought it was a cleverly crafted fake. The Platypus again confounded scientists when they discovered it had mammary glands but was also found to lay eggs. This improbable animal was neither a hoax nor an evolutionary link between reptiles and placental mammals.

Although the Platypus is the only living member of the Ornithorhynchidae family, recent fossil finds indicate that different species of platypuses have existed during the past 120 million years. Its unique body and aquatic lifestyle have made the present-day platypus a winner in the survival stakes.

Habitat

Found over much of the east coast of Australia, the Platypus inhabits tropical regions from as far north as Cooktown to the southern high-altitude watercourses of the Alps and Tasmanian highlands. Historically it enjoyed a wider distribution, even extending into South Australia, where it is now locally extinct.

The Platypus is aquatic and can be found in freshwater creeks, rivers, dams, lakes and streams. It prefers to live in less disturbed habitat but is also found in agricultural areas and streams with relatively poor water quality. When it is not foraging, grooming or sleeping, the Platypus rests in a burrow above the water level. The burrow has one or two dome-shaped entrances, usually concealed by tree roots.

Although solitary, several Platypuses may share overlapping ranges if necessary.

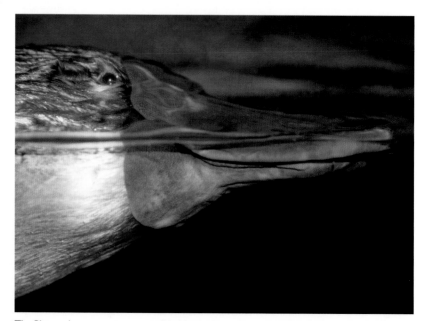

The Platypus's ear openings are well hidden in the groove behind the eyes on either side of the head. When underwater, both eyes and ears are closed.

Behaviour

The Platypus spends up to 12 hours a day in the water, mostly between dusk and dawn. Its smooth swimming style is powered by alternate strokes of the front legs and the over-sized webbing on the front feet. Its broad tail acts as a rudder and its hind feet are used to steer and brake. When walking or digging, the Platypus folds the web extensions back over the soles of its front feet and supports itself on its knuckles.

The Platypus is meticulous about grooming its fur. Its thick coat has an inner layer of fine hairs that traps air to insulate the body. The outer layer of long, flat hairs that streamlines the body and repels water moults continually. Grooming keeps the coat in good condition.

FACTS

- A Platypus egg is 17 mm long and has a sticky coating.

- A Platypus hatchling is about 15 mm long.

- Females supplying milk to larger nestlings can consume their body weight in food each day.

- Adult males become more aggressive and their venom glands enlarge during the mating season.

Above: Female Platypuses excavate complex breeding burrows into the banks of streams, with the chamber above the water level. **Below:** A Platypus egg, although tiny, contains a partially developed embryo inside it when it is laid.

The Platypus typically avoids confrontation. However, if challenged, the male Platypus is able to retaliate using a remarkable structure that is unique among mammals. Like the male echidna, it has a spur on its hind legs, but the Platypus's spur is more interesting for being venomous. No other living mammal has this venomous spur structure. The venom is produced in a gland in the Platypus's upper leg. The spur's function is thought to assist in male–male interaction when gaining access to mates.

During the breeding season, pairs engage in an elaborate aquatic courtship that lasts several days. After mating takes place in the water, the male resumes his solitary habits while the female digs a complex burrow, up to 30 metres long, about half a metre above the water's surface. The snug egg chamber is lined with damp vegetation and the tunnel is sealed with plugs of mud ready to block off floodwater and predators.

She lays one to three eggs and curls up to incubate them between her tail and belly. The eggs hatch in about 10–12 days. The mother warms and suckles her young for the first few days. When she leaves the nest to hunt, she bundles the babies into a protective cocoon of vegetation. The young are two-thirds adult size by the time they are weaned and independent at around four months.

A SIXTH SENSE

- A Platypus's rubbery bill is covered with thousands of tiny pores. Some pores have nerves that are sensitive to touch; others detect electrical fields generated by moving prey. This kind of sensory information may give them an image of their underwater hunting grounds.

Diet

When it dives to hunt underwater, the Platypus closes its eyes, ears and nostrils. It detects prey by waving its sensitive bill from side to side approximately two or three times a second. Worms, shrimps, insect larvae and other small animals are collected from the bottom or snapped up in passing and stored in cheek pouches. The Platypus then returns to the surface where it floats, spread-eagled, as it grinds up its food between the horny ridges that replace the early teeth in adults. Alternatively, they may return to their burrow to grind their food. A voracious feeder, a platypus can consume between 13–28% of its body weight in food in a single evening.

LOCATION TIPS

- Eungella NP, Qld
- Upper Murray River, Vic
- Bombala River, NSW
- Lake Dobson, Mt Field NP, Tas.

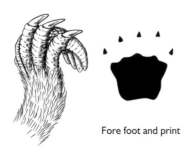

Finding Platypus

To find a platypus in the wild, you must be very still because it is an extremely shy animal. Active mainly around dawn and dusk, it is very quiet and spends a lot of time under water. When it surfaces, only the top of the bill, back and tail are visible.

Dawn and dusk or overcast winter days are the best times to look for a Platypus. Find a spot on a high bank overlooking a freshwater creek, lake or dam as the Platypus prefers to make its burrows about 50 centimetres to a metre above the water line, beneath overhanging banks that create a purchase in the river bank for burrowing. Scan the surface, preferably with binoculars, for its distinctive V-shaped wake or a series of circular ripples, which indicate one has just dived out of view.

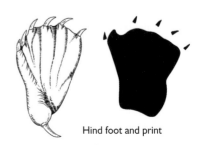

Fore foot and print   Hind foot and print

PLATYPUS *Ornithorhynchus anatinus*

QUICK REFERENCE	
Average lifespan	8–12 years
Diet	Carnivore
Reproduction period	Aug–Oct
Number of offspring	1–3
Offspring maturity	2 years
Length HT ♂	400–630 mm
Length HT ♀	370–550 mm
Weight ♂	0.8–3 kg
Weight ♀	0.6–1.8 kg
Status	Near Threatened

The world's only species of Platypus is found in eastern Australia from Cooktown to Tasmania and along the Murray River system through Victoria to the South Australian border.

Habitat: East coast tropical rainforest to alpine heath with permanent, freshwater lakes, dams, creeks or rivers. **Behaviour:** Amphibious, solitary, mostly nocturnal. **Diet:** Predominantly freshwater invertebrates, and occasionally small fish and frogs. **Breeding:** August through October depending on latitude; females can be mature at 2 years. **Features:** Thick, soft fur is waterproof, dark brown on top, cream belly sometimes tinged red. Rubbery, charcoal grey bill has two obvious nostrils. Broad, flat tail. Ears have no external extensions. Webbed feet have 5 toes with long claws. Male has a sharp spur on hind leg ankles capable of injecting venom. **Threats:** Habitat destruction, pollution, injuries from rubbish and fish and yabby traps.

ECHIDNA

FAMILY: TACHYGLOSSIDAE

It is impossible to confuse the unique Short-beaked Echidna with any other Australian mammal. It is however, sometimes mistaken for a hedgehog or porcupine. Its most obvious features are the sharp spines that protrude from its brownish coat. Small, beady eyes face forward above its pronounced, elongated snout.

Scientists remain unsure whether the Short-beaked Echidna has colour vision, although there are a small amount of cone receptors in the retina, as well as rod types. The Echidna does have external ear openings (pinnae) but in most these are hard to distinguish through the thick spines. Tasmanian individuals, however, often have visible ear openings.

Echidnas were a food source for Aborigines and their spines were used to make jewellery and other decorations.

Habitat

The Short-beaked Echidna is one of the few native mammals to live in all parts of Australia. It seems equally at home in habitats ranging from tropical rainforests to arid grasslands.

The Echidna has a home range, but makes no claim to a permanent den. Home ranges vary from as little as nine hectares (on Kangaroo Island, South Australia) to as many as 93 hectares or more (in southern Queensland) and may overlap in hot regions where there is a high density of Echidnas.

Echidnas camouflage well in grass or leaf litter and are hard to spot. Rotting tree stumps and hollow logs make suitable retreats and provide the added benefit of plenty of ants or termites. They may also occupy abandoned rabbit warrens or wombat burrows.

Although termites are 77% water, Echidnas still need to drink.

Behaviour

Echidnas are not fighters and rely on their spines and evasive action to escape inexperienced or desperate predators. An Echidna's initial reaction is to freeze and hunch its shoulders to raise its spines. On hard ground it may simply roll up into a spiky ball or it can wedge itself into a crevice or hollow log by raising its spines and spreading its limbs. On soft ground, the Echidna seems to sink below the surface as it digs furiously in a horizontal position. An Echidna cannot throw its spines, but it does shed them once a year.

The Short-beaked Echidna spends a considerable amount of time grooming its unusual hair. The Echidna's spines are simply a modified type of keratin, the protein that makes up all mammal hair, but between the needle-like protrusions is softer fur that ranges in colour depending on distribution. To groom between the spines, the echidna employs the use of another modification — the elongated curved claw on the second 'toe' of the hind foot. By raking this claw through the fur, the Echidna can rid itself of tangles, burrs and parasites. The Echidna's flexibility and the structure of its hind legs (which, although they face backwards, can be rotated around to face the front) allow it to scratch even the most difficult to reach places between the spines, such as behind the head.

FACTS
• A female has only one functional ovary.
• A young Echidna consumes about 20% of its body weight in milk at each feed.
• Echidna milk is pink because it contains a large amount of iron-laden haemoglobin.
• A baby Echidna weighs 0.5 g at birth.
• The record lifespan of a captive Echidna is 49 years.

During the winter breeding season a female may find herself being trailed for several days by up to 11 males. She selects the most persistent male, which digs a shallow trench under her to avoid being spiked while mating. About two weeks after mating, the female lays a single, 15 millimetre-long, leathery-shelled egg that is incubated in a temporary pouch on her belly for about 10 days at 32°C. Certain females prepare a nesting burrow about one metre long during the incubation period; others shelter in dense clumps of vegetation.

Above left: Extraordinary musculature allows the echidna to contort itself into a ball to protect its vulnerable underside, snout and limbs. **Above right:** 'Trains' made up of up to 11 males may follow a single female during breeding periods.

After hatching, the baby remains in the pouch until it is covered with short spines. It is then left in a nursery burrow, often found at the base of a termite mound or between tree roots. The mother returns to suckle the baby every one to two days. The young is thought to begin exploring the outside world after three months, but is seldom seen until it is about a year old. During this time it is vulnerable to predators, such as Dingos and goannas.

Diet

While its habitat requirements are minimal, the Echidna is a specialist when it comes to food. It feeds exclusively on ants and termites. With more than 1,300 ant species and nearly 350 termite species living in Australia, it has plenty of choice.

The Echidna is a very vigorous forager that snuffles about and pokes its nose into the ground, logs and mounds as it ignores the bubbling mucous that sometimes seeps from its snout.

An Echidna tracks prey by scent and by using sensors in the tip of its snout to detect electrical impulses in the moving muscles of its prey. It opens up termite and ant nests or underground trails with its claws and snout then inserts its long, sticky tongue to collect its meal. The insects are crushed between horny plates on the back of the tongue and roof of the mouth.

Sometimes, an Echidna will lie on an ant track with its tongue out to trap unsuspecting prey. As it feeds, the Echidna consumes a lot of soil and nesting materials, which pass through its body, forming a large part of distinctive cylindrical droppings.

QUEENSLAND MUSEUM

Top and above left: The Echidna's long, sticky tongue can be up to 18 cm long and is rapidly flicked out over termite mounds to lap up the insects. **Above right:** A Short-beaked Echidna generally hunts for ants and termites at dawn or dusk, seeking out its prey with its highly sensitive snout.

Finding Echidnas

The Echidna avoids temperature extremes and is most active at dawn and dusk, although in southern states it may be found foraging in the middle of the day. It can be very difficult to see when it is inactive, hiding in grass tussocks or beneath leaf litter.

Signs to look for include conical holes in breached ant nests, mating trenches, shed spines and smooth, cylindrical scats usually containing parts of insects they have eaten. Tracks showing the distinctive hind foot of the Short-beaked Echidna, with its long grooming claws, are also a good indicator of an Echidna's whereabouts.

LOCATION TIPS

▶ Found all over Australia in forests and woodlands, heath, grasslands and arid environments where suitable food and shelter are available.

Fore foot and print

Hind foot and print

SHORT-BEAKED ECHIDNA *Tachyglossus aculeatus*

The Echidna may not be as intelligent as its competitors and predators, but a specialised diet and a repertoire of escape strategies even the odds when it comes to survival.

Habitat: Any habitat with suitable food and shelter. **Behaviour:** Terrestrial, solitary, active day or night depending on temperature. **Diet:** Ants, termites. **Breeding:** July and August. **Features:** Light to dark brown fur. Dark-tipped cream spines on back and sides. Long, tubular snout. Front foot has 5 toes with broad claws. Long claws on 2nd and 3rd toes of hind foot. Walks with a distinctive waddle. Male has ankle spurs. Female has temporary pouch. **Threats:** Vehicle strike, habitat destruction.

QUICK REFERENCE	
Average lifespan	Up to 50 years
Diet	Insectivore
Reproduction period	Jul–Aug
Number of offspring	1
Offspring maturity	5–12 years
Length	300–450 mm
Weight	2–7 kg
Status	Least Concern

Once covered in spines, the Echidna puggle is left in a burrow and suckled sporadically every 5–10 days until old enough to fend for itself.

MARSUPIALS

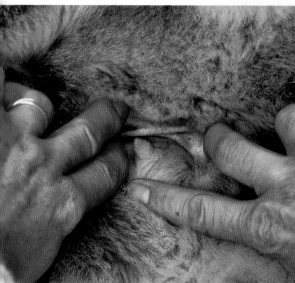

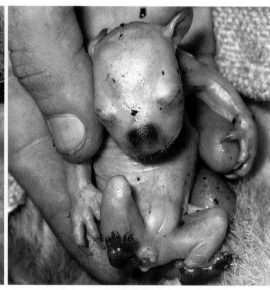

Above left: The Koala's pouch faces backwards, towards the animal's cloaca.
Above right: A koala joey before starting to grow hair.
Opposite: Eastern Grey kangaroo and joey.

Marsupials are the most successful and diverse group of native mammals in Australia. There are about 140 species, and at least one of these amazing animals can be found in almost every part of the continent. Their ecological roles range from predatory carnivore to grazing herbivore, just as those of placental mammals do in other countries.

The way marsupials reproduce sets them apart from other mammals. They are not monotremes because they do not lay eggs and they are not placental mammals because their newborn is only partially developed.

Unlike placentals, marsupials are born in an embryonic state after a brief period of gestation and continue development attached to a teat on the mother's belly, usually within the protection of a pouch.

Marsupial reproduction is just as successful as the placental method and, even though bandicoots and the Koalas have a placenta, their newborns are no more advanced than those of other marsupials. While the group gets its name from the word 'marsupium', meaning pouch, not all female marsupials have one.

Marsupials were the only mammals, other than primates, to develop opposable digits. These have been retained by tree-climbing species but reduced or lost in the ground dwellers. Many terrestrial marsupials, however, have a unique hind foot structure with an extra long fourth toe and fused grooming toes. Like monotremes, marsupials have a slower metabolism and smaller brain than placental mammals.

CARNIVOROUS MARSUPIALS

ORDER: DASYUROMORPHIA

FACTS

- Carnivorous marsupials are little known and many species can be confused with rodents.

- Dasyurids have sharp incisors as compared to the wedge-shaped teeth of rats and mice.

- Dasyurids can be terrestrial (ground-dwelling), arboreal (tree-dwelling) or both.

- The earliest fossilised member of the Dasyuridae family dates from the Miocene Epoch (23-5.3 million years ago).

- Aboriginal people revered the larger carnivorous marsupials, but it is likely that the smaller species were a food source, particularly in arid areas.

- Carnivorous marsupials range from a tiny 2.6 grams to a hefty 35 kilograms.

There are 56 living species of carnivorous marsupials belonging to the order **Dasyuromorphia**. While they vary in size and appearance, they all have squat, triangular heads, and with the exception of the Kultarr, their front and hind legs are about equal in length.

Living members of this group are divided into two families. The **Dasyuridae** family includes the Tasmanian Devil, four quolls and 50 smaller species. The Numbat is the sole member of the **Myrmecobiidae** family and, from an evolutionary perspective, is the least similar to those in the other families. Unlike its dasyurid relatives, this termite eater is active during the day and has small, peg-like teeth.

Most marsupials in this order are endemic to Australia and the continent's offshore islands, although radiation was aided by a land bridge that once connected Australia to New Guinea, most recently during the Pleistocene (two million to 10,000 years ago). As such, two species (*Sminthopsis archeri* and *S. virginiae*) are also distributed in New Guinea and recent studies suggest that the New Guinean Bronze Quoll (*Dasyurus spartacus*) could be a subspecies of the Western Quoll (*D. geoffroii*), which inhabits mainland Australia.

Right: The Numbat is the least like others within its order and has no similar living relatives, appearing to be a sister clade of the Dasyuridae.

Certain species exist only in Tasmania, but fossil evidence indicates that they were once present on the mainland. Ongoing evolutionary isolation has since led to changes in Tasmanian savanna and woodland species, making them differ slightly from their mainland counterparts, as evidenced by genetic studies.

Captain Cook made the first European record of a dasyurid when he reported weasel or polecat footprints around Botany Bay, thought now to be the tracks of a quoll. When he reached the Endeavour River in Queensland and actually saw a quoll, it was again referred to as 'resembling a polecat'. Many explorers, naturalists and settlers commented on the dasyuroids' superficial resemblance to placental mammals, such as rats, cats, shrews, wolves or weasels. In *The Voyage of Governor Phillip to Botany Bay* (1789), an illustration of an Eastern Quoll (*Dasyurus viverrinus*) was labelled the Spotted Opossum (on account of its pouch), while the Spotted-tailed Quoll (*Dasyurus maculatus*) was called the Spotted Martin.

Significant evolutionary distinctions between the Dasyuromorphia and other marsupial orders indicate that these pugnacious, voracious little 'pouched predators' are among the most primitive and ancient 'modern' marsupials to inhabit the Australian continent. Dasyuroids, despite a few charismatic 'mascots', are little-known carnivorous and insectivorous marsupials that vary in size from the now extinct Tasmanian Tiger, which weighed about 35 kilos, to the dog-sized Tasmanian Devil, cat-sized quolls and finally the ferocious tiny mouse-sized Long-tailed Planigale capable of attacking prey as large, if not larger, than itself.

- The Tasmanian Devil is the best known dasyurid and was made famous by a deranged Looney Tunes cartoon character.

- Dasyuroid digestion is very fast, taking just several hours (much faster than in marsupial herbivores).

- Several dasyurid species can reduce their body temperature for hours at a time to conserve energy during periods of cold or food shortage.

- Dasyurids make several vocalisations, including squeaks, barks, hisses, growls and screeches. They also use body language and scent to communicate.

- In most species the tail is shorter than the body and can be used to store fat reserves.

- At least eight dasyurid species are known to play, which helps develop survival and social skills.

- The lifespan of a carnivorous marsupial is brief, especially when compared to placental mammals of similar size; some males live less than one year.

An impressive set of teeth set Dasyurids apart from other Australian mammals — the primarily herbivorous marsupials — Koalas, kangaroos, wallabies, wombats, possums and gliders, which only have two pairs of lower incisors. Dasyurids have four pairs of pointy upper incisors, three lower pair, well-developed upper and lower canines, and a variety of razor-sharp upper and lower molars. These tools allow them to attack and consume their prey quickly and efficiently to satisfy their formidable appetite for food which is only surpassed by their sexual appetite.

Useful Role

The first Europeans saw the larger dasyurids, particularly the quolls, as a great pest and a threat to their poultry and rabbits and bounties were placed on their heads. When dasyurid numbers started to decrease, cat, rat, and rabbit numbers began to rise to significant and damaging proportions. Those numbers are still high and the introduction of foxes, dogs, toads, cattle and sheep continue to contribute to the demise of many dasyurids.

TASMANIAN TIGER

At least six species of Thylacine-like animals roamed Australia about 10,000 years ago. The last known Thylacine, a close relative of the dasyurids, was captured in 1933 and died at Hobart Zoo on the 7th September in 1936. National Threatened Species Day is held in Australia on this date each year, commemorating the extinction of the species.

Unable to compete with the Dingo, the Thylacine had disappeared from the mainland about 2,000 years earlier. European settlers in Tasmania labelled it a sheep killer and hunting for bounty contributed to its extinction.

Early naturalist John Gould produced this illustration of a pair of Thylacines in about 1850–1851.

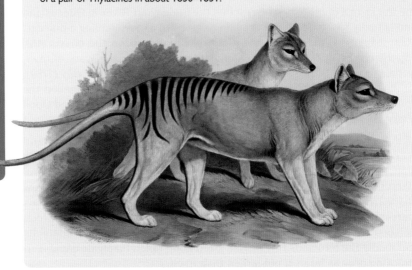

Opposite: The Spotted-tailed Quoll is the largest carnivorous marsupial on the mainland.

QUOLLS

SUPERFAMILY: DASYUROIDEA
FAMILY: DASYURIDAE

The elegantly furred quoll brings a certain panache to the art of predation. This nocturnal predator strikes with lightning speed, delivering a killer bite to the back of its prey's neck or head. It fastidiously cleans its paws and snout after eating and sometimes leaves the skin of its prey neatly everted (inside out).

Quolls are great opportunists. They make the most of food sources on and above the ground. Their varied diet includes fruit, insects, reptiles, birds, rodents and even other marsupial carnivores. They also scavenge and males will challenge females for their catches.

Quolls are efficient nocturnal hunters with keen senses and the dasyurid's characteristic mouthful of teeth: three pairs of lower incisors and four upper pairs are used for tearing, two pairs of canines for stabbing, while blade-like premolars and ridged molars handle the shearing and grinding.

They are not capable of shearing through bone to the same extent as the larger Tasmanian Devil. Instead, quolls tear flesh off a carcass and leave a 'midden' of stripped, polished bones when finished.

FACTS

- Quolls use one or more dens within their home range. These are found in hollow logs, rock crevices and burrows.

- Toxoplasmosis, a disease caused by a cat parasite, may have decimated quoll populations in the late 1800s.

- When threatened, the Western Quoll makes a noise that sounds like its Aboriginal name, *Chuditch*.

- Quolls living in overlapping home ranges may leave their droppings at a shared 'latrine' site.

- The Northern Quoll sometimes shelters in termite mounds.

- A male Spotted-tailed Quoll will defend the nursery den and feed his mate while she cares for their offspring.

- A female Eastern Quoll can give birth to as many as 30 babies, but has only 6 nipples.

- The male Northern Quoll lives for 1 or 2 years. The Spotted-tailed Quoll lives for up to 5 years.

- Captain James Cook's 1770 expedition in the *Endeavour* collected quolls and recorded this word as their Aboriginal name.

IAN MORRIS

Spotted-tailed Quolls hunt by day on occasion to take advantage of nocturnal possums asleep in tree hollows.

IAN MORRIS

Top: A mother Eastern Quoll nurses her litter of four on a bed of grass in captivity. **Above:** As soon as quolls are born, they crawl like small pink slugs from the mother's cloaca to the pouch.

Breeding

The Eastern Quoll is no bigger than a grain of rice at birth, which occurs after just two to three weeks in the womb. By the time it leaves the pouch about 10 weeks later, it has barely opened its eyes and its 20 gram body has a scant covering of fur. It continues to grow in the safety of a nursery den and, when big enough, will cling to the mother's back as she hunts. A mother will retrieve a youngster that slips off if she hears its cries.

At about five months, the young are weaned and take up their independence with little or no parental assistance. This new generation of quolls may breed a year after their birth. The stress of their predatory lifestyle and marathon mating sessions means most will breed for one or two years only.

39

Distribution

Australia's four quoll species were common and widespread at the time of European settlement. Loss of habitat, viruses, parasites, predation by Red Foxes, dogs and feral cats, as well as competition from other introduced animals, have diminished their chances of survival.

The Eastern Quoll was widely distributed from south-east South Australia, throughout Victoria and Tasmania to eastern New South Wales until the late 19th century.

The Western Quoll now occupies only about 5% of its former range, which included all mainland states. It is now considered extinct in the wild on the mainland, although captive-bred individuals have been released in fauna parks and reserves. Eastern and Spotted-tail Quolls are still common in Tasmania, but face an uncertain future should Red Foxes become established on the island.

On the mainland, some populations of Spotted-tail and Northern Quolls are being devastated by the invasion of Cane Toads into their habitat. Quolls that prey on these poisonous toads do not live to hunt again.

Above: Northern Quoll tracks on a sandy beach.
Right: Hollow logs, caves and tree roots make excellent den sites for quolls.

Finding Quolls

Quolls are active at night, but look for basking quolls on winter days. Check for tracks beside creeks and at the base of trees, rocks and termite mounds. Look for latrine sites with long or twisted cylindrical scats containing fur, feathers, bone or insect skeletons.

LOCATION TIPS

▶ Cradle Mountain–
   Lake St Clair NP, Tas.

▶ Kakadu NP, NT

▶ The Hills Forest, WA

Fore foot and print of a Spotted-tailed Quoll

Hind foot and print of a Spotted-tailed Quoll

WESTERN QUOLL *Dasyurus geoffroii*

The Western Quoll, or Chuditch, once claimed Australia's arid and semi-arid regions as its domain. It is now restricted to south-western WA and the total population estimated to be under 6,000.

Habitat: Eucalypt forest and woodland, mallee shrubland. **Behaviour:** Mostly terrestrial, nocturnal. **Diet:** Insects, reptiles, birds, small mammals. **Breeding:** May to early July, mature by 1 year. **Features:** Sturdy body, brown with white spots above and creamy-white below. Sparsely furred tail with dark feathery tip and no spots. Hind foot has 5 toes and grained sole. Female has pouch and 6 teats. **Threats:** vehicle strike, illegal shooting, predation.

M & I MORCOMBE

QUICK REFERENCE	
Average lifespan	3 years
Diet	Carnivore
Reproduction period	May–Jul
Number of offspring	Up to 6
Offspring maturity	1 year
Length HB ♂	310–400 mm
Length T	250–350 mm
Length HB ♀	260–360 mm
Length T	210–310 mm
Weight ♂	710–2185 g
Weight ♀	615–1130 g
Status	Vulnerable

NORTHERN QUOLL *Dasyurus hallucatus*

QUICK REFERENCE	
Average lifespan	1–3 years
Diet	Omnivore
Reproduction period	Late June
Number of offspring	7
Offspring maturity	11 months
Length HB ♂	270–370 mm
Length T	222–345 mm
Length HB ♀	249–310 mm
Length T	202–300 mm
Weight ♂	340–1120 g
Weight ♀	240–690 g
Status	Endangered

This is the smallest and most aggressive of the four quoll species. It occurs in most habitats across northern Australia, but its populations have been drastically reduced, in part because of the spread of Cane Toads. As with many of the small dasyurids, most of the males die after their first breeding season.

Habitat: Rock outcrops in open eucalypt forest and grassy woodland, human dwellings. **Behaviour:** Mostly arboreal, nocturnal. **Diet:** Invertebrates, reptiles, small mammals, fruit. **Breeding:** Late June, mature by 1 year. **Features:** Grey-brown to brown with large white spots, cream to white below. Pointed snout, large eyes and large pointed ears. Hind foot has ridged pads and 5 toes. Female has 6–8 teats and develops temporary skinfolds. **Threats:** Poisoning by cane toads, predation, vehicle strike.

SPOTTED-TAILED QUOLL *Dasyurus maculatus*

QUICK REFERENCE	
Average lifespan	5 years
Diet	Carnivore
Reproduction period	May–Aug
Number of offspring	5
Offspring maturity	1 year
Length HB ♂	380–759 mm
Length T	370–550 mm
Length HB ♀	350–450 mm
Length T	340–420 mm
Weight ♂	1.5–5 kg
Weight ♀	0.9–2.5 kg
Status	Endangered

This agile climber spends most of its time on the ground where it dens in caves, rock crevices and hollow logs. It is the largest carnivorous marsupial on the mainland.

Habitat: Rainforest, eucalypt forest and woodland, coastal heath. **Behaviour:** Partly arboreal, nocturnal but may bask or hunt during day. **Diet:** Insects, birds, medium-sized mammals, carrion. **Breeding:** Late May to early August, mature by 1 year. **Features:** Stocky body. Chocolate brown fur with irregular white spots on body and long tail; cream to yellow below. Short face with pointed snout. Hind feet have ridged soles and a clawless opposable first toe for climbing. Female has 6 teats arranged in 2 rows, temporary pouch. **Threats:** Habitat destruction and fragmentation, poisoning by Cane Toads, competition from introduced predators, human persecution.

EASTERN QUOLL *Dasyurus viverrinus*

QUICK REFERENCE	
Average lifespan	Up to 5 years
Diet	Omnivore
Reproduction period	May–Jun
Number of offspring	6
Offspring maturity	1 year
Length HB ♂	320–450 mm
Length T	200–280 mm
Length HB ♀	280–400 mm
Length T	170–240 mm
Weight ♂	900–1900 g
Weight ♀	700–1100 g
Status	Endangered

Once widespread in south-east mainland Australia, there have been no recorded mainland sightings of this swift and graceful predator since 1963. The species is still common in Tasmania. While the female hunts near her dens, the male will travel up to one kilometre in search of prey.

Habitat: Eucalypt forest, scrub, heath, farmland. **Behaviour:** Mostly terrestrial, solitary, nocturnal. **Diet:** Insects, ground-nesting birds, small mammals, carrion, grass, fruit. **Breeding:** May to June, mature at 11 months. **Features:** Thick, soft fur with irregular white spots on back and sides. Can be black with brown belly or fawn with white belly. Tail has no spots. Four toes on hind foot. Large rounded ears. Female has 6 teats, develops temporary skinfolds. **Threats:** Vehicle strike, predation by cats and foxes.

TASMANIAN DEVIL

SUPERFAMILY: DASYUROIDEA
FAMILY: DASYURIDAE

The genus names of this species, Sarcophilus, literally means 'flesh-lover' in Greek — an apt name for this charismatic, carrion-devouring carnivore. This famous fighter with the bad reptutation is found only in Tasmania, but is far less 'devilish' than many reports suggest. In the early days of European settlement it was persecuted relentlessly until granted protection in 1941.

FACTS

- The Tasmanian Devil lives up to 8 years in captivity.

- The Tasmanian Devil once lived throughout Australia and is thought to have become extinct on the mainland around 400 years ago.

- Devil Facial Tumour Disease (a form of cancer) has wiped out more than two-thirds of the total Devil population since 1995.

- The Tasmanian Devil was hunted almost to extinction. It was not protected until June 1941.

- A Tasmanian Devil's ears turn deep red when it is agitated.

- A Devil's bounding run gives it a top speed of about 13 km/h.

Tasmanian Devil foraging.

Angry Tasmanian Devils have red ears due to increased blood flow.

A Devil's Playground

Just over 400 years ago, the Tasmanian Devil joined the Thylacine, or Tasmanian Tiger, as an exile in Tasmania. Subsequent European settlement of the island not only provided the Devil with new food sources and habitats, but also elevated it to the role of top native carnivore by contributing to the extinction of the Thylacine.

The Devil is now widespread but its future is not guaranteed. Predation and competition from introduced animals, extermination by people who regard it as a pest species, and also disease may see the Tasmanian Devil follow the Thylacine's path to extinction.

The Tasmanian Devil's home range is 10–20 hectares. Although territories overlap, it lives and hunts alone. The Devil follows well-worn trails through the bush as it searches for food between dusk and dawn. It can travel up to 16 kilometres in a night when food is scarce.

During the day it retreats to dens in dense bush, hollow logs, caves or often, a deserted wombat burrow. The Devil is not territorial, except near a breeding den.

Young Tasmanian Devils are notoriously boisterous, wrestling, biting and play fighting for hours at a time.

Breeding

A female Tasmanian Devil begins breeding at two years of age. She bears two young in her first season and then three or four annually for the next three years. Like most Dasyurids, she produces more babies than her four nipples can accommodate.

The Tasmanian Devil mates in March and the young are born three weeks later. They remain in their mother's backward-facing pouch for 15 weeks and then are left in a den. By October the cubs are weaned and have begun following their mother, sometimes catching a lift on her back.

Young Tasmanian Devils indulge in noisy, boisterous play. They wrestle and tumble with each other, snapping and gaping their jaws in imitation of adults guarding food. They also are very agile and can scramble up sloping branches in search of roosting birds.

Meal times are beset by squabbling, squalling and blood-curdling screaming, and operate under a strict hierarchy.

Diet

With its blood-curdling scream and bone-crushing jaws, the Tasmanian Devil looks and sounds like a ferocious predator. But while Australia's largest and most famous marsupial carnivore will prey on animals as big as wallabies and wombats, this expert scavenger would rather feed on carrion or steal prey from its smaller relatives, the quolls.

When more than one Devil scents out the same carcass, they champ, growl and shriek at one another. Once the ritualised squabbling is out of the way, they settle down to a shared meal.

A Devil's powerful jaws and sharp teeth make short work of large mammal carcasses. A thick wombat skull may defeat it, but it will hold a kangaroo leg bone in its paws and chomp away as if eating a carrot. The only evidence of its nocturnal feasts is usually some fur and the intestines, which it delicately removes from the stomach cavity.

Fore foot and print

Hind foot and print

LOCATION TIPS

- ▶ Cradle Mountain–Lake St Clair NP
- ▶ Freycinet NP
- ▶ Mt William

Finding Devils

During the day look for foraging trails, burrow entrances, tracks and droppings. The broken or twisted cylindrical scats are grey, smelly and contain bone fragments and fur. The Devil's awkward gait leaves a distinctive one-two-one pattern of squarish paw prints. At night, listen for calls or wait quietly near fresh road-kill.

TASMANIAN DEVIL *Sarcophilus harrisii*

QUICK REFERENCE	
Average lifespan	6 years
Diet	Carnivore
Reproduction period Number of offspring Offspring maturity	March 2 2 years
Length HB ♂ Length T	652 mm 258 mm
Length HB ♀ Length T	570 mm 244 mm
Weight ♂	8–14 kg
Weight ♀	5–9 kg
Status	Endangered

Australia's largest living carnivorous marsupial lives only in Tasmania. Once widespread on the mainland, the arrival and spread of the Dingo and climate change may have contributed to its extinction there.

Habitat: All habitats — eucalypt forest, woodlands, heath and farmland.
Behaviour: Terrestrial, nocturnal. **Diet:** Insects, mammals up to wombat size, carrion.
Breeding: March, females mature at 2 years. **Lifespan:** About 6 years. **Features:** Compact, muscular body with short, broad head and small eyes. Black with white streak across chest, sometimes white patch on rump. Sparsely furred snout and ears. 5 toes on front foot; 4 toes on long hind foot. Male larger with broader head and thicker neck. Female has 4 teats and a pouch. **Threats:** Disease, persecution, car strike. **Status:** Endangered.

Above: Young Tasmanian Devils spend much of their time sleeping, when not wrestling with siblings.
Opposite: This Tasmanian Devil displays its powerful jaws and sharp teeth.

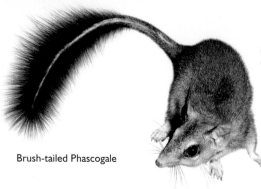

Brush-tailed Phascogale

SMALL DASYURIDS

SUPERFAMILY: DASYUROIDEA
FAMILY: DASYURIDAE

Within Australia's forests, woodlands and deserts live 50 species of flesh-eating marsupials renowned for their ferocity and voracious appetites. They hunt under cover of darkness, relying on speed and agility to pursue and kill prey. These small, secretive members of the Dasyuridae family weigh between 2.6 and 300 grams. Their size belies their aggressive nature and these feisty, pocket-sized predators often take on prey larger than themselves. When threatened, they respond with bared teeth, hisses, growls and shrieks.

Strong legs and long hind feet with ridged soles give these predators the power and traction they need when running or climbing. Tree-dwelling species also have a thumb-like inner toe on each hind foot for extra grip.

FACTS

- Very small dasyurid females ovulate only once a year because they don't have the energy required to ovulate more often.

- The Brown Antechinus male dies at the end of its 2-week mating season.

- The female Fawn Antechinus may give birth to 16 young but has only 10 nipples.

- The female Sandstone Pseudantechinus has no pouch.

- The tiny Long-tailed Planigale, weighing as little as 2.6 g, is the world's smallest marsupial and second smallest mammal.

- A newborn Kowari is 3 mm long.

- Fat-tailed Dunnarts huddle together in nests to keep warm in winter.

- The Mulgara gets all the water it needs from the spiders, insects and rodents it eats.

- The bristles on the Hairy-footed Dunnart's feet give traction on sand.

The fat stored in the Fat-tailed Dunnart's tail is a source of energy for leaner times.

Arid Land Hunters

Desert-dwelling marsupial carnivores have many features and strategies for staying alive in difficult conditions. They are most active at night and avoid the heat of the day by sheltering in burrows, rock crevices and cracks in the ground. They can slow down their metabolism to save energy when temperatures are extreme. Some produce concentrated urine to reduce water loss.

When food is scarce, they can call on stored body fats and delay breeding. Their ability to produce and raise young quickly during brief wet spells gives them an advantage over competitors.

Breeding

Small marsupial carnivores are prolific breeders. The females give birth to more young than their nipples can accommodate and some produce more than one litter per season. Such fecundity has its price and few live more than two to three years.

A female Brush-tailed Phascogale uses a tree hollow with a small entrance as a nursery.

The males of several antechinus and phascogale species do not survive beyond their first breeding season. They use enormous amounts of energy pursuing females, fighting other males and engaging in mating sessions that last up to 12 hours. Their frenetic sexual behaviour causes their immune systems to break down and they die before their offspring are born.

It is first in, first served when a mother has more babies than nipples. The blind and furless newborns that succeed in finding a nipple remain attached for about five weeks. Those not protected by a pouch risk being dislodged as the mother forages for enough food to keep up her milk supply.

When they are too big to be dragged beneath her belly, the young are left in a nest or cling to their mother's back. They are weaned within three to five months and most are sexually mature by 10 months.

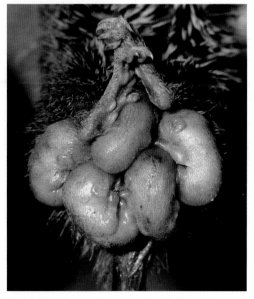

Tiny, hairless young cluster on a female dasyurid's teats.

BRUSH-TAILED MULGARA *Dasycercus blythi*

QUICK REFERENCE	
Average lifespan	6 years
Diet	Carnivore
Reproduction period Number of offspring Offspring maturity	May–Jun 6 11 months
Length HB ♂ Length T	135–165 mm 75–100 mm
Length HB ♀ Length T	120–140 mm 60–90 mm
Weight ♂	75–110 g
Weight ♀	60–90 g
Status	Vulnerable

Although originally described in 1904, the Brush-tailed Mulgara was later considered to be a subspecies of *Dasycercus cristicauda*, the Crest-tailed Mulgara. Taxonomically, it remained so for four decades, ignoring obvious differences in tail shape until reclassified in 2000.

Habitat: Spinifex grassland; burrows in sand dunes. **Behaviour:** Terrestrial, solitary, mostly nocturnal. **Diet:** Insects, spiders and small vertebrates. **Breeding:** Mid-May to mid-June; mature at 10 months. **Features:** Five toes on front and hind feet; short, swollen tail covered in bristly black hairs along most of length; fur sandy, grey–brown with rusty colouring at tail base. **Threats:** Feral cats, foxes, habitat destruction, altered fire regimes.

CREST-TAILED MULGARA *Dasycercus cristicauda*

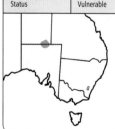

QUICK REFERENCE	
Average lifespan	7 years
Diet	Carnivore
Reproduction period Number of offspring Offspring maturity	May–Oct Up to 8 10 months
Length HB ♂ Length T	130–230 mm 80–125 mm
Length HB ♀ Length T	120–170 mm 80–110 mm
Weight ♂	110–185 g
Weight ♀	65–120 g
Status	Vulnerable

IAN MORRIS

Crest-tailed Mulgaras are fast efficient hunters that move with a bounding gait. They dig burrows with tunnels, shafts and pop-up holes in and between sand dunes. The Mulgara produces a small amount of highly concentrated urine, allowing it to survive on water obtained from its prey.

Habitat: Inland sandy deserts. **Behaviour:** Terrestrial, solitary, mostly nocturnal. **Diet:** Insects, spiders, scorpions, small vertebrates. **Breeding:** Mid-May to October. Mature at 10–11 months. **Features:** Fine, soft fur is light sandy brown above, creamy white below. Tail has reddish base and black crest. Rounded ears are sparsely furred. Front and hind feet have 5 toes. Female has pouch and 8 teats. **Threats:** Predation by introduced predators.

KOWARI *Dasyuroides byrnei*

QUICK REFERENCE

Average lifespan	1–2 years
Diet	Carnivore
Reproduction period	May–Dec
Number of offspring	6
Offspring maturity	9 months
Length HB ♂	140–180 mm
Length T	110–160 mm
Length HB ♀	135–160 mm
Length T	110–160 mm
Weight ♂	85–175 g
Weight ♀	70–140 g
Status	Vulnerable

These solitary hunters use urine and scent glands on their chests to mark their burrows and home ranges. They chatter and hiss at interlopers, switching their tails and raising one front foot as a threat. Fewer than 10,000 breeding individuals are thought to exist.

Habitat: Gibber plains. **Behaviour:** Terrestrial, solitary, nocturnal. **Diet:** Insects, small vertebrates, carrion. **Breeding:** May through December. May produce two litters per season. Mature at 9 months. **Features:** Light grey-brown to sandy brown above and greyish white below. Eyes are large. Snout and thin ears are sparsely furred. Black, bottlebrush tail-tip. 4 toes on hind foot. **Threats:** Habitat destruction, predation.

DIBBLER *Parantechinus apicalis*

M & I MORCOMBE

QUICK REFERENCE

Average lifespan	1–3 years
Diet	Insectivorous
Reproduction period	March
Number of offspring	8
Offspring maturity	10 months
Length HB ♂	145 mm
Length T	105–115 mm
Length HB ♀	140 mm
Length T	95 mm
Weight ♂	60–125 g
Weight ♀	40–73 g
Status	Endangered

The Dibbler was first discovered in 1884 and was not seen again until 1967. Thriving populations exist on Boulanger and Whitlock Islands, but mainland distribution seems limited to Fitzgerald River and Torndirrup National Parks, Western Australia.

Habitat: Coastal heath. **Behaviour:** Partly arboreal, nocturnal. **Diet:** Insects, possibly nectar. **Breeding:** Mates in March. Mature at 10–11 months. **Lifespan:** 1–3 years. Most males die after their first breeding season. **Features:** Coarse fur, grey-brown flecked with white above, greyish white below, sides tinged yellow. White-ringed eye. Short, hairy, tapered tail. 5 toes on hind foot. Female has shallow pouch and 8 teats. **Threats:** Habitat destruction, altered fire regime.

SANDSTONE PSEUDANTECHINUS *Pseudantechinus bilarni*

QUICK REFERENCE	
Average lifespan	1–3 years
Diet	Insectivore
Reproduction period Number of offspring Offspring maturity	Jun–Jul 4–5 1 year
Length HB ♂ Length T	90–115 mm 90–125 mm
Length HB ♀ Length T	90–115 mm 90–120 mm
Weight ♂	20–40 g
Weight ♀	15–35 g
Status	Near Threatened

IAN MORRIS

Although well known to Arnhem Land Aborigines, this marsupial first came to scientific attention in 1948. Its high metabolic rate often drives it from shelter in search of late afternoon snacks. This species is more diurnal than most dasyurids, basking in the morning sun.

Habitat: Sandstone escarpments, prefers boulder slopes with grassy eucalypt forest, may move to monsoon forest in dry season. **Behaviour:** Terrestrial, mostly nocturnal. **Diet:** Insects and other small invertebrates. **Breeding:** Late June to early July. Mature at 12 months. **Features:** Grey-brown above and pale grey below. Forehead is marked with darker fur. Pointed snout is almost hairless. Reddish patches behind large, thin ears. Tail is long, slender and scaly. Female has 6 teats and no pouch. **Threats:** Predation, altered fire regime.

FAT-TAILED PSEUDANTECHINUS *Pseudantechinus macdonnellensis*

QUICK REFERENCE	
Average lifespan	7 years (captivity)
Diet	Insectivore/ Carnivore
Reproduction period Number of offspring Offspring maturity	Jul–Sept 6 1 year
Length HB ♂ Length T	95–105 mm 75–80 mm
Length HB ♀ Length T	95–105 mm 75–85 mm
Weight ♂	25–45 kg
Weight ♀	20–40 g
Status	Least Concern

KEN STEPNELL

This marsupial shelters in crevices or termite mounds and comes out to bask on winter days. Fat is stored in the base of its short tail when insect prey is plentiful.

Habitat: Sparsely vegetated arid land with rocky outcrops. **Behaviour:** Terrestrial, mostly nocturnal. **Diet:** Insects and other small invertebrates. **Breeding:** July through September. Mature by 12 months. **Features:** Greyish brown fur with chestnut patches behind large ears. Large eyes and broad hind feet. Short tail. Female has 6 teats and develops temporary skin folds. **Threats:** Cats, owls and snakes may prey on this species, but otherwise it has few threats. **Status:** Least Concern (IUCN).

FAWN ANTECHINUS *Antechinus bellus*

IAN MORRIS

QUICK REFERENCE	
Average lifespan	1 year
Diet	Insectivore/ Carnivore
Reproduction period Number of offspring Offspring maturity	Late Aug Up to 10 < 1 year
Length HB ♂ Length T	121–148 mm 105–126 mm
Length HB ♀ Length T	110–130 mm 93–110 mm
Weight ♂	42–66 g
Weight ♀	26–41 g
Status	Vulnerable

The Fawn Antechinus is common but rarely seen in its northern tropical habitat. It is one of the largest antechinus species and relies on tree and log hollows for shelter.

Habitat: Open eucalypt forest and woodland with grassy or shrubby undergrowth.
Behaviour: Shelters and hunts on the ground and in trees, crepuscular. **Diet:** Insects, small geckos. **Breeding:** Late August. Up to 10 young, which are weaned in January.
Features: Pale to medium grey fur, sometimes with brownish tinge; belly cream to pale grey. Chin and paws white. Tail is shorter than combined head and body length. Female has 10 teats.
Threats: Cane Toads and habitat changes by other introduced species, such as Buffel grass.

YELLOW-FOOTED ANTECHINUS *Antechinus flavipes*

QUICK REFERENCE	
Average lifespan	1 year
Diet	Omnivore
Reproduction period Number of offspring Offspring maturity	Jul–Sept Up to 12 < 1 Year
Length HB ♂ Length T	93–165 mm 70–151 mm
Length HB ♀ Length T	86–127 mm 65–107 mm
Weight ♂	26–79 g
Weight ♀	21–52 g
Status	Least Concern

This inquisitive creature darts over the ground, bulldozing through leaf litter and pouncing on prey. It runs along the underside of branches when hunting in trees.

Habitat: The most widespread antechinus; inhabits rainforest, mulga, woodland, swamps, vine forest and suburban gardens. **Behaviour:** Arboreal and terrestrial, gregarious, nocturnal. **Diet:** Insects, small birds, rodents, flowers, nectar. **Breeding:** Late winter to spring. Up to 12 young carried in pouch for 5 weeks. **Features:** Slate grey head with white-ringed eyes grading to orange-brown sides, rump, belly and feet. Throat and chest white. Tail has black tip. Female has 8 nipples and develops temporary skinfolds.
Threats: Predation from owls, snakes and feral cats.

BRUSH-TAILED PHASCOGALE *Phascogale tapoatafa*

QUICK REFERENCE	
Average lifespan	1–3 years
Diet	Omnivore
Reproduction period Number of offspring Offspring maturity	May–Jun 6–8 11 months
Length HB ♂ Length T	160–261 mm 175–234 mm
Length HB ♀ Length T	148–223 mm 160–226 mm
Weight ♂	175–311 g
Weight ♀	106–212 g
Status	Near Threatened

Sharp claws and hind feet that rotate 180° make this dasyurid a nimble climber that leaps up to two metres between trees. This social creature often shares a nest and alerts others to danger by tapping on branches.

Habitat: Open eucalypt woodland with sparse undergrowth. They prefer to forage on rough-barked trees. **Behaviour:** Mostly arboreal, gregarious, nocturnal. **Diet:** Insects, spiders, small vertebrates, nectar. **Breeding:** Mid May–early June. Mature by 11 months. **Features:** Grey fur flecked with black on head, back and sides; cream below. Large ears and eyes. Dark stripe down centre of face. Black, bottlebrush tail; hairs up to 40 mm long. Short fifth toe on hind foot. Female has 8 teats and develops temporary skinfolds. **Threats:** Habitat destruction; predation by owls, foxes and cats.

COMMON PLANIGALE *Planigale maculata*

QUICK REFERENCE	
Average lifespan	Not known
Diet	Insectivore
Reproduction period Number of offspring Offspring maturity	Oct–Jan 8–12 < 1 year
Length HB ♂ Length T	51–90 mm 48–84 mm
Length HB ♀ Length T	51–83 mm 44–73 mm
Weight ♂	4–22 g
Weight ♀	3–17 g
Status	Least Concern

IAN MORRIS

Despite being common and widespread, little is known about the Common Planigale. This planigale has a tenacious grip and fearlessly attacks insects larger than itself. It shelters during the day in crevices, under rocks and in hollow logs, and forages at night on the ground in dense vegetation and leaf litter.

Habitat: Rainforest, eucalypt forest, grassland, marshes, rocky outcrops, suburban gardens. **Behaviour:** Mostly terrestrial, nocturnal. **Diet:** Insects. **Breeding:** Late spring and summer in the east, all year elsewhere. **Features:** Cinnamon to grey-brown fur sometimes speckled with white. Pale underbelly and white chin. Large, notched ears. Thin tail is shorter than head and body. Female has pouch and 8–12 nipples. **Threats:** Predation from cats, dogs, cane toads and owls.

WONGAI NINGAUI *Ningaui ridei*

JIRI LOCHMAN/LOCHMAN TRANSPARENCIES

QUICK REFERENCE	
Average lifespan	18–24 months
Diet	Carnivore
Reproduction period	Oct–Jan
Number of offspring	5–8
Offspring maturity	8–10 months
Length HB	57–75 mm
Length T	59–71 mm
Weight	6.5–10.5 g
Status	Least Concern

This very small, feisty dasyurid inhabits states that make up inland arid Australia — WA, NT, Qld and Victoria.

Habitat: The shrubs, sparse trees and spinifex hummock grasslands on dunes and sandplains. **Behaviour:** Nocturnal and solitary. Builds nests under spinifex clumps, in borrowed shallow tunnels or hollow logs. It attacks its prey viciously. Quickly and repeatedly biting it on the head. Goes into torpor during unfavourable conditions. **Diet:** Small vertebrates including grasshoppers, cockroaches, beetles, spiders and moths. **Breeding:** Females have litters of 5–8 young once a lifetime. **Features:** Males and females are the same size. Grizzled buff-brown to greyish-brown spiky fur with black guard hairs above, yellowish sides and whitish underneath. Ginger face and ears. Narrow snout, sharp teeth, little close-set black eyes, smallish ears. **Threats:** No major threats.

SOUTHERN NINGAUI *Ningaui yvonneae*

HANS & JUDY BESTE/LOCHMAN TRANSPARENCIES

QUICK REFERENCE	
Average lifespan	14 months
Diet	Carnivore
Reproduction period	Oct–Nov
Number of offspring	5–7
Length HB	48–81 mm
Length T	53–71 mm
Weight	6–14 g
Status	Least Concern

The tiny Southern Ningaui (aka Mallee Ningaui) inhabits the semi-arid southern regions of WA, SA, Victoria and NSW.

Habitat: Low heathlands, sandy plains, open and low mallee scrub with a preference for spinifex (*Triodia*) hummocks. **Behaviour:** Nocturnal. Spends most of its time in and around hummocks. They forage in leaf litter for their prey which they bite on the head and consume head first. **Diet:** Mostly invertebrates. **Breeding:** Breeding occurs Oct–Nov. Females have litters of 5–7 young once a lifetime, rarely twice. **Features:** Males are larger than females. Orange- to yellowish- or greyish-olive spiky fur with black guard hairs above, and pale grey underneath. Cinnamon patch under the ears. **Threats:** Sheep grazing, changed fire regimes, mining.

KULTARR *Antechinomys laniger*

QUICK REFERENCE	
Average lifespan	1–2 years
Diet	Insectivore
Reproduction period	Jul–Feb
Number of offspring	6–8
Offspring maturity	8 months
Length HB ♂	80–100 mm
Length T	100–150 mm
Length HB ♀	70–95 mm
Length T	100–140 mm
Weight ♂	30 g
Weight ♀	20 g
Status	Least Concern

M & I MORCOMBE

Long hind legs and a bounding gait give the Kultarr extra manoeuvrability. Recognisable calls allow a mother to retrieve unweaned young that stray or fall from her back.

Habitat: Stone and sand plains in grassland, shrubland or woodland. **Behaviour:** Terrestrial, solitary, nocturnal. **Diet:** Insects, spiders. **Breeding:** July to February. Can produce 2 litters per season. Mature at 8 months. **Features:** Fawn-grey to sandy brown above, white below. Dark stripe from crown to nose. Large ears. Protruding eyes with dark rings. Long, thin tail with dark brush. Very long hind foot with 4 toes. Female has 6–8 teats and temporary skinfolds. **Threats:** Habitat degradation by introduced livestock, predation by cats and foxes.

FAT-TAILED DUNNART *Sminthopsis crassicaudata*

QUICK REFERENCE	
Average lifespan	2–3 years
Diet	Insectivore
Reproduction period	Jul–Feb
Number of offspring	8–10
Offspring maturity	5 months
Length HB	60–90 mm
Length T	40–70 mm
Weight	10–20 g
Status	Least Concern

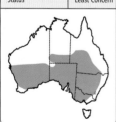

IAN MORRIS

In cold weather, the Fat-tailed Dunnart will huddle with others in a communal nest. Fat stored in the tail becomes a source of energy when food is scarce. The Fat-tailed Dunnart gains enough water from the invertebrates it preys upon and hence does not need to drink.

Habitat: Wide range from coastal areas to arid inland — woodland, grassland, shrubland, farmland and gibber plains. **Behaviour:** Terrestrial, solitary, completely nocturnal. **Diet:** Insects and other invertebrates. **Breeding:** July to February. May produce 2 litters per season. **Features:** Greyish brown above, light grey to white below. Large ears. Round, protruding eyes. Short fat tail. Hind foot has grainy, raised pads. Female has pouch and 8–10 teats. **Threats:** This species has few threats and has probably increased in range since settlement.

LITTLE LONG-TAILED DUNNART *Sminthopsis dolichura*

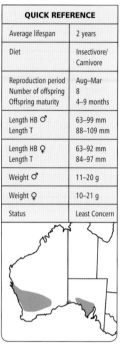

QUICK REFERENCE	
Average lifespan	2 years
Diet	Insectivore/ Carnivore
Reproduction period Number of offspring Offspring maturity	Aug–Mar 8 4–9 months
Length HB ♂ Length T	63–99 mm 88–109 mm
Length HB ♀ Length T	63–92 mm 84–97 mm
Weight ♂	11–20 g
Weight ♀	10–21 g
Status	Least Concern

Previously considered a form of Common Dunnart, this species was described in its own right in 1984. Population fluctuations of this species can be linked to seasonal conditions and fire ecology. Little else is known about the reproductive biology of the Little Long-tailed Dunnart.

Habitat: Arid and semi-arid areas of southern Australia; woodlands, shrublands, heaths and grassland. **Behaviour:** Active, terrestrial, nocturnal. **Diet:** Insects, and small vertebrates. **Breeding:** August to March; up to 8 young; may have 2 litters per year. **Features:** Upper body has grey fur, slightly grizzled in appearance; white underneath and on feet; cinnamon-brown on face, cheeks and behind ears. Face lacks dorsal stripe; eye encircled by thin black ring. Long, naked ears; elongated, thin tail. Lack of granular toe pads on hind feet distinguish adults from similar species. **Threats:** Probably secure, predation by foxes and cats.

STRIPE-FACED DUNNART *Sminthopsis macroura*

QUICK REFERENCE	
Average lifespan	4–11 years (in captivity)
Diet	Insectivore/ Carnivore
Reproduction period Number of offspring Offspring maturity	Jun–Feb 8 4–9 months
Length HB Length T	70–100 mm 80–110 mm
Weight	15–25 g
Status	Least Concern

The Namoi Aboriginal people referred to this species as the Toon-moo-ra-la-ga, according to notes made by naturalist John Gilbert and a citation in Gould. The Stripe-faced Dunnart has the shortest gestation period (11 days) of any marsupial.

Habitat: Saltbush and bluebush shrublands, Spinifex grasslands, Acacia shrublands, tussock grasslands, salt lakes and rocky ridges. **Behaviour:** Strictly nocturnal, very mobile. **Diet:** Mainly invertebrates supplemented by lizards and rodents. **Breeding:** June to February, two litters with 8 young in each. **Features:** Superficially hard to identify in the wild; 3 genetically distinct species may be 'lumped' in with this species. Prominent dark stripe on top of head and very long tail (1.25 times head-body length) fattened at the base are both distinctive. **Threats:** Stock grazing may destroy habitat.

COMMON DUNNART *Sminthopsis murina*

QUICK REFERENCE	
Average lifespan	< 2 years
Diet	Insectivore
Reproduction period Number of offspring Offspring maturity	Aug–Mar Up to 10 5 months
Length HB ♂ Length T	76–104 mm 70–99 mm
Length HB ♀ Length T	64–92 mm 68–92 mm
Weight ♂	16–28 g
Weight ♀	10–22 g
Status	Least Concern

STANLEY BREEDEN/LOCHMAN TRANSPARENCIES

Also called the Slender-tailed Dunnart, and previously comprising several subspecies, the Common Dunnart was reclassified in 1984 when all but two subspecies were separated out. It seems to benefit from periodic burning of its habitat, with higher densities recorded two to four years after a fire.

Habitat: East coast; woodland, open forest and heathland. **Behaviour:** Nocturnal, competitive. **Diet:** Insects; prefers beetles and larvae. **Breeding:** August to March; females have 8 to 10 teats and can give birth to 2 litters. **Features:** Difficult to distinguish from other dunnarts; mouse-grey above, mainly white below; slender, pointed muzzle, large ears and eyes. Lacks dark dorsal stripe of *S. macroura* and striated footpads of *S. crassicaudata*. Tail equal to body length. **Threats:** Habitat destruction; drought; predation by cats and foxes.

RED-CHEEKED DUNNART *Sminthopsis virginiae*

QUICK REFERENCE	
Average lifespan	1–2 years (Estimate)
Diet	Insectivore/ Carnivore
Reproduction period Number of offspring Offspring maturity	All year 6–8 4–6 months
Length HB ♂ Length T	96–135 mm 100–135 mm
Length HB ♀ Length T	90–133 mm 90–122 mm
Weight ♂	31–58 g
Weight ♀	18–34 g
Status	Least Concern

IAN MORRIS

The Red-cheeked Dunnart proved elusive after it was discovered in 1847, and every time it was rediscovered it was given a new name. This species is one of the most colourful and attractive among its genus. It is found in Australia's north and New Guinea.

Habitat: Tropical savanna woodland near creeks and billabongs. **Behaviour:** Terrestrial, solitary, nocturnal. **Diet:** Insects, small reptiles. **Breeding:** All year; 6 to 8 young; mature at 4 to 6 months. **Features:** Spiky, dark grey fur flecked with white, white to cream below. Red cheeks. Dark stripe from forehead to nose. Eyes and ears are large and round. Thin tail almost furless. Hind foot has 4 long toes and 1 short inner toe. Female has pouch and 8 teats. **Threats:** Populations may be affected by fire and rainfall.

NUMBAT

SUPERFAMILY: DASYUROIDAE
FAMILY: MYRMECOBIIDAE

This marsupial carnivore armed with more teeth than any other native land mammal is a fearsome prospect for any prey. But 25 pairs of teeth are of little use when most of them lie below the gum line. A 100 millimetre-long tongue that moves faster than the human eye can see is, however, a formidable weapon for a predator that feeds exclusively on termites.

The Numbat sniffs out its prey then scratches open its log nests or shallow underground runways. Its sticky, flickering tongue traps the termites, which are then swallowed whole along with any ants that might take advantage of the feeding opportunity the Numbat's activity offers. The Numbat hunts during the day when termites are most active. In winter, both the termites and the Numbat remain in their nests on cold mornings. When summer temperatures drive termites deeper underground, the Numbat bides its time in shady retreats.

FACTS

- The Numbat is the sole member of its family.
- A Numbat's tongue is about half as long as its head and body combined.
- The Numbat's pouch is a flap of skin, below which its offspring dangle while the mother forages.
- Fewer than 1,000 Numbats are thought to survive in the wild.
- The Numbat lines its nests with shredded bark and leaves.
- The Numbat is diurnal, i.e. active during the day.
- The Numbat is Western Australia's faunal emblem.
- The Numbat will not share its territory with members of the same sex.
- A Numbat eats up to 20,000 termites a day.
- Land clearing and foxes are the biggest threats to the Numbat's survival.

Sharp claws, a good sense of smell and a superbly adapted sticky tongue facilitate its diet.

Habitat

The Numbat is the only living member of the **Myrmecobiidae** family. At the time of European settlement it could be found in woodlands and forests across southern Australia to western New South Wales. It is now confined to isolated pockets of Jarrah and Wandoo forest in the south-west. These eucalypt forests provide old trees, fallen timber and shrubby undergrowth that shelter the Numbat and termites.

While foraging, the Numbat moves along at a brisk trot, tail raised in a bristling arc above its back. It stops frequently to stand and sniff the air or scrabble in leaf litter and rotting logs. It takes a lot of termites to support such a high energy animal and a Numbat's territory can range from 25 to 50 hectares. It maintains several nests in logs, burrows and tree hollows within its home range and beds down in the nearest one at dusk.

SHARON WORMLEATON

Above left: Within months of being left in the nest the curious youngsters begin to emerge tentatively from the burrow by day. **Above right:** The Numbat's pouch is merely a flap of skin, below which its offspring dangle while the mother forages.

Breeding

Breeding is a fairly synchronised event for the Numbat. The January mating season is brief and a female only has a 48-hour window of opportunity to conceive. Most of the young are born in late January and early February after 14 days' gestation. The female Numbat has no pouch, merely a flap of skin, and her long belly hairs offer minimal protection to her under-developed babies.

By late July the young no longer need to suckle constantly and they are left in a nursery chamber at the end of a burrow one to two metres long. They begin exploring the outside world in September and within a few weeks have learned to feed themselves. At the age of 10 months, they leave home to find their own territories.

Defensive behaviour

The Numbat relies on camouflage to deceive the eyes and minds of its daytime predators. The Numbat's colours and stripes break up its body outline and help it blend into its open forest habitat.

When standing still, the Numbat becomes part of a confusing image of light and shadow. When a Numbat runs, its flashing white stripes create a flicker effect that dazzles the eye and is difficult to process. While a predator's other senses are overriding its visual confusion, the Numbat may have just enough time to escape to a nearby bolt-hole.

A cornered Numbat can only hope that its dark eye stripes will make its head a less conspicuous target than its bushy tail. A predator that goes for the tail may be left with a mouthful of hair as the rest of its dinner heads off in the opposite direction.

SHARON WORMLEATON

Finding Numbats

Try a late afternoon walk in a Wandoo or Jarrah forest. Check the ground for shallow, funnel-shaped holes. Look for dark, shiny cylindrical droppings on logs. Tracks are similar to the Western Quoll, but the front foot has longer claws and the hind foot has only 4 toes.

Top to bottom: Numbats are excellent climbers, able to climb quickly to evade predators or in the search for termites; A Numbat remains alert to danger as it excavates shallow holes in search of termites; The Numbat's cryptic colouring helps it blend into the light and shadow of its home on the forest floor.

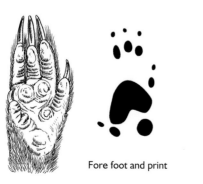

Fore foot and print

Hind foot and print

LOCATION TIPS

▶ Dryandra State Forest, WA

▶ Perup Forest, WA

▶ Dragon Rocks Nature Reserve, WA

▶ Boyagin Nature Reserve, WA

NUMBAT *Myrmecobius fasciatus*

QUICK REFERENCE	
Average lifespan	2–3 years
Diet	Insectivore
Reproduction period Number of offspring Offspring maturity	January 4 1–2 years
Length HB ♂ Length T	222–290 mm 125–207 mm
Length HB ♀ Length T	200–267 mm 140–213 mm
Weight ♂	405–752 g
Weight ♀	305–647 g
Status	Vulnerable

The Numbat's population and range have drastically declined since European Settlement. They are being reintroduced to suitable habitats in nature reserves and national parks where control programs reduce the threat of feral predators.

Habitat: Eucalypt forest and woodland with shrubby undergrowth. **Behaviour:** Mostly terrestrial, territorial, solitary, diurnal. **Diet:** Termites. **Breeding:** January. Females mature at 1 year, males at 2 years. **Features:** Coarse, reddish brown fur with darker, sometimes black rump; pale below. 4–11 transverse white stripes between shoulders and base of tail. Narrow head with large ears. White eyebrows and white patch below dark eye stripe running from nose to ear. Bushy tail with long hairs. Hind foot has 4 toes. Female has 4 teats and no pouch. **Threats:** Predation by foxes and cats, habitat destruction, changed fire regimes. **Status:** Vulnerable (EPBC); Endangered (IUCN).

M & I MORCOMBE

One of the most beautiful and vulnerable Australian marsupials, the Numbat is also the faunal emblem of Western Australia and is confined to just a small range in the South-West of the State.

BANDICOOTS & BILBY

ORDER: PERAMELEMORPHIA
SUPERFAMILY: PERAMELOIDEA

BANDICOOTS

FAMILY: PERAMELIDAE

Bandicoots belong to the order Peramelemorphia, which is divided into two existing families. The Peramelidae family includes 'typical' bandicoots, and the family Thylacomyidae with the Bilby as its sole living representative. It may surprise you that 'bandicoot' is not an Aboriginal word. It comes from the Telegu language of southern India, where 'pandi-kokku' (which means pig-rat) is the name given to a large rodent, *Bandicoota bengaliensis*. The navigator George Bass first used the word to refer to this order of marsupials in 1799.

Bandicoots are terrestrial marsupials that rely on thick undergrowth of shrubs and grasses for food and shelter. They spend the day in camouflaged nests of leaf litter scraped into a pile in a shallow depression. Sometimes a layer of soil is kicked over the top for waterproofing.

They emerge at night to forage over territories ranging from one to six hectares. Insects, worms and other invertebrates are a bandicoot's preferred foods, but it also eats fruit and fleshy plant roots. It locates underground food by smell and leaves distinctive 10-centimetre-deep, cone-shaped holes where it digs.

FACTS

- The Bandicoots and Bilbies originally consisted of 11 species; 2 species are now extinct and another species is probably extinct.

- Male bandicoots are larger and more aggressive than females.

- Bandicoots have the second shortest gestation period of any mammal — 12.5 days (the Stripe-faced Dunnart is the shortest at 11 days).

- Bandicoots have an average lifespan of 3 years.

- A newborn Long-nosed Bandicoot weighs 0.25 g and is about 13 mm long.

- Unlike all other marsupials, bandicoots have knee caps and lack a collar bone.

Bandicoots give birth to litters of up to five young.

M & I MORCOMBE

This 'beach-bunny' Western Barred bandicoot could very well be searching for eggs in a Green Turtle nest to snack on.

Diet

Bandicoots are equipped with well muscled forearms and robust claws, which are used to excavate soil and root in the earth for bulbs and underground fruiting fungi. Their elongated, conical snouts probe and shovel the earth for spiders, insects, fungi, truffles, bulbs and tubers. Roots, fruit, berries, some vegetation and eggs are also opportunistically consumed, as are juvenile mice and rodents, although the latter are generally not a large part of most bandicoots' diets.

Bandicoots have developed a taste for the fruiting bodies of subterranean fungi and researchers undertaking trapping studies on Long-nosed Bandicoots have recently found that expensive truffle oil attracts more bandicoots than traditional baits of peanut butter mixed with oats. Some species visit suburban backyards and, because they have a fondness for lawn pests such as cockshafer beetles and army worms, they can be of benefit to gardeners. Campsites and picnic areas may also be visited at night by bandicoots seeking an easy meal.

Breeding

Bandicoots are aggressive territorial animals. When paths cross, there is a brief exchange of hisses, grunts and squeals, a bit of pouncing and chasing then each goes its separate way. Mating encounters are equally brief. On the other hand, breeding seasons are long and a female may produce two or three litters a year. Unlike most other marsupials, bandicoots have rudimentary placentas. The placental cords provide attachment to the womb for the embryonic young, but there is no transfer of nutrients or wastes.

Bandicoots have a very short gestation period — 12.5 days. Though bandicoots have eight teats, usually up to five young are born and carried in the female's backward-opening pouch for about seven weeks. A nursing female can become pregnant during the week it takes to wean her young. She gives birth to another litter within days of the previous brood leaving to find their own territories.

A Missing Link?

Some scientists believe bandicoots are an evolutionary link between marsupial carnivores and herbivores. A bandicoot has the teeth of a typical dasyurid carnivore, except its incisors are flat-edged and point slightly outwards to suit its mixed diet. The hind legs and feet resemble those of a plant-eating macropod. Like kangaroos, the hind foot has an extra long fourth toe and joined second and third toes that are used for grooming. The bandicoot has a bounding gait and its strong leg muscles allow it to bounce into the air and leap distances of up to a metre.

Eastern Barred Bandicoots are rare on the mainland but fairly common in Tasmania.

Finding Bandicoots

Try spotlighting at night after listening for telltale scuffles and snuffles in the garden. Look on the ground for domed piles of leaf litter used as nests and 10-centimetre-deep, conical excavations. Scats are brown or black smooth cylindrical pellets containing soil, plant fibres and insect remains. Front-foot prints usually show only three toes.

LOCATION TIPS

▶ Freycinet NP, Tas.

▶ Fitzgerald River NP, WA

▶ Kakadu NP, NT

▶ Lamington NP, QLD

Fore foot and print of
Long-nosed Bandicoot

Hind foot and print of
Long-nosed Bandicoot

LES HALL

Hind foot of an Eastern
Barred Bandicoot

GOLDEN BANDICOOT *Isoodon auratus*

JIRI LOCHMAN/LOCHMAN TRANSPARENCIES

QUICK REFERENCE	
Average lifespan	3 years
Diet	Omnivore
Reproduction period	Dec–Jan/Aug
Number of offspring	2–3
Offspring maturity	< 1 year
Length HB	190–295 mm
Length T	84–121 mm
Weight	250–670 g
Status	Vulnerable

A Golden Bandicoot can cover up to 10 hectares a night while foraging. While it is the most common mammal on Barrow Island, off the coast of Western Australia, it is restricted to isolated populations on the mainland.

Habitat: Arid and semi-arid grassland and grassy woodland, monsoon forest.
Behaviour: Terrestrial, territorial, solitary, nocturnal. **Diet:** Insects, plant roots and tubers, small reptiles and mammals, turtle eggs (Barrow Is). **Breeding:** All year, peaking in summer and August. More than 1 litter per year. Usually 2 young per litter. **Features:** Black-flecked, golden brown guard hairs over grey underfur. White belly. Rounded ears. Long, slender tail. Female has 8 teats and rear-opening pouch. **Threats:** Predation by feral cats; Black Rats may also limit populations.

NORTHERN BROWN BANDICOOT *Isoodon macrourus*

QUICK REFERENCE	
Average lifespan	3 years
Diet	Omnivore
Reproduction period Number of offspring Offspring maturity	Aug–Apr 1–7 (4) 4 months
Length HB ♂ Length T	300–470 mm 90–215 mm
Length HB ♀ Length T	300–410 mm 80–185 mm
Weight ♂	500–3100 g
Weight ♀	500–1700 g
Status	Least Concern

This bandicoot is a common, nocturnal visitor to suburban backyards along Australia's east coast. Males are larger and more aggressive than the females, and use scent glands behind their ears to mark their territories. They often lose their tails in territorial disputes.

Habitat: Forest, woodland, grassland, suburban gardens. **Behaviour:** Terrestrial, territorial, solitary, nocturnal. **Diet:** Insects, spiders, worms, fruit, grass seeds. **Breeding:** August to April, all year in south-east Queensland. 1–2 litters per season. Females mature at 3–4 months. **Features:** Coarse, dark brown fur speckled with black; belly is greyish white. Small, pointed ears and short, pointed tail. Female has 8 teats and rear-opening pouch. **Threats:** Predation by foxes, cats and dogs (especially in urban areas); grazing; altered fire regimes.

SOUTHERN BROWN BANDICOOT *Isoodon obesulus*

QUICK REFERENCE	
Average lifespan	3 years
Diet	Omnivore
Reproduction period Number of offspring Offspring maturity	Jun–Jan 1–6 (3) 4–5 months
Length HB ♂ Length T	300–360 mm 96–145 mm
Length HB ♀ Length T	280–330 mm 90–128 mm
Weight ♂	500–1850 g
Weight ♀	400–1200 g
Status	Endangered

The Southern Brown Bandicoot prefers habitats with sandy soils and scrubby undergrowth where occasional fires renew plant and insect food sources. It is territorial and aggressively defends its two to seven hectare home range.

Habitat: Dry eucalypt forest, woodland, shrubland. **Behaviour:** Terrestrial, territorial, solitary, nocturnal. **Diet:** Insects, other invertebrates, fungi, plant roots. **Breeding:** Winter to summer. 2–3 litters per season. Of 1–6 young born, 2–3 survive to weaning. Mature at 4–5 months. **Features:** Solid body with hunched posture. Brownish grey fur flecked with yellow and brown, creamy white below. Bristly guard hairs cover upper body. Short, pointed tail and upper surface of hind feet usually dark brown. Small, rounded ears. Female has 8 teats and rear-opening pouch. **Threats:** Introduced predators, inappropriate fire regimes and clearing of habitat for pastoral purposes.

WESTERN BARRED BANDICOOT *Perameles bougainville*

JIRI LOCHMAN/LOCHMAN TRANSPARENCIES

QUICK REFERENCE	
Average lifespan	4 years
Diet	Omnivore
Reproduction period	Apr–Oct
Number of offspring	1–3
Offspring maturity	< 1 year
Length HB ♂	179–226 mm
Length T	81–100 mm
Length HB ♀	173–222 mm
Length T	84–106 mm
Weight ♂	168–280 g
Weight ♀	165–379 g
Status	Endangered

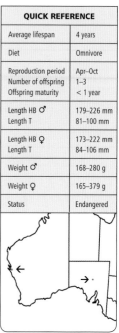

The Western Barred Bandicoot is found only on Bernier and Dorre Islands off the WA coast. Prior to European settlement it existed in a variety of habitats across southern Australia. They spend the day in well-hidden nests built in a hollow in the ground and covered with vegetation or concealed beneath a shrub.

Habitat: Coastal scrub and grassland. **Behaviour:** Terrestrial, territorial, solitary, nocturnal.
Diet: Insects and other small animals, plant roots, leaves, berries and seeds.
Breeding: April to October. More than 1 litter per season. Usually 2 young per litter.
Features: Light grey to greyish-brown above with 2–3 pale stripes on rump. Underside and feet are white. Large, slightly pointed ears. Female has 8 teats and rear-opening pouch.
Threats: Competition with sheep and predation from native and introduced predators.

EASTERN BARRED BANDICOOT *Perameles gunnii*

QUICK REFERENCE	
Average lifespan	2–3 years
Diet	Omnivore
Reproduction period	Jul–Nov
Number of offspring	1–5 (2)
Offspring maturity	3–5 months
Length HB	270–350 mm
Length T	70–110 mm
Weight	500–1450 g
Status	Vulnerable/ Endangered

With prominent barring on the hindquarters, this is perhaps the most attractive bandicoot species. Eastern Barred Bandicoots have a bounding gait and stand to sniff the air when alarmed. They are more common in Tasmania, but on the mainland are restricted to a few colonies in western Victoria that are derived from captive-bred animals.

Habitat: Open grassland, grassy woodland, pastures with areas of dense groundcover.
Behaviour: Terrestrial, solitary, nocturnal. **Diet:** Insects, larvae, worms, bulbs, tubers, fruit, fungi. **Breeding:** July to November, 1–2 litters per season. Females mature at 3 months; males at 4–5 months. **Features:** Greyish fawn fur with 3–4 pale bars on hindquarters. Belly is pale grey to white. Short, pointed tail is pale with a dark base. Slender snout and large, pointed ears. **Threats:** Competition with sheep and rabbits and predation by foxes; disease.

LONG-NOSED BANDICOOT *Perameles nasuta*

QUICK REFERENCE	
Average lifespan	3 years
Diet	Omnivore
Reproduction period Number of offspring Offspring maturity	All year 1–5 5 months
Length HB Length T	310–445 mm 120–160 mm
Weight	520–1330 g
Status	Least Concern

A remarkably long snout distinguishes this bandicoot from other east coast species. It is probably the most common member of the Perameles genus. Suburban gardeners may be familiar with its cone-shaped excavations (up to 30 centimetres deep) and shrill squeaks.

Habitat: Rainforest, eucalypt forest, woodland, grassland, suburban gardens. **Behaviour:** Terrestrial, aggressive, solitary, nocturnal. **Diet:** Insects, larvae, plant roots, fungi, seeds, fruits and tubers. **Breeding:** All year. 1–5 young (usually 2 or 3). More than 1 litter per season. Females mature at 5 months. **Features:** Greyish brown fur with darker flecks, creamy white below. Some have bands on rump. Front paws and upper surface of hind feet are creamy white. Long, slender snout and long, pointed ears. Female has 8 teats and rear-opening pouch. **Threats:** Habitat destruction, predation by cats, foxes and dogs.

LONG-NOSED ECHYMIPERA *Echymipera rufescens*

QUICK REFERENCE	
Average lifespan	Not Known
Diet	Omnivore
Reproduction period Number of offspring Offspring maturity	Nov–May 1–4 4–5 months
Length HB ♂ Length T	278–480 mm 75–107 mm
Length HB ♀ Length T	215–415 mm 75–91 mm
Weight ♂	525–2225 g
Weight ♀	300–1200 g
Status	Least Concern

GREG RICHARDS

This rainforest-dwelling bandicoot is the only member of its sub-family (Echymiperinae) to live in Australia. Also called the Long-nosed Echymipera, this New Guinean species was first discovered on Cape York Peninsula in 1932. Also known as a Rufous Spiny Bandicoot.

Habitat: Rainforest, open forest, grassy woodland, coastal heath. **Behaviour:** Terrestrial, nocturnal, solitary. **Diet:** Insects, fungi, fruit, seeds, bulbs. **Breeding:** November to May. 1–4 young; up to 3 litters per season. **Features:** White flecks on blackish head and rufous body, pale underneath. Broad, stiff guard hairs. White front feet. Tapered, cylindrical head with elongated muzzle. Short, furless tail. Only 4 pairs of upper incisors. Female has 8 teats and rear-opening pouch. **Threats:** Species has been little affected by European settlement.

BILBY

FAMILY: THYLACOMYIDAE

The pale, rabbit-eared, silver-furred Bilby is arguably the most charismatic living Australian bandicoot. It is also the sole remaining member of its family, although its relative, the Lesser Bilby, once also shared this continent. Both are bandicoots, despite belonging to the distinct Thylacomyidae family. They have silkier hair that is longer on the tail tip compared with other Bandicoots in the family Peramelidae.

The two species of bilbies once occupied 70% of mainland Australia, with the exception of some areas east of the Great Dividing Range and the Top End, but even the Bilby has now vanished from more than 90% of its historical range, and the Lesser Bilby is almost certainly extinct. The Bilby's profile has benefited enormously from its promotional role as 'Australia's Easter Bunny'; however, it is still at risk.

FACTS

- The Greater Bilby was known as Urgata and the Lesser Bilby as Urpila in dialects of the Indigenous people of the central deserts.

- Australia once had two bilby species; the Lesser Bilby hasn't been seen since 1931 and is presumed extinct.

- The Bilby is Australia's largest bandicoot.

- A Bilby's faeces can consist of up to 90% sand because they incidentally consume a lot of sand along with their food.

- Aboriginal people hunted bilbies for food and used their tails for ceremonial purposes.

FACTS

- Bilby tucker includes witchetty grubs, Honeypot Ants, termites and wild onion bulbs.

- A Bilby may have up to 12 burrows within its home range.

- Foxes, feral cats, Dingos and owls prey on Bilbies.

- Bilbies make cone-shaped holes up to 25 cm deep when digging up food.

- A female Bilby has 8 nipples but only raises 1 or 2 babies per litter.

- Young Bilbies spend 75 to 80 days in their mother's backward-opening pouch.

- At night, a female leaves her young in the burrow, returning at intervals to feed them.

Habitat

In the 1920s, Bilbies were common in the arid and semi-arid woodland and grassland that covered 70% of mainland Australia. Today there are only scattered populations in the central and western deserts and a small area of Queensland's channel country.

In 2001, 100 Bilbies were released in a 25-square-kilometre fenced enclosure built by volunteers with money from the Save the Bilby Fund at Currawinya National Park in south-west Queensland. As a result of several consecutive wet seasons, the fence eroded away and in 2012 feral cats entered and devoured 80 Bilbies.

The Bilby can survive in one of Australia's harshest and most unforgiving environments. Its silky fur and deep burrows insulate it from extreme temperatures. It does not need to drink and, instead of sweating out precious moisture, it seems that the Bilby's large thin ears packed with blood vessels allow excess body heat to escape.

Opportunistic breeding and a rigid social structure help balance population numbers with food supply. When food becomes scarce during lengthy dry periods, Bilbies abandon their burrows and move to a new territory.

Very few Bilbies are left in the wild as they are easy prey for feral cats and foxes.

Behaviour

The Bilby is the only Australian species of bandicoot that makes underground shelters. A Bilby burrow spirals downwards one to two metres and can be up to three metres long. The single entrance is usually concealed at the base of a termite mound, grass clump or shrub. A Bilby maintains several burrows where it can shelter during the day.

Above left: The Bilby, if restrained, will emphatically hiss for its release and may even bite savagely if given the opportunity. **Above right:** Bilby burrow entrances under a spinifex plant.

This energetic excavator usually begins foraging around midnight. It has poor vision, but a keen sense of smell leads it to food. With tail aloft and nose to the ground, it licks up grass and acacia seeds and unearths insects, spiders, bulbs and fungi. It will take on small mammals and lizards when other food is scarce.

The Bilby lives alone or in small family groups and forages within its home range. In ideal conditions, a square kilometre of habitat can support up to 16 Bilbies. When territories overlap, males and females establish separate pecking orders. A male's eligibility to mate depends on his rank in the hierarchy. Breeding also depends on the availability of food, even though females can mate throughout the year. During a good year, a female may produce four litters of one to two young.

Conservationists working for the Australian Wildlife Conservancy maintain suitable Bilby habitat at Yookamurra Sanctuary.

Conservation

Despite their notorious fertility, Bilby numbers have plummeted over the past 200 years. Predation by feral cats and foxes, soil degradation from livestock trampling and competition with rabbits for food and burrowing spaces have all amounted to the decline of the Bilby. In recent times, feral cats have thwarted conservation efforts by decimating reintroduced Bilby populations.

In Queensland, a 25-square-kilometre enclosure allows the Bilby, whose populations are dangerously low, to breed in an area free of stock and feral animals. Captive breeding and re-release programs have also reintroduced the Bilby to feral-free habitats within their former range in South Australia.

Finding Bilbies

The Bilby's hind foot prints are slightly pigeon-toed, its scats can be tinged red and its burrow entrances may be found at the base of termite mounds and grass tussocks.

LOCATION TIPS

▶ Currawinya NP, Qld

▶ Diamantina NP, Qld

▶ Dryandra Woodland SF, WA

▶ Venus Bay Conservation Park, SA

BILBY *Macrotis lagotis*

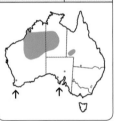

QUICK REFERENCE	
Average lifespan	5 years
Diet	Omnivore
Reproduction period	All year
Number of offspring	1–3
Offspring maturity	6 months
Length HB ♂	300–550 mm
Length T	200–290 mm
Length HB ♀	290–390 mm
Length T	200–278 mm
Weight ♂	1000–2500 g
Weight ♀	800–1100 g
Status	Vulnerable

This arid land marsupial lives in the Tanami, Gibson and Great Sandy Deserts and in south-west Queensland. It is the only bandicoot that burrows underground, digging tunnels three metres long and up to two metres deep. The tips of Bilbies' tails, which are thought to be used to communicate with other Bilbies, were once used for decoration by Aboriginal people. This endearing species now holds pride of place as Australia's 'Easter Bunny'.

Habitat: Arid and semi-arid tussock grasslands and Mitchell grass plains, mulga scrub. **Behaviour:** Terrestrial, nocturnal. Bilbies may be found living singly or in pairs. **Diet:** Insects, larvae, fungi, seeds, bulbs, fruit. Bilbies are efficient at processing water and do not require drinking water. **Breeding:** All year. 1–3 young per litter. Mature at 6 months. **Features:** Soft, silky fur is bluish grey on the head and back, tinged with fawn on flanks, and pale on belly. Crested tail black with white tip. Long, slender snout and very large ears. Hind foot lacks first toe. Female has 8 teats and rear-opening pouch. **Threats:** Changing fire regime, competition with livestock and rabbits, predation by foxes and cats particularly in recent times.

HERBIVOROUS MARSUPIALS

ORDER: DIPROTODONTIA

The order **Diprotodontia** encompasses a wide variety of marsupials. They are sometimes referred to as herbivorous marsupials in comparison with the carnivorous Dasyurids and the omnivorous Bandicoots. However, there are several species that feed on insects as well as plants.

Members of this group have only one pair of lower incisor teeth and no lower canine teeth. The single pair of front incisors in the lower jaw is the diagnostic feature that gives the order its name — *di proto* meaning 'two front' and *dont* 'teeth' in Greek. The second and third toes on the hind feet are small and joined together except for the claws, making a grooming and climbing tool known as the syndactyl toe.

The **Diprotodontia** is a very diverse and successful group divided into two suborders. Wombats and the Koala are classified as **Vombatiformes** and their common characteristics include cheek pouches, a short, flap-like tail and the females have permanent, rear-opening pouches with two teats. Possums and macropods, with their long tails and permanent forward-opening pouches, belong to the suborder **Phalangerida**.

Above: The Common Wombat's colour varies from black through to light brown.
Opposite, clockwise from top left: Common Brushtail Possum; Koala; Long-nosed Potoroo; Red Kangaroo.

KOALA

SUBORDER: VOMBATIFORMES
FAMILY: PHASCOLARCTIDAE

The Koala is the evolutionary offspring of an ancient tree-dwelling marsupial that also gave rise to the wombat. While the wombat stayed on the ground, the Koala has spent the last 15 million years or so developing an intimate relationship with Australia's ubiquitous gum trees. It is the sole surviving member of the family **Phascolarctidae**.

The Koala spends most of its time in the treetops and depends almost entirely on eucalypt leaves for food. Long, muscular limbs and grasping paws make it an expert climber while dense, waterproof fur protects it from the elements. The Koala possesses two opposable thumbs on its forelimbs and is the only mammal other than primates with this feature.

The Koala leads a solitary life within a home range of between 2 and 100 hectares. Its low-nutrient diet provides little energy and it usually rests or sleeps for 18 to 20 out of every 24 hours.

FACTS

- A Koala can leap up to 2 m from one branch to another.

- A Koala curls into a ball to keep warm and sprawls out to cool down.

- The Koala can swim.

- A long thigh muscle attached low on the shin gives the Koala's hind legs extra strength.

- The word 'Koala' is an Aboriginal word that means 'no drink'.

- The Koala's fur provides very good insulation and is also waterproof.

- 'Sarah', the oldest known Koala, lived to the age of 23 at Lone Pine Sanctuary in Queensland and has an entry in the Guinness book of World Records.

Koalas and their joeys stay very close together for the first 12 months.

Habitat

The Koala dwells in eucalypt forests and open woodlands that stretch in a belt along the coast and hinterland from Qld to Vic. It does not inhabit WA or Tasmania and has been introduced to Kangaroo Island, SA, with disastrous consequences. In the south, it prefers low-altitude forests and sclerophyll forests on coastal plains and hinterlands. In the north it inhabits mostly coastal woodlands and riverine woodlands. The Koala does not use burrows, dens or nests; it spends its time in the forks of trees and comes to the ground only to change trees.

Breeding

Much of the male Koala's aggressive behaviour is related to breeding. A mature male establishes a territory that encompasses those of several females and younger males. He proclaims his dominance with bellowing calls and marks the ground and tree trunks in his territory with urine and secretions from a chest gland. Rivals may challenge him vocally and physically.

FACTS

- The Koala walks or bounds along the ground when changing trees.

- Like a human, the Koala has fingerprints.

- A newborn Koala weighs 0.5 g and is less than 2 cm long.

- A Koala's eyes open at 22 weeks and its incisor teeth emerge at 24 weeks.

- If a mother does not retrieve a lost joey, it may be adopted by another female.

Koalas are most often seen resting in tree forks.

The males will pursue a female on and above the ground. A mother with a piggybacking young will vigorously fend off unwanted advances. Thirty-five days after mating, a single joey is born. It struggles to the rear-opening pouch and attaches to one of two teats. At five to six months, the joey begins making forays into the outside world. During this time, the mother produces a greenish faecal pap that inoculates the baby with the bacteria necessary for digesting a gumleaf diet, beginning the weaning process.

After leaving the pouch at seven months, the joey clings to its mother's back and sleeps curled in her lap. This is a dangerous time for a young Koala. It risks being taken by a bird of prey or python as it learns to climb and forage. The transition from milk-fed baby to self-fed juvenile is completed by 12 months. The female usually remains in the area where she was born, while the male sets out to find his own home range at two to three years of age.

Diet

The Koala is one of the few mammals able to eat eucalypt leaves, which are tough, toxic and low in nutrition. But not just any eucalypt will do. A Koala's discerning nose picks out those species for which it has developed a chemical tolerance. Favourites include Manna Gum, Swamp Gum, Blue Gum, Forest Red Gum and Grey Gum. Food tree preferences vary for Koalas living in different regions. The fresh shoots or 'tips' are favoured over mature leaves due to their higher water and nutrient content.

Eating takes up many of a Koala's waking hours. Leaves are sniffed carefully before one is selected and placed in the mouth to be ground up and swallowed. Toxic substances are removed in the stomach and filtered out by the liver. Bacterial fermentation in the Koala's two-metre-long caecum completes the process of changing a mass of fibres into digestible nutrients. These bacteria are obtained by a joey from its mother in a process known as 'pap feeding' at around six months of age.

Clockwise from left: Mother and joey feeding; a young Koala reaching for a leaf; a sleepy Koala is a common sight.

What's the Difference?

Male vs Female

The male Koala is taller, up to 50% heavier and has a larger, broader head and bigger nose than the female. Only the male has a brown, sternal (chest) gland for scent-marking. The female has a rounder forehead and proportionally larger ears. Her nose and chin are smaller and more pointed.

North vs South

The Koala that lives in cooler, southern regions is 30% heavier than its cousin in the north. Its coat is darker and shaggier with thicker fur around the face and ears, providing more warmth than the shorter, lighter fur of the northern Koala.

The Koala as a Commodity

The Koala features in a number of Aboriginal Dreaming stories and has various local names including *cullawine, karbor, koolah, colo, boorabee* and *burrenbong*. For certain Aboriginal people, the Koala has cultural significance and for others it was a valued source of meat and pelts. During the late 1800s, the Koala became an Australian export commodity. Since shooting spoiled the fur, the animal was trapped, clubbed or poisoned with cyanide. One million skins were taken in the 1919 Queensland season and in 1927, more than 580,000 pelts were exported, mostly to the USA. Public outrage and a ban on imports by the USA finally ended the Koala fur trade in the late '20s.

FACTS

- The Koala's caecum is similar to the human appendix.

- A Koala eats around 400 g (or a shopping bag full) of leaves a day to meet its energy needs.

- A eucalypt leaf may contain 50% water, 18% fibre, 13% tannins, 8% fat, 5% carbohydrates, 4% protein and 2% minerals.

- The Koala gets water from its food and rarely needs to drink.

- The Koala occasionally eats bark and soil. It is thought it obtains extra nutrients by doing this.

Threats

Deforestation, agriculture and development, as well as increasing human population growth, have further marginalised this once widespread mammal. Two of its greatest threats are car strikes and dog attacks. In some areas housing covenants prohibit dog ownership to prevent attacks. Koala corridors joining sections of fragmented bushland are important for allowing Koalas to disperse. The Koala is also at risk of infection from Chlamydia, a sexually transmitted disease that can cause blindness and female infertility. Other threats include bushfire, drought, eucalyptus dieback and climate change.

LOCATION TIPS

- ▶ Kangaroo Island, SA
- ▶ Grampians NP, Vic.
- ▶ Brisbane Forest Park, Qld
- ▶ Myall Lakes NP, NSW

Finding Koalas

The Koala can be difficult to spot in the wild, often looking like part of the tree in which it is sitting. During the day, look up into forked branches. Check smooth tree trunks for pock marks and short, parallel tear-shaped gouges. Look on the ground for tracks with wide-soled, five-digit prints or at the base of trees for brown or reddish brown droppings that are hard, ridged and cylindrical. Track Koalas at night by their loud bellows, snore-like grunts, wails and screams.

Fore foot and print   Hind foot and print

KOALA *Phascolarctos cinereus*

QUICK REFERENCE	
Average lifespan	18 years
Diet	Herbivore
Reproduction period Number of offspring Offspring maturity	Sept–Feb 1 2 years
Length ♂	750–820 mm
Length ♀	680–730 mm
Weight ♂	9.5–15 kg
Weight ♀	7–11 kg
Status	Vulnerable

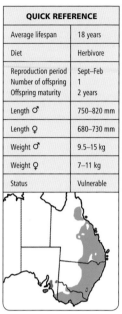

The Koala is one of Australia's best-known marsupials, but it is often overlooked in the wild because of its cryptic behaviour and colouration.

Habitat: Tropical to temperate eucalypt forest and woodland. **Behaviour:** Arboreal, solitary, mostly nocturnal. **Diet:** Eucalypt leaves. **Breeding:** September to February. Females breed at 2 years; males usually at 3–4 years. **Features:** Woolly fur light to dark grey with brown and white patches; cream belly. Broad head with small eyes, large furry ears and rectangular naked nose. Tail not visible. 5 toes on each foot; front foot has 2 opposable digits; hind foot has clawless opposable first toe and fused second and third toes. Female has 2 teats. Male has scent gland in pale fur on chest. **Threats:** Habitat destruction, car strike, dog attack, disease.

WOMBATS

SUBORDER: VOMBATIFORMES
FAMILY: VOMBATIDAE

The shambling, muddle-headed wombat of storybook fame is a creature of fiction. People who have spent time with them describe wombats as playful, stubborn and quick to learn. They have the most well-developed brain of any marsupial. Since wombats avoid people and are mainly nocturnal, their intelligence is not generally appreciated.

There are only three members of the **Vombatidae** family, separated into two genera. They are primarily grazers with a preference for native grasses. Wombats feed at night and spend their days in burrows which may be lined with vegetation for insulation and comfort.

A Southern Hairy-nosed Wombat enjoying a good scratch.

The nocturnal Common Wombat will venture out of its burrow before dark on certain occasions.

The biggest burrower

The wombat is the largest burrowing herbivorous mammal in the world. A stout body, blunt head and broad paws with strong claws make it a powerful earth-mover. An industrious wombat can excavate up to two metres a night. It loosens the soil with its forepaws and uses all four limbs to push it backwards. It lies on its side to scratch out the walls and roof, making a tunnel about 50 centimetres high and 50 centimetres wide.

Burrows provide wombats with protection from predators, weather and bushfires. A major burrow may be 30 metres long and form part of a network with several entrances. It usually takes more than one generation of wombats to create a large warren.

Wombats spend about two-thirds of their life underground, carrying out regular tunnel maintenance and resting in leaf-lined sleeping chambers. A burrow sometimes has a vestibule just inside the entrance from which the wombat can observe outdoor conditions before emerging to forage at night or on overcast days.

FACTS
• When a wombat is resting in its burrow, its metabolism slows to two-thirds its normal rate to conserve energy and water.
• Wombats can visit between 1 and 6 burrows each night.

A Common Wombat busy at work maintaining its burrow.

Breeding

Female wombats build separate nursery burrows in which they give birth and raise their young. Between 20 and 30 days after mating, a female gives birth to a bean-sized baby weighing one gram. The blind and furless young uses its front legs to pull itself into its mother's backward-facing pouch. It remains attached to one of two nipples until it weighs about three kilograms. The joey learns to forage and burrow at its mother's heels as it is being weaned. If a colony's home range cannot support another adult, the young wombat is forced to move.

Diet

Wombats leave their burrows at dusk to search for food. They graze on native grasses, sedges and rushes, and will gnaw on the roots of trees and shrubs. Wombats are equipped with one pair of upper and one pair of lower incisors and five pairs of flat grinding molars. A unique stomach gland helps them cope with a diet high in fibre but low in nutrients.

A wombat's home range can vary from five to 23 hectares depending on the availability of food. It will travel up to four kilometres during its nocturnal wanderings and visit between one and four burrows. A wombat is very territorial when it comes to food. It uses scent posts and prominently displayed droppings to mark its feeding area. It warns off interlopers with an aggressive display of head shaking, gnashing teeth and guttural growls.

Wombats are equipped with a variety of teeth — from sharp incisors to crushing molars — that allow them to slice through grasses, herbs and sedges and gnaw on roots, tree bark and shrubs.

Wombats can move deceptively quickly when the need arises.

Threats

Dingos, foxes and domestic dogs prey on wombats, but humans are the biggest threat to their survival. Land clearing for grazing and agriculture has reduced the range of suitable wombat habitats, while cattle and sheep compete with them for food. Since the 1860s many landholders have regarded wombats as vermin. Their burrows can undermine buildings and be a hazard to machinery. They also breach fences, which allows Dingos to prey on stock, and kangaroos to graze on pastures. Between 1955 and 1965, the Victorian government paid bounties on 63,000 wombat scalps. Wombats are now protected species in all states, except for parts of eastern Victoria.

Sarcoptic mange is an infection from a parasitic mite which predominantly affects the Common Wombat and to a lesser degree the Southern Hairy-nosed Wombat. It can be debilitating and very painful for infected animals, which can become blind, deaf, emaciated and die a slow death as a result of the infection.

The Southern Hairy-nosed Wombat was once common, but its home ranges are now sparsely scattered in semi-arid and arid regions in south-west New South Wales, South Australia and south-east Western Australia. Habitat degradation and competition from feral herbivores are threats to its survival.

The Northern Hairy-nosed Wombat is critically endangered with an estimated population in 2010 of 163 individuals. Efforts to save this species include research, fire and predator management, erection of a predator-proof fence and reintroduction of the species to former parts of its range.

FACTS

- The wombat's decline was predicted by Gould in 1863.

- The range of the critically endangered Northern Hairy-nosed Wombat is less than 400 ha.

- A predator following a wombat into a burrow may be crushed against the walls or roof by the wombat's rump.

- A wombat will abandon its burrow if a snake moves in.

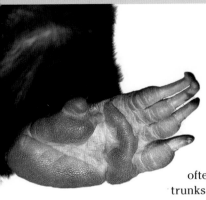

Finding Wombats

Look along dry watercourses, gullies and on sloping hills above creeks on cloudless evenings. Try overcast winter days in the snow country. A cluster of entrance holes fronted by piles of rubble is the most obvious sign. Wombats have large flat feet and a pigeon-toed gait, and leave distinctive tracks. Look for large cube-shaped droppings on prominent logs and rocks. Wombats often leave hair on smoothly polished rubbing posts, such as tree trunks, logs and stumps.

LOCATION TIPS

- Kosciuszko NP, NSW
- Wilsons Promontory NP, Vic.
- Messent CP, SA
- Cradle Mountain– Lake St Clair NP, Tas.
- Nullarbor Plain, SA & WA

Fore foot and print

Hind foot and print

COMMON WOMBAT *Vombatus ursinus*

QUICK REFERENCE	
Average lifespan	15 years
Diet	Herbivore
Reproduction period	All year
Number of offspring	1
Offspring maturity	2 years
Length HB	840–1150 mm
Weight ♂	22–39 g
Status	Least Concern

Also known as the Bare-nosed Wombat, this species was often called a 'badger' by early settlers. The Common Wombat prefers to feed in open grassy areas at night. In winter and in alpine habitats it can be found basking or foraging during the day.

Habitat: Eucalypt forest, open woodland, coastal scrub and heath. **Behaviour:** Terrestrial, gregarious but feeds alone, nocturnal in summer. **Diet:** Native grasses, sedges, rushes, shrub and tree roots. **Breeding:** All year. 1 young per season. Mature at 2 years. **Features:** Coarse, thick fur can be cream, brown or black. Large head has short, rounded ears and a naked nose. Hind foot has clawless opposable inner toe. Female has 2 teats and a rear-opening pouch. **Threats:** Habitat destruction, persecution, mange, predation by wild dogs, competition with livestock, drought, car strike.

NORTHERN HAIRY-NOSED WOMBAT *Lasiorhinus krefftii*

TINA JANSSEN

QUICK REFERENCE	
Average lifespan	20 years
Diet	Herbivore
Reproduction period Number of offspring Offspring maturity	Nov–Apr 1 3 years
Length ♂	1028–1130 mm
Length ♀	1037–1125 mm
Weight ♂	28.6–33.4 kg
Weight ♀	28.9–34.9 kg
Status	Critically Endangered

Epping Forest National Park in central Queensland is home to the main surviving colony of Northern Hairy-nosed Wombats. A second insurance population was established by reintroduction at Richard Underwood Nature Refuge near St George in south-central Queensland in 2009. The two populations are protected by Dingo-proof fences.

Habitat: Semi-arid open woodland with deep, sandy soil. **Behaviour:** Terrestrial, sometimes share burrows, feed alone, nocturnal. **Diet:** Mainly native grasses, some introduced grass. **Breeding:** November to April. Females breed every 2 years. **Features:** Long, silky fur is mainly grey-brown or grey mottled with fawn or black. Relatively long, pointed ears with tufts of white hairs along edges. Broad, square muzzle covered with short brown hair. May have dark patches around eyes. Female has 2 teats and a rear-opening pouch. **Threats:** inbreeding, drought, competition with livestock, predation by Dingos, fire and the spread of unpalatable Buffel grass.

SOUTHERN HAIRY-NOSED WOMBAT *Lasiorhinus latifrons*

QUICK REFERENCE	
Average lifespan	>15 years
Diet	Herbivore
Reproduction period Number of offspring Offspring maturity	Jul–Dec 1 3 years
Length HB Length T	840–1110 mm 25–60 mm
Weight	17.5–32 kg
Status	Least Concern

The smallest of the three wombat species, the Southern Hairy-nosed Wombat is found mostly on the semi-arid sandy plains of Australia's southern central coastal region where annual rainfall is 200–500 mm. It is very well adapted to living in a harsh, unpredictable environment where free water is rarely available.

Habitat: Eucalypt and acacia woodland, shrubland, heath. **Behaviour:** Terrestrial, feed alone, sometimes share burrows, nocturnal. **Diet:** Prefer young shoots of native grasses. **Breeding:** July to December; 1 young, do not breed during drought. Mature at 3 years. **Features:** Silky fur varies from reddish brown to grey. Short face with pointed ears. Can have white hair on nose and chest. Female has 2 teats and a rear-opening pouch. **Threats:** Habitat destruction, competition with livestock, drought, mange.

POSSUMS & GLIDERS

ORDER: DIPROTODONTIA

FACTS

- Urban-dwelling Common Brushtail Possums use roof cavities for dens.

- Sugar Gliders live in groups consisting of up to seven adults and their offspring.

- Secretions from a male Common Brushtail's chest gland stain its fur red.

- A Common Ringtail Possum may have up to eight nests in its home range.

- The Rufous Owl preys on ringtail possums in tropical rainforest.

- Rock Ringtail Possums form a guard around their young when moving between feeding sites.

Australia has 27 species of climbing marsupials commonly referred to as possums. They are grouped into four separate superfamilies, then six families within the suborder **Phalangeriformes**. While their bodies are as diverse as their lifestyles, all possums have a single pair of front lower incisors and the second and third toes on the hind foot are fused except for the claws. They also have long, flexible tails and the females have forward-opening pouches.

Habitat

Possums are found in forest, woodland and heath around Australia where rainfall is regular. Most arboreal species shelter in tree hollows, although some prefer to perch in clumps of leaves or even the roof cavities of buildings. The ground-dwellers make use of crevices in piles of boulders. Many possums line their shelters with shredded bark and other vegetation, making spherical nests.

Possums are quite possessive about their home areas. Some declare their feeding and breeding rights with raucous calls and physical aggression. Others mark their territories with secretions from chest, head or anal glands. Those that live in groups also mark each other, making it easier to identify and dispatch interlopers. Not having any scent glands, the sociable Leadbeater's Possum scents clan members with saliva.

IAN MORRIS

Above: Rock Ringtail Possums mark their territories with strong smelling, rust-coloured secretions from chest and anal glands. **Opposite:** Common Ringtail Possum in its drey.

This Long-tailed Pygmy-possum scurries down the branch, using its tail and feet to grip even on vertical sections.

Behaviour

Possums are adept climbers with slender, jointed toes and sharp, curved claws. Their hind feet have opposable first toes that provide a pincer-like grip. Several species also have 'thumbs' on their front feet that come in handy when climbing or holding food. Possums with prehensile tails have not only the additional security of a fifth limb, but also the means to carry nesting material.

Australia has six species of possums that volplane, or glide, from tree to tree. A flexible membrane, the patagium, extends between the front and back legs on each side of the body. Gliders can adjust the position of each membrane for stability and directional control while gliding.

Binocular vision, such as humans have, allows gliders to judge distances fairly accurately.

The Squirrel Glider **(left)** and the Common Brushtail Possum **(right)** using their prehensile tails as a fifth limb.

CHRIS & SANDRA POLLITT/ANTPHOTO.COM

A Squirrel Glider in full glide with paws raised in preparation for landing.

The larger, bushy-tailed gliders push off from a branch and stretch out their bodies to plane down towards the next tree. They finish with an upward swoop to land on all four feet.

The Greater Glider can make 90° turns in the air and glide up to 100 metres. They are often seen perched in the treetops preparing for takeoff when moderate winds and bright moonlight create optimum gliding conditions.

The Feathertail Glider is the world's smallest gliding mammal. It has relatively small membranes, but a flat tail edged with stiff bristles provides increased surface area and helps it steer and brake. It usually makes a direct approach, but can spiral around a tree trunk before landing.

The ability to glide gives possums greater access to scattered and seasonal food sources, as well as a means of escaping predators, such as pythons, quolls and cats.

A Herbert River Ringtail Possum

Leadbeater's
Possum

Diet

Whether they live on or above the ground, possums and gliders rely mainly on plants for food. Some are herbivorous, feeding on leaves, flowers, fruit and tree sap while others also eat insects, small birds and eggs, making them omnivores.

Possums have only two lower front teeth for tearing and biting, but several ridged molars for grinding. They also have serrated premolars for cracking hard seeds and insect exoskeletons. The Eastern Pygmy-possum, Feathertail Glider and Honey Possum use slender, brush-tipped tongues to feed on nectar and pollen.

The relationship between possums and plants is not a one-sided affair. In exchange for food, shelter and nesting material, possums provide plants with a means of dispersing genetic material when they carry pollen and seeds on their fur.

Possums foraging (clockwise from top left): Squirrel Glider; Green Ringtail; Common Brushtail; Eastern Pygmy-possum.

Usually found in wet tropical rainforest, the Striped Possum also forages in eucalypt woodland.

Finding Possums

There is at least one species of ringtail or brushtail possum to be found in most coastal towns and cities. Listen for guttural calls, soft snorts, rustling and crashing in trees, and thumping on roof tops. Scratch marks on tree trunks and scats shaped like jellybeans may indicate where they rest or feed. They will raid bird feeders and can be enticed with fruit. Look for gliders on relatively windy, moonless nights. During the day look on tree trunks for scratch marks and the V-shaped gouges of sap feeding sites. Several species of possums and gliders can be identified by the colour of their reflected eyeshine.

Fore foot and print of a Common Brushtail Possum

Hind foot and print of a Common Brushtail Possum

Tiny Eastern Pygmy Possums feeding on banksia pollen and nectar.

PYGMY-POSSUMS

SUBORDER: PHALANGERIFORMES
SUPERFAMILY: BURRAMYOIDEA
FAMILY: BURRAMYIDAE

Five species of pygmy-possums, belonging to the **Burramyidae** family, live in eastern and southern Australia in habitats ranging from rainforest to boulder-strewn alpine peaks.

They are usually found at night on or near the ground where they dart around the undergrowth in search of insects and flowers.

These small, nimble possums have sparsely furred, prehensile tails and padded feet with flexible toes. Most also have an opposable first toe on their hind foot. Three or four pairs of smoothly ridged molar teeth are more than adequate to deal with their omnivorous diet.

Pygmy-possums are fairly prolific breeders with some species producing three litters a year. A brief gestation period of about two weeks is followed by an average pouch life of 30 days. The young then continue development within the security of a nest and, depending on the species, are weaned and independent at 45–90 days old. The female Western Pygmy-possum hurries things along by mating one or two days after giving birth. She gives birth a second time 50 days or more later, when her first litter has been weaned.

During cold weather or food shortages pygmy-possums curl up, tuck in their ears and reduce their metabolic rate. This energy-saving torpor can last a few hours or several days. The alpine Mountain Pygmy-possum goes beyond the torpid state and actually hibernates for up to seven months of the year.

FACTS

- The Eastern Pygmy-possum feeds mostly on pollen and nectar from banksias, eucalypts and bottlebrushes.

- A Mountain Pygmy-possum's body temperature drops to 2 °C during hibernation.

- Female pygmy-possums build spherical nests of shredded bark, leaves or grass.

- It can take 20 minutes for a torpid Little Pygmy-possum to become fully active.

- Pygmy-possums use several nests within their home range.

GREG HARM

The quick and agile Mountain Pygmy-possum has an excellent sense of smell.

MOUNTAIN PYGMY-POSSUM *Burramys parvus*

QUICK REFERENCE	
Average lifespan	2–5 years
Diet	Omnivore
Reproduction period Number of offspring Offspring maturity	Oct & Nov 4 per litter 90–120 days
Length HB ♂ Length T	110 mm 138 mm
Length HB ♀ Length T	111 mm 136 mm
Weight ♂	30–75 g
Weight ♀	30–82 g
Status	Critically Endangered

The only three known populations of Mountain Pygmy-possums in the Australian Alps comprise less than 2,600 adults. They nest on the ground among boulders and often travel over a kilometre in a night's foraging.

Habitat: Heath and shrubby woodland with boulder heaps, above 1,400 metres altitude. **Behaviour:** Terrestrial, hibernates, nocturnal. **Diet:** Insects and other arthropods, seeds, fruit. **Breeding:** October and November. Usually 4 per litter. Mature by 1 year. **Features:** Fine, thick fur, grey-brown above, may be darker from top of head to middle of back. Pale brown to cream below. Dark ring around eye. Tail long, thin and scaly. Female has 4 teats. **Threats:** Climate change may reduce its snowy habitat.

The Mountain Pygmy-possum eats berries and seeds most of the year but gorges itself on Bogong Moths during the summer months.

LONG-TAILED PYGMY-POSSUM *Cercartetus caudatus*

QUICK REFERENCE	
Average lifespan	5 years
Diet	Omnivore
Reproduction period Number of offspring Offspring maturity	2 seasons 1–4 per litter 45 days
Length HB Length T	103–108 mm 128–151 mm
Weight	25–40 g
Status	Least Concern

This pygmy-possum is seldom seen because of its nocturnal habit. It has been found on the ranges and coastal plains between Townsville and Cooktown, and also lives in Papua New Guinea. These possums nest in logs, fern clumps and tree hollows. Females will stand over their young and hiss if disturbed.

Habitat: Rainforest, fringing forest of eucalypt, melaleuca and casuarina.
Behaviour: Mainly arboreal, may share nests and feeding sites, nocturnal.
Diet: Nectar, insects. **Breeding:** 2 seasons: January to February, August through October.
1–4 young per litter. **Features:** Brownish grey above and pale grey below. Distinct black eye patches and thin, crinkly ears. Long hairless tail except for small areas at thick base onto which body fur extends. Female has 4 teats.

WESTERN PYGMY-POSSUM *Cercartetus concinnus*

QUICK REFERENCE	
Average lifespan	5 years
Diet	Omnivore
Reproduction period Number of offspring	All year 6 per litter
Length HB Length T	64–106 mm 53–101 mm
Weight	8–21 g
Status	Least Concern

JIRI LOCHMAN/LOCHMAN TRANSPARENCIES

The Western Pygmy-possum feeds in low shrubs and on the ground. It shelters during the day in tree hollows and the crowns of grass-trees. They are prolific breeders, which helps keep populations from being decimated by cats.

Habitat: Heath, dry eucalypt forest and woodland with shrubby undergrowth. **Behaviour:** Mainly arboreal, solitary, nocturnal. **Diet:** Insects, nectar. **Breeding:** All year. 2 to 3 litters per year. 6 young per litter. **Features:** Fawn or reddish brown above, white below. Tapered tail has fine scales with some fur at the base. Short claws on toes of front foot. Opposable first toe on hind foot. Female has 6 teats. **Threats:** Owls and feral cats. When confronted, will freeze and sit stock still to avoid attack.

LITTLE PYGMY-POSSUM *Cercartetus lepidus*

Australia's smallest possum weighs in at an average of 7 g. It was thought to exist only in Tasmania, where it occupies most habitats except rainforest, but has since been found in north-west Victoria, south-east South Australia and on Kangaroo Island, South Australia.

DAVE WATTS/LOCHMAN TRANSPARENCIES

Habitat: Wet and dry eucalypt forest, mallee woodland. **Behaviour:** Nests and feeds on or above ground, nocturnal. During winter, becomes torpid. **Diet:** Nectar, pollen, insects and other arthropods. **Breeding:** September through January. Usually 3–4 per litter. **Features:** Soft, thick fur is pale fawn above, grey below. Large ears. Furred, prehensile tail tapers from thick base. Has a fourth pair of upper and lower molars. Female has 4 teats. **Threats:** Cats (both feral and domestic), owls, snakes and probably quolls. Backburning of protective undergrowth could also affect this pygmy-possum.

QUICK REFERENCE	
Average lifespan	5 years
Diet	Omnivore
Reproduction period Number of offspring	Sept–Jan 3–4 per litter
Length HB Length T	50–73 mm 60–75 mm
Weight	6–10 g
Status	Least Concern

EASTERN PYGMY-POSSUM *Cercartetus nanus*

QUICK REFERENCE	
Average lifespan	4 years
Diet	Omnivore
Reproduction period Number of offspring Offspring maturity	All year 4 per litter 5 months
Length HB Length T	70–110 mm 75–105 mm
Weight	15–43 g
Status	Least Concern

This little possum extracts nectar and pollen with the help of a brush-tipped tongue. Nesting females are sometimes found in tree hollows, under loose bark and in abandoned bird nests.

Habitat: Swampland, eucalypt forest, heath. **Behaviour:** Arboreal, mostly solitary, nocturnal. During winter, becomes torpid. **Diet:** Nectar, pollen, fruit, insects. **Breeding:** Late spring to early autumn on mainland. Late winter to early spring in Tasmania. 2 litters of 4 young per season. Mature at 5 months. **Features:** Soft, dense fur is fawn-grey to olive-brown above, light grey to white below. Large round ears. Sparse-haired tail with fat base tapering to point. Female has 4 teats. **Threats:** Cats. Unsuitable fire regimes could destroy understorey.

Striped Possum

WRIST-WINGED GLIDERS, STRIPED POSSUM & LEADBEATER'S POSSUM

SUBORDER: PHALANGERIFORMES
SUPERFAMILY: PETAUROIDEA
FAMILY: PETAURIDAE

There are six species of possums in Australia that belong to the **Petauridae** family. They all have long, chisel-like lower incisors. Other characteristic features include a dark stripe that runs from the forehead along the back, and a long, thickly furred prehensile tail. The four gliding species have membranes that extend from the fifth toe on the front foot to the first toe on the hind foot.

Most of these possums live in groups of three to 10 and scent marking is used to identify one another. The male Striped Possum and Mahogany Glider prefer a solitary existence except in the breeding season. They all use tree hollows for shelter.

Petaurid possums give birth to one or two young and species with extended breeding seasons may produce two litters a year. The young spend two and a half to three months in the pouch and then another two to three months as nestlings. They often cling to their mother's back while learning to forage.

As a family, these possums are known for their vocal repertoire, which includes gurgles, snorts, hisses, shrill yaps and territorial shrieks and screams.

FACTS

- A female Mahogany Glider may use up to 10 nests within a 20 ha home range.

- The Yellow-bellied Glider's home range is about 35 ha and it may travel 4 km a night foraging

- Leadbeater's Possums build communal nests of shredded bark in tree hollows 6–30 m above the ground.

- The Striped Possum sometimes sleeps in clumps of epiphytic ferns.

- Squirrel Gliders and Sugar Gliders have interbred in captivity, producing fertile offspring.

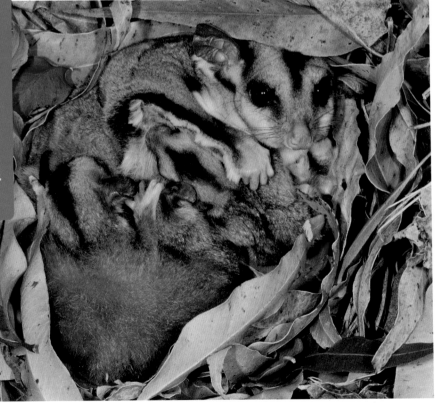

Sugar Glider families love to snuggle in tight bunches.

STRIPED POSSUM *Dactylopsila trivirgata*

The Striped Possum is noisy, smelly and erratic. It races, leaps, crashes and snorts its way through the rainforest canopy looking for food or chasing rivals. The sharp claw on the long fourth toe extracts wood-boring insect larvae.

Habitat: Rainforest and adjacent eucalypt forest and woodland.
Behaviour: Mainly arboreal, solitary, nocturnal. **Diet:** Ants, termites and other insects, leaves, fruit.
Breeding: All year, with a peak in autumn and early winter. **Features:** Variable pattern of black and white stripes with white, Y-shaped marking on forehead. Single black stripe on each leg. Belly white. Tail-tip often white. Rounded ears. Toes lightly furred. Elongated fourth toe on front foot. Female has 2 teats. Dull red eyeshine.
Threats: Scrub Pythons and other reptiles, but no major threats.

QUICK REFERENCE	
Average lifespan	5 years
Diet	Omnivore
Reproduction period Number of offspring	All year 2 per litter
Length HB Length T	256–270 mm 310–345 mm
Weight	310–545 g
Status	Least Concern

LEADBEATER'S POSSUM *Gymnobelideus leadbeateri*

QUICK REFERENCE	
Average lifespan	5 years
Diet	Omnivore
Reproduction period Number of offspring Offspring maturity	See text 1–2 per litter 10–15 months
Length HB Length T	150–170 mm 145–180 mm
Weight	100–166 g
Status	Endangered

This possum was presumed extinct until it was rediscovered in 1961. It is found only in Victoria's highland Mountain Ash forest. Groups of up to eight live in communal nests lined with shredded bark in tree hollows. Colonies defend their home nests against intruders. These nimble climbers can leap up to two metres.

Habitat: Highland eucalypt forest with acacia understorey. **Behaviour:** Arboreal, gregarious, nocturnal. **Diet:** Insects and other arthropods, plant sap and wattle gum.
Breeding: Spring and autumn. 1–2 young per litter. **Features:** Similar to Sugar Glider but without gliding membranes. Soft fur is grey to greyish brown above with dark stripe from crown to rump, pale below. Club-shaped tail. Large, thin, ears have white base. Ridged foot pads, retractable claws and one opposable toe on front foot. Female has 4 teats.

YELLOW-BELLIED GLIDER *Petaurus australis*

QUICK REFERENCE	
Average lifespan	10 years
Diet	Omnivore
Reproduction period	See text
Number of offspring	1
Offspring maturity	2 years
Length HB	240–310 mm
Length T	380–460 mm
Weight	435–725 g
Status	Vunerable

This noisy and gregarious glider chews V-shaped notches in eucalypt trees to get at the sap. It can run along the underside of branches and glide up to 150 metres. It lives in small groups dominated by an adult male that scent-marks his den mates.

Habitat: Eucalypt forest.
Behaviour: Arboreal, territorial, gregarious, nocturnal. **Diet:** Eucalypt sap, pollen, nectar, insects.
Breeding: August to September in the south; May to September in the north. 1 young per year. **Features:** Dark to pale grey above with dark stripe on forehead and thighs. White, cream or yellow below. Black paws with white claws. Gliding membranes extend from wrists to ankles. Large, bare ears. Long, thick, bushy tail. Female has 2 teats and pouch is divided into two compartments. **Threats:** Habitat destruction and fragmentation, logging, barbed wire.

SUGAR GLIDER *Petaurus breviceps*

QUICK REFERENCE	
Average lifespan	6 years
Diet	Omnivore
Reproduction period	See text
Number of offspring	2 per year av.
Offspring maturity	See text
Length HB	160–210 mm
Length T	165–210 mm
Weight ♂	115–160 g
Weight ♀	95–135 g
Status	Least Concern

These small gliders live in groups of up to 10. If an adult male dies, an outsider is recruited to the clan. Sugar Gliders can volplane up to 50 metres.

Habitat: Rainforest, eucalypt forest and woodland with shrubby undergrowth.
Behaviour: Arboreal, territorial, gregarious, nocturnal. **Diet:** Wattle gum, eucalypt sap, pollen, nectar, insects. **Breeding:** June to July in south-east. All year in north, 2 litters per year. 1–2 young per year. Females mature at 8–15 months, males at 12 months.
Features: Blue-grey to brown-grey, dark stripe from forehead to mid-back, cream to pale grey below. Dark patches at base of large, pointed ears. Tail grey to black, sometimes white tipped. Female has 4 teats. Dull mauve eyeshine. **Threats:** Carpet Pythons, monitor lizards, kookaburras, Powerful Owls, barbed wire, cats and foxes.

MAHOGANY GLIDER *Petaurus gracilis*

It wasn't until 1986 that this silent and elusive glider was rediscovered by science and recognised as a different species from the Squirrel Glider. The Mahogany Glider has a longer body and tail and distinct differences in skull structure. Its average glide is 30 metres.

Habitat: Medium to low woodland between Ingham and Tully, including coastal paperbark swamps and grass-tree woodland. **Behaviour:** Arboreal, mostly solitary, nocturnal. **Diet:** Nectar, sap and gum from eucalypts, acacias and grass-trees, acacia seeds, insects. **Breeding:** Births occur between April and October. 1 litter per season. 1–2 young per litter. **Features:** Varies from mahogany brown to predominantly grey above, buff to apricot belly. Dark stripe from forehead along back. Dark tail-tip. Female has 4 teats. **Threats:** Agricultural land clearing, barbed wire, car collision, cats, birds of prey and pythons.

QUEENSLAND MUSEUM/BRUCE COWELL

QUICK REFERENCE	
Average lifespan	5–6 years
Diet	Omnivore
Reproduction period	Apr–Oct
Number of offspring	1–2
Offspring maturity	12–18 months
Length HB ♂	230–275 mm
Length T	335–395 mm
Length HB ♀	225–270 mm
Length T	345–405 mm
Weight ♂	330–500 g
Weight ♀	310–454 g
Status	Endangered

SQUIRREL GLIDER *Petaurus norfolcensis*

QUICK REFERENCE	
Average lifespan	3–4 years
Diet	Omnivore
Reproduction period	Apr–Nov
Number of offspring	1–2 per litter
Offspring maturity	1 year
Length HB	180–230 mm
Length T	220–300 mm
Weight	190–300 g
Status	Least Concern

The Squirrel Glider is similar in appearance and behaviour to its smaller relative, the Sugar Glider. While they coexist in some habitats, the Squirrel Glider generally occurs in drier forest and woodland. It lives in family groups of up to 10 in home ranges of 20–30 hectares. In spite of its scientific name, it does not occur on Norfolk Island.

Habitat: Dry eucalypt forest and woodland, coastal forest and wet eucalypt forest in north. **Behaviour:** Arboreal, gregarious, nocturnal. **Diet:** Insects, wattle gum and seeds, eucalypt sap, nectar, pollen. **Breeding:** April to November. 1 to 2 per litter. Mature by 12 months. **Features:** Similar coloration to Sugar Glider. Belly fur is cream or white. Tail is bushier and never white-tipped. Snout is longer and more pointed. Ears are larger and narrower. Molar teeth are larger. Female has 4 teats. **Threats:** Barbed wire, land clearing, cats, birds of prey, pythons, and car collisions.

Daintree River
Ringtail Possum

THE GREATER GLIDER & RINGTAIL POSSUMS

SUBORDER: PHALANGERIFORMES
SUPERFAMILY: PETAUROIDEA
FAMILY: PSEUDOCHEIRIDAE

The Australian side of the **Pseudocheiridae** family is represented by the Greater Glider and seven species of ringtail possums. They are accomplished climbers having two opposable toes on each front foot and a slender prehensile tail. Unlike the wrist-winged gliders, the gliding membrane of the Greater Glider extends only to its elbow.

These leaf-eating possums have one pair of long, blade-like lower incisors and several pairs of ridged molars for chopping and grinding their fibrous food. They also have a specialised digestive system. Nutrients are released from the leaf fibres by fermentation in the large appendix-like caecum and then slowly absorbed in the extra-long intestine.

As a group, these possums display varying degrees of social behaviour. Some are solitary, meeting only to mate; others live in small family units. In between are the species where males and females feed and den together from courtship through to the weaning of their offspring. The Common Ringtail male is known to assist with the transport, grooming and defence of his unweaned nestlings.

Most of these possums are forest inhabitants that shelter and raise their young in tree hollows. The females give birth to one or two young per litter and, depending on the species, the young spend three to four months in the pouch. During the weaning, which takes two to four months, the young may be left in a nest or carried on the mother's back.

FACTS

- The prehensile tail of the Rock Ringtail Possum cannot support the possum's full body weight.

- A Western Ringtail Possum weighs about 550 g when it is weaned by 7 months of age.

- Some tropical rainforest ringtails park their unweaned young on low branches while they forage.

- Fig leaves are the Green Possum's favourite food.

- The Common Ringtail Possum builds basketball-sized nests lined with shredded bark or grass.

- When separated from its mother, a young Lemuroid Ringtail Possum makes a squeaky, hissing sound.

Above: The largest glider, the Greater Glider, eats only eucalyptus leaves.
Opposite: A pair of Common Ringtail Possums inside a tree-hollow.

LEMUROID RINGTAIL POSSUM *Hemibelideus lemuroides*

QUICK REFERENCE	
Average lifespan	4 years
Diet	Herbivore
Reproduction period Number of offspring Offspring maturity	Aug–Nov 1 6 months
Length HB ♂ Length T	315–360 mm 320–365 mm
Length HB ♀ Length T	313–400 mm 300–373 mm
Weight ♂	810–1060 g
Weight ♀	750–1140 g
Status	Near Threatened

HANS & JUDY BESTE/LOCHMAN TRANSPARENCIES

The Lemuroid Ringtail is an agile climber that spends most of its time in the rainforest canopy. It is the only ringtail to make freefall leaps of 2–3 m between branches.

Habitat: Highland tropical rainforest above 450 m. **Behaviour:** Arboreal, gregarious, nocturnal. **Diet:** Leaves, flowers, fruit. **Breeding:** August to November. 1 young. **Features:** Soft, thick fur is chocolate brown and dark grey above, yellow tinged belly. Creamy white colour form found in 30% of population above 1100 m. Short face with light eye rings. Bare-tipped tail. Female has 2 teats. Bright green to gold eyeshine. **Threats:** Global warming, pythons, Spotted-tailed Quolls and owls.

GREATER GLIDER *Petauroides volans*

QUICK REFERENCE	
Average lifespan	6 years
Diet	Herbivore
Reproduction period Number of offspring Offspring maturity	Mar–June 1 9 months
Length HB Length T	350–460 mm 450–600 mm
Weight	900–1700 g
Status	Vunerable

This is Australia's largest gliding possum; individuals may weigh three times as much as the Yellow-bellied Glider — the next largest glider. It usually follows established gliding routes between feeding trees, making up to 100-metre glides with its forearms tucked beneath its chin.

Habitat: Eucalypt forest and woodland. **Behaviour:** Mostly arboreal, solitary, nocturnal. **Diet:** Eucalypt leaves. Normally does not need to drink. **Breeding:** March to June. 1 young. Mature at 9 months. **Features:** Colour varies from rich brown through grey to mottled cream. Belly is creamy white. Sometimes head and tail are pale. Large ears have furred fringe. Very long, furry tail is not prehensile. Gliding membranes extend between elbows and ankles. Female has 2 teats. **Threats:** Logging, foxes, Dingoes and Powerful Owls.

ROCK RINGTAIL POSSUM *Petropseudes dahli*

IAN MORRIS

QUICK REFERENCE	
Average lifespan	Not known
Diet	Herbivore
Reproduction period Number of offspring Offspring maturity	2 seasons 1 per season 7 months
Length HB ♂ Length T	334–375 mm 200–220 mm
Length HB ♀ Length T	349–383 mm 207–266 mm
Weight	1.2–2 kg
Status	Least Concern

Rock Ringtails live in small family groups and the male will defend its mate and young with much grunting and tail slapping. Unlike other ringtails, it is not known to build a nest and, during the day, rests on rock ledges and shelters in rock crevices, climbing among trees and shrubs to feed at night.

Habitat: Rocky outcrops with deep crevices and boulders in eucalypt woodland and vine forest. **Behaviour:** Semi-terrestrial, territorial, gregarious, nocturnal. **Diet:** Leaves, flowers, fruit. **Breeding:** 2 seasons per year. 1 young per season. **Features:** Thick, woolly fur is grey to red-tinged brownish grey, dark stripe from forehead to rump. White belly. White around eyes and under ears. Pointed snout and small round ears. Short tail tapers to almost naked tip, most of underside is bare. Female has 2 teats. **Threats:** Altered fire regime, predation by Dingoes, pythons, owls, cats and dogs.

GREEN RINGTAIL POSSUM *Pseudochirops archeri*

This possum's camouflage-green coat is actually a combination of black, white and yellow hairs. Instead of using a nest or den, the Green Ringtail finds a suitable branch and curls into a ball to sleep. Its young ride on the female's back after emerging from the pouch possibly for the longest time of all ringtails.

QUICK REFERENCE	
Average lifespan	Not known
Diet	Herbivore
Reproduction period Number of offspring Offspring maturity	All year 1 1 year
Length HB ♂ Length T	344–371 mm 309–372 mm
Length HB ♀ Length T	285–377 mm 315–333 mm
Weight ♂	880–1190 g
Weight ♀	670–1350 g
Status	Least Concern

Habitat: Highland tropical rainforest above 300 m. **Behaviour:** Mostly arboreal, solitary, nocturnal.
Diet: Leaves, figs. **Breeding:** All year, peaking in July. 1 young. **Features:** Thick, soft fur is greyish green to lime-green with two silvery stripes along back from shoulder to rump. White belly. Pointed snout, pink nose, small rounded ears. White around eyes and ears. Relatively short tail has thick base. Female has 2 teats. Dull yellow-red eyeshine.

DAINTREE RIVER RINGTAIL POSSUM *Pseudochirulus cinereus*

QUICK REFERENCE	
Average lifespan	Not known
Diet	Herbivore
Reproduction period Number of offspring	Apr–May 2
Length HB ♂ Length T	346–360 mm 320–395 mm
Length HB ♀ Length T	335–368 mm 325–362 mm
Weight ♂	830–1450 g
Weight ♀	700–1200 g
Status	Least Concern

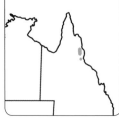

The Daintree River and Herbert River Ringtails were thought to be the same species until 1989. Having 16 pairs of chromosomes compared to the Herbert River's 12 pairs was enough to see it classified as a separate species.

Habitat: Highland tropical rainforest above 450 m. **Behaviour:** Mostly arboreal, solitary, nocturnal.
Diet: Leaves, figs. **Breeding:** April to May peak. 2 young. **Features:** Pale caramel to brown above grading to creamy white belly. Dark stripe from forehead to lower back. Tail has naked pink skin on underside and usually has white tip. Female has 2 teats.
Threats: Spotted-tailed Quolls, Lesser Sooty Owls, Grey Goshawks, Scrub Pythons and Dingoes. Global warming could diminish its rainforest home.

HERBERT RIVER RINGTAIL POSSUM *Pseudochirulus herbertensis*

QUICK REFERENCE	
Average lifespan	3–6 years
Diet	Herbivore
Reproduction period Number of offspring Offspring maturity	Apr–May 2 4.5 months
Length HB ♂ Length T	350–400 mm 360–470 mm
Length HB ♀ Length T	301–376 mm 335–410 mm
Weight ♂	810–1530 g
Weight ♀	800–1230 g
Status	Least Concern

Herbert River Ringtails are cautious climbers and rarely come down from the branches to the ground. They sleep in tree hollows and clumps of epiphytic ferns or sometimes build a nest in a forked branch.

Habitat: Highland tropical rainforest and fringing eucalypt forest above 350 m.
Behaviour: Arboreal, solitary, nocturnal. **Diet:** Leaves. **Breeding:** April to May peak.
2 young. **Features:** Adults dark brown to black above, varying amounts of white on chest, belly and fore limbs. Long, tapering tail usually white-tipped. Pointed snout, small ears and bulging reddish brown eyes with white rims. Juveniles same colour as Daintree River Ringtail. Female has 2 teats. Pinkish orange eyeshine.

WESTERN RINGTAIL POSSUM *Pseudocheirus occidentalis*

Western Ringtails are most at risk from land clearance and predation by foxes. They have small home ranges and may use up to 8 sleeping sites in a year.

Habitat: Eucalypt forest with Peppermint Gum, Marri or Jarrah. **Behaviour:** Mostly arboreal, solitary, nocturnal. **Diet:** Leaves. **Breeding:** All year with winter peak. Usually 1 young. Females mature at 8 months. **Features:** Dark brown or grey above, cream or grey belly. Slender, white-tipped tail. Medium-sized, rounded ears. Female has 2 teats. **Threats:** Foxes, feral cats and pythons. Habitat loss from land clearing.

JIRI LOCHMAN/LOCHMAN TRANSPARENCIES

QUICK REFERENCE	
Average lifespan	6 years
Diet	Herbivore
Reproduction period	All year
Number of offspring	1 average
Offspring maturity	7 months
Length HB	300–400 mm
Length T	300–410 mm
Weight	700–1300 g
Status	Vunerable

COMMON RINGTAIL POSSUM *Pseudocheirus peregrinus*

QUICK REFERENCE	
Average lifespan	6 years
Diet	Herbivore
Reproduction period	Apr–Nov
Number of offspring	2
Offspring maturity	6 months
Length HB	300–350 mm
Length T	300–350 mm
Weight	700–900 g
Status	Least Concern

The Common Ringtail Possum of eastern Australia is probably a group of four subspecies. They have adapted well to urban life, using exotic flowers and fruit as alternative food sources.

Habitat: Rainforest, eucalypt forest, woodland, shrubland, suburban gardens. **Behaviour:** Mostly arboreal, gregarious, nocturnal. **Diet:** Leaves, flowers, fruit. **Breeding:** April to November. 2 young. **Features:** Colour varies from reddish brown through grey to almost black above, paler below. Face, flanks and limbs may be red-tinged. Pale patches under ears. Long tail tapers to white tip with naked underside. Medium-sized, rounded ears. Female has 4 teats. **Threats:** Cats and foxes.

A rare cream-coloured Brushtail Possum.

BRUSHTAIL POSSUMS, CUSCUSES & THE SCALY-TAILED POSSUM

SUBORDER: PHALANGERIFORMES
SUPERFAMILY: PHALANGEROIDEA
FAMILY: PHELANGERIDAE

In Australia there are two species of cuscuses and four species of possums that belong to the **Phalangeridae** family. They all have soft, thick fur and an area of bare skin around the nostrils.

The members of this family are primarily herbivores that feed on a variety of plant material with the help of one pair of large, chisel-edged lower incisors and several pairs of ridged molars. The cuscuses, with their impressive canines, and the Common Brushtail, with its sharp triangular premolars, are known to indulge occasionally in animal protein, such as arthropods and small birds and their eggs.

Phalangerids have a prehensile tail, an opposable first toe on the hind foot and, except for the brushtails, are also equipped with two opposable toes on the front foot. They are agile but careful climbers, likely to stretch rather than leap across gaps.

Most of these marsupials have a gestation period of about 17 days. Twins are common in the cuscuses, but the possums usually rear only one young at a time. Depending on the species, a newborn spends four to six and a half months in its mother's forward-opening pouch. During the weaning period, which ends at about eight months of age, a young possum alternates time in the nest with foraging trips on its mother's back. Not having a nest or den, the Spotted Cuscus carries its young until they get too heavy.

The brushtail possums are the most vocal members of this group, using a variety of snorts, hisses and guttural sounds to announce their presence and defend their den and feeding sites. They also mark their areas with secretions from chin, chest and anal glands.

FACTS

- Common Brushtail Possums shelter in tree hollows, clumps of leaves, fallen logs, termite mounds, rock crevices and roof cavities.

- Initially, Mountain Brushtails produce mostly male offspring; towards the end of their reproductive life they give birth to more females.

- Two of the world's 17 species of cuscuses live in Australia.

- The Scaly-tailed Possum's Aboriginal name is Ilangurra.

Copper-coloured Brushtail Possum feeding at night.

SOUTHERN COMMON CUSCUS *Phalanger mimicus*

This cuscus is a slow, deliberate climber that shelters in tree hollows. It bounds over the ground at human walking speed.

PAVEL GERMAN/AUSCAPE

Habitat: Tropical rainforest on eastern Cape York Peninsula.
Behaviour: Mostly arboreal, solitary, nocturnal. **Diet:** Fruit, flowers, buds, leaves; possibly insects, birds and eggs.
Breeding: Possibly all year. 1–2 young.
Features: Greyish brown flecked with white. Dark stripe from crown to rump. Off-white below. Male has yellow chest patch and yellow tinge to sides of neck. White claws. Sparsely furred head with long snout and white patch behind ear. Large canine teeth. Most of tail is naked. 2 opposable toes on front foot. Female has 4 teats. Bright red eyeshine.
Threats: Pythons.

QUICK REFERENCE	
Average lifespan	Not known
Diet	Omnivore
Reproduction period	All year
Number of offspring	1–2
Length HB	350–400 mm
Length T	280–350 mm
Weight	1.5–2.2 kg
Status	Least Concern

COMMON SPOTTED CUSCUS *Spilocuscus maculatus*

QUICK REFERENCE	
Average lifespan	Up to 11 years
Diet	Omnivore
Reproduction period	All year
Number of offspring	1–2
Length HB	348–580 mm
Length T	310–435 mm
Weight	1.5–4.9 kg
Status	Least Concern

The Spotted Cuscus has no fixed shelter. It rests on tree branches, sometimes making a temporary platform of leafy twigs. The males are aggressive and will attack each other.

Habitat: Tropical rainforest, mangroves, open eucalypt forest. **Behaviour:** Mostly arboreal, solitary, mainly nocturnal. **Diet:** Fruit, flowers, leaves, insects, small birds, bird eggs.
Breeding: Possibly all year. 1–2 young. **Features:** Solidly built with dense, woolly fur, grey above and cream below. Males have pale spots on back and females sometimes have white rumps. Very small ears. Large red-rimmed eyes. Snout is sparsely furred showing yellowish pink skin. Large canine teeth. Two-thirds of prehensile tail is naked. 2 opposable toes on front foot. Female has 4 teats.

SHORT-EARED BRUSHTAIL POSSUM *Trichosurus caninus*

QUICK REFERENCE	
Average lifespan	See text
Diet	Herbivore
Reproduction period	Mar–May
Number of offspring	1
Offspring maturity	Up to 18 mths
Length HB	400–500 mm
Length T	340–420 mm
Weight ♀	2.5–4.5 g
Status	Least Concern

The Short-eared Brushtail is found on the Great Dividing Range from south-east Queensland to central New South Wales. Its southern relative, the Mountain Brushtail *T. cunninghami* has longer ears and feet, and a shorter tail. Until recently, these were thought to be the same species.

Habitat: Subtropical rainforest, eucalypt forest. **Behaviour:** Mainly arboreal, solitary, nocturnal. **Diet:** Leaves, fruit, flowers, seeds, fungi, lichen, bark. **Breeding:** March to May. 1 young. Females mature at 2 years. **Lifespan:** Females up to 17 years, males up to 12 years. **Features:** White-flecked dark grey to black above, whitish below. Short, round ears. Bushy tail has strip of naked skin on underside. 5 toes on front paws are evenly spread.

MOUNTAIN BRUSHTAIL POSSUM *Trichosurus cunninghami*

QUICK REFERENCE	
Average lifespan	Up to 17 years
Diet	Herbivore
Reproduction period	Apr–May
Number of offspring	1
Offspring maturity	2 years
Length HB	490–540 mm
Length T	340–370 mm
Weight	2.6–4.2 kg
Status	Least Concern

Once believed to be a subspecies of the Short-eared Brushtail Possum, this possum, also known as the Bobuck, was declared to be a different species in 2002 based on its longer hind foot, longer ears and shorter tail. It prefers to live in wetter, high-altitude sclerophyll forests in the continent's far south-east and does not enter urban areas.

Habitat: Densely forested ranges along the coast of eastern Australia and along the Great Dividing Range and has a habitat association with Silver Wattle. **Behaviour:** Semi-terrestrial, nocturnal. The most sought-after drey sites are in tree hollows, although they are tolerant of nest boxes and will use them. **Diet:** Leaves, fungi, fruiting truffles. **Breeding:** April to May. 1 young. Mature at 2 years. **Lifespan:** Females up to 17 years. **Features:** Although also similar to the Common Brushtail, this species is distinguished by denser fur, smaller ears, a flatter snout and larger size. Males and females look very similar in size and colouring.

COMMON BRUSHTAIL POSSUM *Trichosurus vulpecula*

Australia's most familiar and widespread possum is actually a group of four subspecies that vary in colour and length of fur depending on their geographic location.

Habitat: Rainforest, eucalypt forest, woodland, urban areas. **Behaviour:** Mostly arboreal, solitary, nocturnal. **Diet:** Leaves, flowers, fruit, seeds, insects, occasionally small birds, eggs. **Breeding:** Autumn and spring; all year in northern regions. 1 young. Females mature at 1 year; males by 2 years. **Lifespan:** Average 6–7 years, up to 11 years. **Features:** Most commonly silver-grey above, off-white to cream below. Dark patches on snout. Light grey paws. Large, oval ears. Bushy tail has naked undersurface. 5 evenly spaced toes on front feet. Female has 2 teats. In the north-west, reddish grey short hair; in north Queensland, coppery short hair; in Tasmania, woolly fur may be blackish.

QUICK REFERENCE	
Average lifespan	6–7 years
Diet	Omnivore
Reproduction period	See text
Number of offspring	1
Offspring maturity	See text
Length HB	350–550 mm
Length T	250–400 mm
Weight ♂	1.3–4.5 kg
Weight ♀	1.2–3.5 kg
Status	Least Concern

SCALY-TAILED POSSUM *Wyulda squamicaudata*

JIRI LOCHMAN/LOCHMAN TRANSPARENCIES

QUICK REFERENCE	
Average lifespan	Not known
Diet	Omnivore
Reproduction period	Mar–Aug
Number of offspring	1
Offspring maturity ♀	2 years
Length HB	310–395 mm
Length T	300 mm
Weight	0.9–2 kg
Status	Data Deficient

The unusual Scaly-tailed Possum is found in rugged sandstone country near the Kimberley coast. It shelters in rock piles and crevices, emerging after dusk to forage in trees.

Habitat: Eucalypt and monsoon forest in rocky country. **Behaviour:** Semi-terrestrial, solitary, nocturnal. **Diet:** Flowers, fruit, leaves, possibly insects. **Breeding:** March to August. 1 young. Females mature at 2 years. **Features:** Pale grey tipped with black, cream below. Dark stripe from crown to rump. Base of tail is tinged red. Rest of tail covered with small knobby projections. Two opposable toes on front foot. **Threats:** Feral cats, inappropriate fire regimes and mining.

HONEY POSSUM

SUBORDER: PHALANGERIFORMES
SUPERFAMILY: PETAUROIDEA
FAMILY: TARSIPEDIDAE

FACTS

- A Honey Possum's tongue is 18 mm long.

- A newborn Honey Possum weighs about 5 mg.

- Like kangaroos, a female carries dormant embryos that resume development shortly before her first litter is weaned.

- Honey Possums may become torpid during cold weather or when food is scarce.

- Male Honey Possums have the longest sperm of any mammal.

The unique Honey Possum of Australia's south-western heathland is the only member of the **Tarsipedidae** family.

This diminutive marsupial darts from blossom to blossom probing each with its slender snout to gather pollen and nectar on its brush-tipped tongue. A keen sense of smell and full-colour vision help it find suitable flowers.

The Honey Possum is one of the few arboreal mammals to climb without the aid of claws. Like primates such as the Tarsier, the broad-tipped toes of its front feet have short, flat nails instead of curved claws. It relies on flexible joints, rough toe pads and a long, prehensile tail for grip.

Honey Possums are social creatures that live in groups dominated by the largest females. They shelter in hollow trunks of grass-trees or abandoned bird nests. Mating occurs throughout the year, but most births occur from early autumn to spring. A female will mate with more than one male and offspring in the same litter can have different fathers.

The young spend about two months in the pouch and are weaned by five months of age.

M & I MORECOMBE

HONEY POSSUM *Tarsipes rostratus*

M & I MORECOMBE

QUICK REFERENCE	
Average lifespan	1–2 years
Diet	Herbivore
Reproduction period Number of offspring Offspring maturity	All year Up to 4 6 months
Length HB Length T	65–90 mm 70–100 mm
Weight	7–16 g
Status	Least Concern

The Honey Possum is found only in southern Western Australia. This nectarivorous nomad does not have a permanent home range, preferring to follow the seasonal flowering of heathland plants. In cold weather or when food is scarce, it may become torpid for up to 10 hours at a time, conserving energy.

Habitat: Coastal sandplain heaths. **Behaviour:** Arboreal, gregarious, mostly nocturnal. **Diet:** Nectar, pollen. **Breeding:** All year with seasonal peaks. 2–3 young. 1–2 litters per year. Mature at 6 months. **Features:** Light brown or grey with three darker stripes along back, cream belly. Long pointed snout. Long, tapering tail is sparsely furred. Hind foot has clawless opposable first toe and fused grooming toes with claws. Broad-tipped toes on front foot are evenly spaced. Female has 4 teats and well-developed pouch. **Threats:** Foxes and cats.

Feathertail Glider

FEATHERTAIL GLIDER

SUBORDER: PHALANGERIFORMES
SUPERFAMILY: PETAUROIDEA
FAMILY: ACROBATIDAE

The Feathertail Glider is the only member of the Acrobatidae family found in Australia. Its relatively small gliding membranes extend from the elbow to the knee on each side of the body. The distinctive feather-like tail provides extra surface area and assists with steering and braking.

These omnivores forage between ground level and the upper canopy, collecting nectar and pollen with a brush-tipped tongue and crunching insects between their ridged molars. They are fast, agile climbers with sharp claws and large serrated toe pads that provide grip even on smooth surfaces.

Feathertails feed and nest in loosely associated groups of up to 20. They may use one or more spherical nests, or dreys, that are constructed in any suitably enclosed space.

During their long breeding season, females often produce more than one litter of three to four young. The young emerge from the pouch after 65 days and are weaned at just over three months of age. High-pitched calls and scent marking help the mother and young recognise one another in the communal nest. Like the Honey Possum, female Feathertails mate within days of giving birth and delay development of the embryos until a few weeks before her first lot of young is weaned.

FACTS

- Feathertail Gliders sometimes nest in electricity meter boxes and telephone junction covers.

- The Feathertail Glider is the smallest gliding mammal in the world.

- Special toe pads provide traction for Feathertail Gliders to climb a vertical pane of glass.

- The Feathertail Glider can glide more than 20 m.

- Huddling together and brief periods of torpor help Feathertail Gliders reduce their energy needs on cold days.

M & I MORCOMBE

The Feathertail Glider spends most of its time in trees above 15 m and glides an average of 14 m.

BROAD-TOED FEATHERTAIL GLIDER *Acrobates frontalis*

QUICK REFERENCE	
Average lifespan	3–4 years
Diet	Omnivore
Reproduction period Number of offspring Offspring maturity	See text 3–4 100 days
Length HB Length T	65–85 mm 70–88 mm
Weight	10–19 g
Status	Least Concern

Up until recently, the Broad-toed Feathertail Glider was believed to be the same as the Narrow-toed Feathertail Glider. While the belly fur of the Narrow-toed Feathertail Glider is both grey and cream, the Broad-toed's belly is all cream-coloured. The latter also has a prehensile tail and heart-shaped rear toe pads. Both species share home ranges along the east coast of Australia from Cape York to south-eastern South Australia and the Broad-toed also inhabits the banks of the Murray River in north-west Victoria.

Habitat: Rainforest, eucalypt forests, parks and gardens of Eastern Australia.
Behaviour: Nocturnal, arboreal, gregarious. **Diet:** Nectar, pollen, eucalypt sap, insects.
Breeding: Late winter through summer; all year in northern regions. 3–4 young. 1–2 litters.
Lifespan: About 3 years. **Features:** Grey-brown above; cream belly. Feather-like tail fringe.
Rear toe pads are heart-shaped. Female has 4 teats. Tip of tail unfurred. **Threats:** Cats.

NARROW-TOED FEATHERTAIL GLIDER *Acrobates pygmaeus*

Common, but difficult to find because of their size, Feathertail Gliders may drop to the ground and freeze when frightened.

Habitat: Rainforest, eucalypt forest and woodland, parks and gardens.
Behaviour: Arboreal, gregarious, nocturnal. **Diet:** Nectar, pollen, eucalypt sap, insects. **Breeding:** Late winter through summer; all year in northern regions. 3–4 young. 1–2 litters. **Features:** Grey-brown above and white to cream below. Fringe of stiff hairs on each side of prehensile tail. Gliding membrane extends between elbows and knees. Pointed snout and relatively large rounded ears. Striated toe pads. Clawless, opposable first toe on hind foot. Female has 4 teats.
Threats: Cats.

QUICK REFERENCE	
Average lifespan	3–4 years
Diet	Omnivore
Reproduction period Number of offspring Offspring maturity	See text 2 per litter 100 days
Length HB Length T	65–80 mm 70–80 mm
Weight	10–15 g
Status	Least Concern

MACROPODS
KANGAROOS & THEIR RELATIVES
ORDER: DIPROTODONTIA

There are three families of marsupials which are commonly referred to as macropods. The Musky Rat-kangaroo of the Hypsiprymnodontidae family, and the potoroos and bettongs of the Potoroidae family are small macropods. The Macropodidae family includes the larger and more familiar kangaroos and wallabies.

This is the largest group of marsupials, with over 70 species. It is also a very diverse superfamily, with species ranging from less than one kilogram in size through to over 90 kilograms. Fossil evidence suggests Australia's macropods evolved from possum-like animals. As they abandoned the treetops for the continent's expanding grassland habitats, most of them developed features more suited to open terrain.

While various models were being tried and tested on the evolutionary roadway, a body plan emerged that became standard equipment for a typical Australian macropod. It included short forelimbs, powerful hindquarters and long hind feet that gave these marsupials a distinctive upright stance and a two-footed hopping gait.

However, not all macropods developed the size or features needed for a life in the open. Several species still rely on densely vegetated habitats for food and shelter, and their compact bodies retain features more commonly found in modern day possums.

FACTS

- A macropod's powerful leg muscles and stretchy tendons store and release energy as an elastic band does.

- When swimming, a macropod can kick its hind legs alternately.

- Tree-kangaroos and the Musky Rat-kangaroo have long forelimbs and can walk on all fours as well as hop.

- A female Eastern Grey Kangaroo holds the marsupial speed record of 64 km/h.

- The high jump record is held by a male Red Kangaroo that escaped hunters by leaping over a 3.1-m-high stack of timber.

- A Red Kangaroo can hop at 40 km/h for up to 2 km.

Features of a Typical Macropod

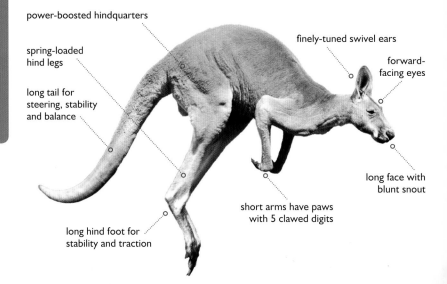

power-boosted hindquarters

spring-loaded hind legs

long tail for steering, stability and balance

finely-tuned swivel ears

forward-facing eyes

long face with blunt snout

short arms have paws with 5 clawed digits

long hind foot for stability and traction

Macropods on the move

On land, most macropods are unable to walk or run on all fours because their hind legs cannot move independently of each other and are much longer than the front limbs. While their 'pentapedal' walk is ungainly, macropods are masters of the two-footed hop.

Hopping is a useful method of locomotion for animals that need to make quick getaways, especially in open country where there are few places to hide. It is an energy-efficient means of travel that uses less oxygen than running or galloping at speeds above 15 kilometres per hour. A hopping macropod also saves on the amount of energy it takes to breathe because air is forced in and out of its lungs as its gut flops up and down.

Eastern Grey Kangaroo

Pentapedal Walk

When a macropod is moving slowly, the front limbs and tail support the body as the hind legs swing forward simultaneously.

Bipedal Hop

When moving at speed, a macropod hops on its two hind legs. The tail acts as a counterbalance and the arms and head are usually positioned to streamline the fore body.

Above left: Eastern Grey Kangaroo. **Above right:** Red Kangaroo.

Keeping cool

A macropod has a split upper lip that channels moisture from the nose into the mouth. To reduce heat stress and conserve body moisture a macropod:

- travels and feeds between dusk and dawn
- rests in the shade during the day
- scrapes away topsoil to lie on cooler ground
- does not sweat
- uses the roof of its mouth and long tongue as evaporative coolers
- licks its chest and arms so the evaporating saliva cools its skin.

A female Red Kangaroo **(Above)** is blue-grey in colour and can be easily mistaken for a Grey Kangaroo, while the males are red in colour.

Diet

For a group of animals usually referred to as herbivores, macropods are surprisingly diverse in their eating habits. Potoroos, the Musky Rat-kangaroo and some of the bettong species depend as much on insects and fungi as they do on plants.

Of the species that are strictly vegetarian, some have a preference for browsing on shrubs and other leafy green plants, while others are predominantly grazers of native and introduced grasses. Regardless of what kinds of vegetation they prefer to eat, all macropods are well equipped to deal with a variety of high fibre, low nutrient food plants.

Top: Lumholtz's Tree-kangaroo. **Above:** Juvenile Red-necked Wallaby encouraging mother to regurgitate stomach flora. **Above right:** An Eastern Grey Kangaroo vocalising a threat.

A typical macropod has two chisel-like lower incisors that fit behind three pairs of upper incisors to create a nipping or shearing mechanism. A gap behind the front teeth allows the tongue to push wads of food back to the grinding molars. Once the food has been swallowed, micro-organisms in the fore stomach ferment the plant fibres into fatty acids that are absorbed by the rest of the digestive system.

Macropods, with the exception of the potoroids, have an unusual adaptation to cope with molars that are worn down by fibrous and abrasive native plants. The four molars on each side of the upper and lower jaws erupt in slow succession and move forward along the jaw as the animal gets older. When a molar at the head of the line wears down, it falls out and the one behind takes its place. A middle-aged macropod may have all 16 molars in use, but after a lifetime of chewing it may be left with only one or two molars in each jaw. The Nabarlek has the additional advantage of having a never-ending supply of moving molars.

Macropods eating **(clockwise from top left):** Red-necked Pademelon; Whiptail Wallaby;
Long-nosed Potoroo; Burrowing Bettong.

Threats

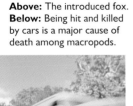

ISSELEE/DREAMSTIME

Above: The introduced fox.
Below: Being hit and killed by cars is a major cause of death among macropods.

The smaller species of macropods and their young (called joeys) are fair game for native and introduced carnivores such as pythons, goannas, birds of prey, quolls, cats, dogs and foxes. Keen senses, multi-directional ears and an upright stance are part of a macropod's inbuilt alert system that helps it pinpoint potential threats. Species that live in groups warn one another of danger by thumping their hind feet, and maternal tutting and clicking help keep vulnerable joeys from straying too far.

While some species use cryptic colouration and behaviour to quietly disappear into their surroundings, a threatened macropod's usual response is to flee. It may, however, escape a predator only to die of a stress-induced heart attack within a very short time. Large male kangaroos sometimes stand their ground and lash out with a disembowelling kick. They've also been seen trying to drown Dingos and dogs that have pursued them into waterholes and rivers.

While some macropod species are common, several of the smaller species require conservation measures to safeguard them from extinction. Since Europeans settled in Australia, 12% of macropod species have already become extinct. Along with predation, the threats to these species include competition from introduced herbivores, car strikes, habitat destruction and fragmentation and degradation of habitats due to agricultural practices.

A Wedge-tailed Eagle swoops in to attack a wallaroo.

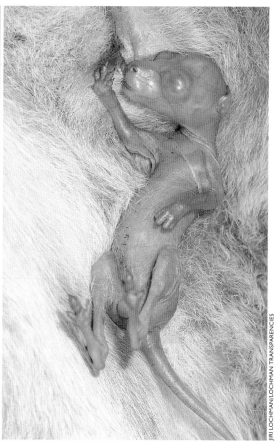

Above left: An unweaned Red-necked Wallaby joey at heel.
Above right: The mother's teat swells in the recently born joey's mouth so it won't slide off.

Reproduction

Most macropods produce young only when conditions favour their survival. The females are fertile throughout the year if food is plentiful, but do not come into breeding condition in times of drought. This is a great advantage to plant-eating animals whose food supply is often limited by irregular rainfall.

The females of most species can also control the rate at which their embryos develop. This phenomenon is called 'embryonic diapause' and is particularly useful in harsh environments where infant mortality is high. A female usually mates again soon after giving birth; however, development of the fertilised egg is suspended while she is carrying a pouch joey.

Development resumes if the joey dies, or a few weeks before it permanently leaves the pouch. The new baby is born after a normal gestation period and takes possession of the pouch.

If conditions are good and the mother mates again, she will have an unweaned joey at heel, a suckling joey in the pouch and an embryonic joey in waiting. Although macropods usually only give birth to one joey at a time, they have four teats in their forward opening pouches and have the remarkable ability to produce different types of milk from different teats at the same time.

FACTS

- A newborn Eastern Grey Kangaroo weighs less than 1 g.

- A newborn Red Kangaroo takes about 3 minutes to crawl from its mother's cloaca to her pouch.

- Almost 50% of Red Kangaroos fail to reach 2 years of age; 90% die before the age of 10.

- A female macropod produces two kinds of milk to suit the different needs of a pouch young and an unweaned 'young at heel'.

JIRI LOCHMAN/LOCHMAN TRANSPARENCIES

MACROPODS ARE IDENTIFIED SCIENTIFICALLY BY:

- measurement of parts of the body (mainly the tail and hindfeet)

- the structure and arrangement of teeth and bones

- DNA and blood protein analysis.

Identifying Macropods

Identifying a macropod species in the wild takes practice, and a good field guide is invaluable. Use the information and distribution maps in this guide to determine the different species that occur in any particular region, then eliminate species by comparing them to your sighting on the basis of:

- preferred habitat
- size
- behaviour

- stance and hopping posture
- shape and size of body parts
- colour and distinctive markings.

The problem with relying only on colouration can be seen at left, where four different photographs of the same species (Whiptail Wallaby *Macropus parryi*) look like four different species.

Kangaroo hopping styles **(clockwise from top left):** Agile Wallaby; Whiptail Wallaby; Red Kangaroo and Eastern Grey Kangaroo.

Posture and Gait

A quick glimpse of a startled macropod fleeing doesn't offer much time to observe details of its appearance. Its hopping gait and posture can offer clues to its identity. Note the length of stride, frequency and height of hops, as well as the position of the head and arms in relation to the torso. The Red Kangaroo *(bottom right & inset)* and Whiptail Wallaby *(top right)* have long legs set well back on the body so the fore body tends to be lower than the arched back. The shorter legged Agile Wallaby *(top left)* and Eastern Grey Kangaroo *(bottom left)* have a shorter stride and lower trajectory. While both have an upright hopping posture, the position of the forelimbs is quite different.

Whiptail Wallabies in a variety of poses.

Common Wallaroos, showing different colours according to age, season, and time of day, could easily be confused with the Antilopine Wallaroo **(top left)**, and Black Wallaroo **(top right)**.

Colour Confusion

It is difficult to identify macropods by fur colour alone. Fur colour and how the human eye perceives it are affected by different angles and intensities of sunlight as lightwaves are absorbed and reflected by the fur's pigments and texture.

There are also genetic variations within a species. Age and gender may determine fur colour and seasonal changes in the weather can be an influence as an animal moults or its coat thickens.

To add to the confusion, Nature tends to favour subtle hues that blend with Australian landscapes. Members of one species may vary in colour in different locations while different species in the one location may look similar in colour.

- Unlike all other macropods, the Musky Rat-kangaroo is unable to hop.

- Thumb-like first toes on its hind feet and ridged foot pads help it climb sloping tree trunks.

- The Musky Rat-kangaroo buries fruit and seeds in leaf litter to come back and eat later.

- The Musky Rat-kangaroo uses its weakly grasping tail to collect nesting material.

- At 19 days, the Musky Rat-kangaroo has the shortest gestation of all macropods.

MUSKY RAT-KANGAROO

SUBORDER: MACROPODIFORMES
SUPERFAMILY: MACROPODOIDEA
FAMILY: HYPSIPRYMNODONTIDAE

Hypsiprymnodontidae is the most ancient family of macropods and contains only one species, the unique Musky Rat-kangaroo. Considered a 'living fossil', the Musky Rat-kangaroo is the smallest macropod species and not likely to be confused with other macropods.

Musky Rat-kangaroo

The genus name Hypsiprymnodon is derived from the Greek hypso or 'high' and prymon 'rump' as well as odon for 'tooth', and refers to the differences in tooth and body structure that distinguish this mammal from members of its superfamily. Its common name refers to its pungent, distinctive odour.

Dwelling in the lush, humid rainforests of north Queensland, the Musky Rat-kangaroo is a diurnal species with a characteristic galloping or bounding gait. It dines mainly on fruit, leaves and leaf litter, and may drop as much as 25% of its body weight when food is scarce.

MUSKY RAT-KANGAROO *Hypsiprymnodon moschatus*

QUICK REFERENCE	
Average lifespan	4 years
Diet	Frugivore
Reproduction period	Oct–Apr
Number of offspring	1–4
Offspring maturity	18 months
Length HB ♂	153–273 mm
Length T	360–680 mm
Length HB ♀	212–252 mm
Length T	123–153 mm
Weight ♂	360–680 g
Weight ♀	453–635 g
Status	Least Concern

Australia's smallest macropod lives in coastal and highland rainforests between Ingham and Cooktown. It forages early in the morning and just before sunset. It uses several nests that may be hidden on the ground or in clumps of vines.

Habitat: Tropical rainforest. **Behaviour:** Primarily terrestrial, uses fallen timber as pathways. Solitary, diurnal. **Diet:** Mostly fruit. Also insects, seeds, fungi. **Breeding:** October to April, 1–4 young. Mature at 18 months. **Features:** Soft, dense fur is rich brown flecked with darker hairs, slightly paler below; sometimes has white patches on chest and throat. Thin tail is dark brown and scaly. Hind foot has opposable first toe. Female has 4 teats. **Threats:** Habitat destruction and fragmentation. Predation by cats and dogs.

POTOROOS & BETTONGS

SUBORDER: MACROPODIFORMES
SUPERFAMILY: MACROPODOIDEA
FAMILY: POTOROIDAE

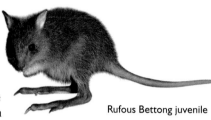

Rufous Bettong juvenile

Potoroos and Bettongs are small macropods that represent an early branch of the macropod family tree. They combine the features of modern kangaroos with those of their long-extinct ancestors.

The Potoroidae prefer habitats with a thick understorey where food and shelter are plentiful. Along with the Musky Rat-kangaroo, they are also the only macropods to build nests, making good use of their weakly prehensile tails to carry nesting material.

These omnivores feed on plants, insects and fungi, most of which are obtained by digging through leaf litter and soil. To cope with this varied diet, their dental equipment includes upper canines and fixed molars, which the herbivorous macropods do not have.

They all have a typical macropod's long hind foot with its fused grooming toes and are speedy little hoppers. Distinguishing bettongs from potoroos can be difficult, although head shape provides some assistance. A potoroo's head is elongated with a longer, thinner snout than that of a bettong.

FACTS

- Two species of the family Potoroidae are now extinct.

- The Long-footed Potoroo eats 30 different kinds of fungi.

- *Bettong* is an Aboriginal word thought to mean 'small wallaby'.

- The Long-nosed Potoroo lives up to 7 years in the wild and 12 years in captivity.

- The Burrowing Bettong builds complex warrens with many entrances and connecting tunnels.

- Bettongs do not need to drink water.

- A Rufous Bettong may travel over 4 km a night when foraging.

LOCATION TIPS

▶ Nightcap NP, NSW

▶ Freycinet NP, Tas.

▶ Dryandra, WA

Cleland Wildlife Park in Adelaide is renowned for its abundance of Long-nosed Potoroos.

RUFOUS BETTONG *Aepyprymnus rufescens*

QUICK REFERENCE	
Average lifespan	7 years
Diet	Omnivore
Reproduction period	All year
Number of offspring	1
Offspring maturity	1 year
Length HB ♂	345–400 mm
Length T	314–407 mm
Length HB ♀	363–480 mm
Length T	322–390 mm
Weight ♂	1.9–3 kg
Weight ♀	1.3–3 kg
Status	Least Concern

The Rufous Bettong has the widest distribution among its family and is the only bettong still common on the mainland. It rests in a cone-shaped nest of dry grass and will hiss and stamp its feet when alarmed.

Habitat: Eucalypt forests and woodland with grassy understorey. **Behaviour:** Terrestrial, gregarious, nocturnal. **Diet:** Mainly roots and tubers. Also flowers, seeds, leaves, sap, fungi, animal bones. **Breeding:** All year; 1 young per mating. Females mature by 11 months, males by 13 months. **Features:** Reddish brown to grey-brown fur flecked with light grey; belly is pale. Head has pointed ears and hairy muzzle. **Threats:** Predation by dogs and foxes, competition with rabbits. Drought, climate change.

TASMANIAN BETTONG *Bettongia gaimardi*

QUICK REFERENCE	
Average lifespan	6 years
Diet	Omnivore
Reproduction period	All year
Number of offspring	1
Offspring maturity	12 months
Length HB	315–332 mm
Length T	288–345 mm
Weight	1.2–2.25 kg
Status	Near Threatened

Although extinct on the mainland, this bettong species has persisted in Tasmania, probably because of the absence of introduced foxes until recent times.

Habitat: Dry, open eucalypt forest with a grassy understory. **Behaviour:** Terrestrial, nocturnal, solitary. **Diet:** Mainly fungi. Also seeds, roots and bulbs. **Breeding:** All year; 1 young; mature at 12 months. Females can produce up to 3 joeys per year. **Features:** Muted brown-grey with a soft white hip-stripe and white-grey belly. Fur is bristly. Tail well furred, and often white-tipped. **Threats:** Recent introduction of the Red Fox to Tasmania. Logging, 1080 baiting and grazing.

BURROWING BETTONG *Bettongia lesueur*

QUICK REFERENCE	
Diet	Omnivore
Number of offspring	1
Offspring maturity	5 months
Length HB	280–360 mm
Length T	207–285 mm
Weight	0.68–1.28 kg
Status	Near Threatened

Also known as the Boodie, this is the only macropod to construct large, complex warrens that shelter dozens of individuals. Found on the mainland until the 1940s it now exists only on four islands off the WA coast (Bernier, Dorre, Barrow and Boodie) and in two re-established populations on the mainland protected by predator-proof fences.

Habitat: Once widespread, except in dense vegetation or high rainfall areas.
Behaviour: Terrestrial, gregarious, nocturnal. **Diet:** Fungi, fruit, seeds, roots, tubers insects.
Breeding: All year; 1 young per mating. Usually 2 young per year. Mature at 5 months.
Features: Yellow-grey above, light grey below. Short, rounded ears. Thick, sparsely furred tail. **Threats:** Predation by cats and foxes. Disease, grazing, climate change.

WOYLIE *Bettongia penicillata*

QUICK REFERENCE	
Average lifespan	6 years
Diet	Omnivore
Reproduction period	All year
Number of offspring	1
Offspring maturity	6 months
Length HB ♂	300–360 mm
Length T	280–350 mm
Length HB ♀	250–360 mm
Length T	250–360 mm
Weight ♂	1–1.8 kg
Weight ♀	0.75–1.5 kg
Status	Endangered

The Woylie, also known as the Brush-tailed Bettong, builds domed nests of shredded bark or grass. Land clearance and predation by foxes restricted its distribution to south-west Western Australia, but it has been successfully reintroduced to areas of West and South Australia.

Habitat: Eucalypt forest and woodland with grassy or shrubby understorey.
Behaviour: Terrestrial, solitary, nocturnal. **Diet:** Fungi, bulbs, tubers, fruit, seeds, bark, insects, resin. **Breeding:** All year; 1 young per mating. Up to 3 young per year. Mature by 6 months. **Features:** White-flecked fur is grey-brown to yellow-grey above, paler below. Tail is dark with black brush at the end. Blunt, naked nose. Medium-sized, slightly pointed ears. Female has 4 teats. **Threats:** Habitat destruction, predation by foxes and cats, grazing, altered fire regimes, competition with rabbits and disease.

NORTHERN BETTONG *Bettongia tropica*

QUICK REFERENCE	
Diet	Omnivore
Reproduction period Number of offspring Offspring maturity	All year 1 1 year
Length HB ♂ Length T	320–430 mm 287–343 mm
Length HB ♀ Length T	295–432 mm 268–350 mm
Weight ♂	1–1.3 kg
Weight ♀	0.9–1.4 kg
Status	Endangered

Also known as the Tropical Bettong, this species is endemic to the drier forests of Queensland's tropical north. Smaller and daintier than its southern kin, it is a dedicated truffle eater that finds underground fungi by smell and digs them up using its sturdy forepaws.

Habitat: Eucalypt woodland with a grassy understory between 800 and 1200 metres. **Behaviour:** Terrestrial. Nocturnal. Solitary. **Diet:** Mainly truffles (underground fruiting bodies of fungi). Invertebrates, and stems of grass, lilies and orchids. **Breeding:** All year. 1 young per mating. Up to 3 young per year. Mature at 10 to 14 months. **Features:** Uniformly grey above, pale underbelly. Naked pink muzzle. Light build, bouncy hopping gait. Short, pale ears. Silver-grey tail ending in short crest. Female has 4 teats. **Threats:** Small population size, climate change, altered fire regimes, competition with feral pigs for food and predation by foxes.

GILBERT'S POTOROO *Potorous gilbertii*

QUICK REFERENCE	
Average lifespan	10 years
Diet	Omnivore
Reproduction period Number of offspring Offspring maturity	All year 1 1–2 years
Length HB ♂ Length T	286–371 mm 215–232 mm
Length HB ♀ Length T	291–343 mm 200–236 mm
Weight ♂	0.8–1.2 kg
Weight ♀	0.7–1.1 kg
Status	Critically Endangered

JIRI LOCHMAN/LOCHMAN TRANSPARENCIES

Probably the continent's most critically endangered mammal, Gilbert's Potoroo only exists in a single population of 30–40 individuals in Western Australia where it was rediscovered in 1994. Fossil evidence and specimens collected by John Gilbert, for whom the species was named, suggest it once enjoyed a much wider distribution.

Habitat: Paperbark-dominated heath with a dense understory of sedges and adjacent woodland. **Behaviour:** Terrestrial. Nocturnal. Gregarious. **Diet:** Over 90% fungi. Occasionally invertebrates and fruit. **Breeding:** All year. 1 young. Mature by 1 year (females) and 2 years (males). **Features:** Dense fur is brown to grey above and paler below. Slightly 'roman' nose, naked only at the very tip. Small, round ears and fluffy cheeks. **Threats:** Small population size, predation by foxes and cats, potentially bushfire.

LONG-FOOTED POTOROO *Potorous longipes*

QUICK REFERENCE	
Average lifespan	8 years
Diet	Omnivore
Reproduction period Number of offspring Offspring maturity	All year 1 2 years
Length HB Length T	380–415 mm 315–325 mm
Weight ♂	2–2.2 kg
Weight ♀	1.6–1.8 kg
Status	Endangered

The Long-footed Potoroo was first recorded in 1980 in East Gippsland. It has since been found in the Victorian Alps and near Rockton, New South Wales. The total population is thought to be less than 2000. This species usually nests in clumps of grass or ferns in the forest understorey.

Habitat: Temperate rainforest, riparian (riverside) forest and wet eucalypt forest. **Behaviour:** Terrestrial, solitary, nocturnal, very secretive. **Diet:** 90% is underground-fruiting fungi. Also plants and invertebrates. **Breeding:** All year, peaking around Spring. I young at a time. Mature at 26 months. **Features:** Grey-brown above; pale grey below. Robust, sparsely furred tail. Hind foot longer than head. Female has 4 teats. **Threats:** Small population size, predation by dogs and foxes, logging, wildfire and competition with feral pigs.

LONG-NOSED POTOROO *Potorous tridactylus*

QUICK REFERENCE	
Average lifespan	10 years
Diet	Omnivore
Reproduction period Number of offspring Offspring maturity	All year 1 1 year
Length HB ♂ Length T	287–410 mm 204–262 mm
Length HB ♀ Length T	259–378 mm 198–254 mm
Weight ♂	0.7–1.65 kg
Weight ♀	0.6–1.35 kg
Status	Vulnerable

The Long-nosed Potoroo in Tasmania has a longer, narrower snout than the Queensland one and is more likely to have a white-tipped tail. This potoroo can be confused with the Southern Brown Bandicoot in places where their habitats overlap.

Habitat: Wet eucalypt forest and coastal heath with thick groundcover. **Behaviour:** Terrestrial, mainly solitary, nocturnal. **Diet:** Mostly fungi. Also fruit, seeds, plant roots and tubers, invertebrates. **Breeding:** All year, but peaks winter to early spring and late summer. I young at a time. Mature at I year. **Features:** Rufous-brown to grey-brown above; paler below. Long, tapered snout with bare patch above nostrils. Tail furred and sometimes white tipped in southern populations. Hind foot shorter than head. Female has 4 teats. **Threats:** Habitat destruction and geographic isolation of populations; predation by cats and foxes.

TREE-KANGAROOS

SUBORDER: MACROPODIFORMES
SUPERFAMILY: MACROPODOIDEA
FAMILY: MACROPODIDAE

Lumholtz's
Tree-kangaroo

Tree-kangaroos are an unusual group of macropods that have returned to their ancestral home in the forest canopy. There are 10 known species of tree-kangaroo, two of which live in Australia. Their success as tree-dwellers probably has more to do with the absence of similar-sized predators and competitors than with their climbing ability.

These medium-sized macropods have longer, more muscular arms and shorter hind feet than a typical kangaroo. Opposable thumbs and recurved claws on the front paws provide grip, while textured soles on the rectangular hind feet give non-slip traction.

A tree-kangaroo's hind legs can move independently of one another, so it can walk on all fours backwards and forwards. When hopping along a branch or on the ground, the long, non-prehensile tail is held behind the body as a counterbalance. A tree-kangaroo descends from a tree tail-first. The front paws move alternately while the hind feet slide against the trunk. About two metres from the ground it pushes off, executes a mid-air twist and finishes with an upright landing.

Tree-kangaroos move through the canopy at night in search of leaves and fruit. The day is spent resting on a sturdy branch. They usually live alone, but are sometimes seen feeding in small groups.

Tree-kangaroos spend 90% of their lives in the treetops.

BENNETT'S TREE-KANGAROO *Dendrolagus bennettianus*

Bennett's Tree-kangaroo is the largest tree-dwelling mammal in Australia. The male occupies a territory of about 20 hectares, which takes in the smaller territories of several females. Though generally a shy animal, the male Bennett's Tree-kangaroo fights savagely to defend his territory.

Habitat: Highland and lowland tropical rainforest, vine forest. **Behaviour:** Mostly arboreal, solitary, nocturnal, cryptic. **Diet:** Mainly leaves, occasionally fruit. **Breeding:** All year. 1 young, independent at 9 months, but stays with mother 2 years. **Features:** Dark brown above, fawn below. Face is grey. Shoulders, and back of head and neck, are rusty brown. Feet are black. Female has 4 teats. **Threats:** Predation by dogs, Dingos and pythons. Habitat destruction, car strike, disease.

ATAGLANCE.COM.AU

QUICK REFERENCE	
Average lifespan	6 years
Diet	Herbivore
Reproduction period Number of offspring	All year 1 young
Length HB ♂ Length T	720–750 mm 820–840 mm
Length HB ♀ Length T	540–705 mm 730–830 mm
Weight ♂	11.5–13.7 kg
Weight ♀	6.3–10.6 kg
Status	Near Threatened

LUMHOLTZ'S TREE-KANGAROO *Dendrolagus lumholtzi*

Known to local Indigenous people as Boongarry, Mabi or Mapee, this tree-kangaroo is found in highland rainforest between Mt Spurgeon and the Cardwell Range in Queensland. It is difficult to spot in the wild due to its excellent camouflage, shy behaviour and habit of staying high in the canopy. Rainforest trees are its main source of food, although it sometimes browses on crops near the forest edges.

Habitat: Highland tropical rainforest, wet sclerophyll forest. **Behaviour:** Diurnal, solitary, arboreal, can leap to ground from heights of 15 m. **Diet:** Rainforest leaves, vines, fruit, flowers. **Breeding:** Sexually mature male sports an orange-coloured pigmentation on its inner thigh. Female produces 1 young; gestation 45 days. Young stays in pouch 8–12 months then with mother for at least 2 years. **Features:** Squat furry kangaroo dark-grey to black above, pale underneath, muscular front and back feet are black, elongated black bear-like face framed with a yellowish-grey chin band, long tail serves to balance, can walk backwards. **Threats:** Dogs, Dingos, pythons, car strikes, habitat destruction.

QUICK REFERENCE	
Average lifespan	6 years
Diet	Herbivore
Reproduction period Number of offspring Offspring maturity	All year 1 young 3+ years
Length HB ♂ Length T	520–710 mm 655–800 mm
Length HB ♀ Length T	420–675 mm 470–740 mm
Weight ♂	5.4–9.85 kg
Weight ♀	5.1–7.75 kg
Status	Not Evaluated

HARE-WALLABIES

SUBORDER: MACROPODIFORMES
SUPERFAMILY: MACROPODOIDEA
FAMILY: MACROPODIDAE

The name 'hare-wallaby' came about because of this compact macropod's reputed similarity to the Hare. Two of the five species are now extinct and only one species is reasonably common.

Hare-wallabies are found in a range of habitats where grass and low shrubs offer protective cover. Their daytime refuges include scraped out hollows under bushes and tunnels made in or underneath tussock or hummock grass. To escape the summer heat, they sometimes dig short burrows that can be up to 700 millimetres deep. They leave their cool retreats at night to browse on leaves, grass tips and fleshy succulents. Their food supplies all the water they need as they produce little urine and do not turn on the body's evaporative cooling system until the air temperature exceeds 30 °C.

Breeding occurs throughout the year, but there are usually two peak periods that coincide with seasonal rain. After a one-month gestation period, the female gives birth and mates again. Development of the resultant embryo is delayed until the current joey vacates the pouch at four to five months of age or, if food is scarce, for the duration of drought conditions.

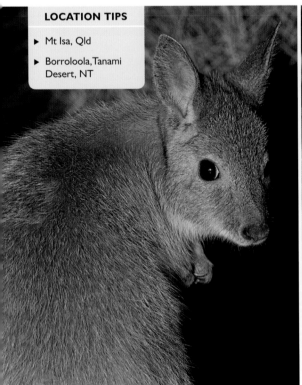

Rufous Hare-wallabies survive thanks to captive breeding programs.

SPECTACLED HARE-WALLABY *Lagorchestes conspicillatus*

Named for the reddish rings around its eyes, it is found in mainland tropical grassland and on Barrow Island, Western Australia. Its populations have declined, not as drastically as other hare-wallabies, but because of habitat change and predation by feral cats.

Habitat: Open forest and woodland shrubs, tussock and hummock grasses. **Behaviour:** Terrestrial, mainly solitary, nocturnal. **Diet:** Shrubs, grasses, fruit. **Breeding:** All year, 1 young. Mature by 1 year. **Features:** Grey-brown flecked with white above, white below, pale stripe on hip. Stocky build with a short neck. Black nose. Orange eye rings. Feet are grey-brown. Sparsely furred tail has dark tip. Female has 4 teats. **Threats:** Grazing, predation by cats and foxes, changing fire regime.

QUICK REFERENCE	
Diet	Herbivore
Reproduction period	All year
Number of offspring	1
Offspring maturity	1 year
Length HB	390–490 mm
Length T	370–530 mm
Weight	1.6–4.75 kg
Status	Least Concern

This species once survived on the Montebello Islands, and on Trimouille and Hermite Islands off the Western Australian coast until feral cats contributed to its eradication.

RUFOUS HARE-WALLABY *Lagorchestes hirsutus*

QUICK REFERENCE	
Diet	Herbivore
Reproduction period	All year
Number of offspring	1
Offspring maturity	5–14 months
Length HB ♂	310–360 mm
Length T	260–315 mm
Length HB ♀	360–390 mm
Length T	245–310 mm
Weight ♂	1.2–1.8 kg
Weight ♀	0.7–1.9 kg
Status	Vulnerable

The Rufous Hare-wallaby, also known as the Mala, was common in the western deserts until the 1930s. Wild populations are now restricted mainly to Bernier and Dorre Islands off Shark Bay, Western Australia. Animals from successful captive breeding colonies are in feral proof enclosures in Watarrka and Uluṟu-Kata Tjuṯa National Parks, NT and in the Dryandra woodlands, WA.

Habitat: Spinifex grassland and coastal shrubland. **Behaviour:** Terrestrial, solitary, nocturnal. **Diet:** Shrubs, herbs, grass, seeds. Occasionally insects. **Breeding:** All year, 1 young. Females mature at 5 months, males by 14 months. **Features:** Reddish fur with grey-brown tinge on back, darker on head. White moustache below black nose. Sparsely furred tail darkens towards tip. Female has 4 teats. **Threats:** Climate change, habitat degradation by cattle, rabbits and camels, predation by cats and foxes, changing fire regimes.

BANDED HARE-WALLABY *Lagostrophus fasciatus*

QUICK REFERENCE	
Average lifespan	6 years
Diet	Herbivore
Reproduction period	All year
Number of offspring	1
Offspring maturity	1 year
Length HB	400–450 mm
Length T	230–360 mm
Weight	1–2.3 kg
Status	Endangered

ATAGLANCE.COM.AU

The Banded Hare-wallaby is in a separate subfamily to the 'true' hare-wallabies and is one of Australia's most fascinating marsupials because mammalogists are still unsure of its place in the family tree. Its ambiguity is even more surprising given it was among the first Australian macropods to be described by Dampier in 1699 and then Péron and Lesueur in 1807.

Habitat: Dense thickets of Sandhill Wattle, Dogwood and Bullock Bush on sand and coastal dunes. Restricted to Bernier and Dorre Islands. **Behaviour:** Nocturnal. Terrestrial. Solitary. **Diet:** Shrubs and grasses. **Breeding:** All year peaking in Autumn. 1 young. Mature at 1 year but rarely breeds before 2 years of age. **Features:** Coarse, shaggy fur with protruding long white guard hairs and obvious transverse bands over the back and rump. **Threats:** Human settlement and agriculture, predation by cats and foxes, drought.

KANGAROOS, WALLAROOS & WALLABIES

SUBORDER: MACROPODIFORMES
SUPERFAMILY: MACROPODOIDEA
FAMILY: MACROPODIDAE

Kangaroos, wallaroos and wallabies belonging to the genus Macropus are Australia's most common and easily recognised macropods. These adaptable, energy efficient herbivores are also the most diverse, abundant and widespread group of marsupials. Several of the open range species have increased in number and distribution in the past 200 years with the agriculture industry providing additional sources of food and water. In some regions they can form enormous mobs of several hundred individuals and are considered a pest by farmers.

Living with the Mob

Many of these macropods live in extended family groups within large mobs. A group usually consists of a dominant male, several females and their young. Young males of breeding age tend to form separate groups, while battle-worn old males often choose to live alone. Adult males challenge one another to establish their rank in the mob hierarchy. The higher a male's status, the more females will mate with him. Sparring involves holding on, raking an opponent's head and chest with sharp claws and kicking with the hind legs.

Even the most solitary species sometimes feed in pairs and family threesomes or, in the case of Red-necked Wallabies, more than 30 individuals may gather at a prime feeding site.

FACTS
• There are 13 living species in the genus Macropus and 1 extinct species (the Toolache Wallaby).
• They range from under 6 kg (Parma Wallaby) up to 92 kg (Red Kangaroo).
• Adult male kangaroos are larger and have longer, more muscular arms than females.
• Eastern and Western Grey Kangaroos sometimes live in the same mob.
• Kangaroos, wallaroos and wallabies are protected by legislation, but in some areas they are considered a pest to crops and pastures and may be culled under permit.

Kangaroos form large mobs when food is plentiful.

Red Kangaroos.

LOCATION TIPS

▶ Namadgi NP, ACT

▶ Alpine NP, Vic.

▶ Litchfield NP, NT

▶ Mount William NP, Tas.

What is the difference?

Kangaroo is a general term for large grazing macropods mainly found on grassy plains. It also is used as a name for the Red, Eastern Grey and Western Grey Kangaroos.

Wallaroos are basically kangaroos that live in hilly or rocky country. They have large, bare, black noses. Wallaroos have a distinctive upright stance with shoulders thrown back, elbows tucked into the sides and wrists raised.

Wallaby is a common word used to distinguish medium-sized macropods from larger kangaroos. Wallabies weigh less than 25 kilograms and, being smaller, most rely on the protective shelter of habitats with dense undergrowth.

Above left: Common Wallaroo. **Above right:** Swamp Wallaby.

AGILE WALLABY *Macropus agilis*

ATAGLANCE.COM.AU

QUICK REFERENCE	
Diet	Herbivore
Reproduction period Number of offspring Offspring maturity	All year 1 12–14 months
Length HB ♂ Length T	715–850 mm 692–840 mm
Length HB ♀ Length T	593–722 mm 587–700 mm
Weight ♂	16–27 kg
Weight ♀	9–15 kg
Status	Least Concern

This common, social wallaby lives in groups of up to 10 and several groups will form a mob when feeding. Sometimes called the Sandy Wallaby, it is known to dig up grass roots from 30 centimetres below the surface.

Habitat: Open forest, woodland, grassland near fresh water. **Behaviour:** Terrestrial, gregarious, active late afternoon to early morning, flighty. **Diet:** Grasses, sedges, leaves, fruit, flowers. **Breeding:** All year, 30 days gestation, pouch life of 7–8 months. Weaned at 10–12 months. Females mature at 12 months, males at 14 months. **Features:** Sandy brown above, whitish below. Dark stripe on forehead. Light stripe on cheeks and thighs. Black-edged ears and tail tip. **Threats:** Bushfires, land clearing, car strikes.

BLACK-STRIPED WALLABY *Macropus dorsalis*

QUICK REFERENCE	
Average lifespan	15 years
Diet	Herbivore
Reproduction period Number of offspring Offspring maturity	All year 1 11–15 months
Length HB ♂ Length T	616–820 mm 656–832 mm
Length HB ♀ Length T	481–617 mm 521–619 mm
Weight ♂	8.7–21 kg
Weight ♀	5.2–7.6 kg
Status	Least Concern

The Black-striped Wallaby rests in groups of 20 or more in permanent camps during the day. It files out at dusk to feed along the forest edges and on open ground. Even when alarmed, the group does not split up.

Habitat: Forest and woodland with dense shrub undergrowth. **Behaviour:** Terrestrial, gregarious, nocturnal, shy. **Diet:** Grasses, leaves. **Breeding:** All year. Gestation 33–35 days, pouch life of 7 months. Females mature at 11 months, males at 15 months. **Features:** Brown above with reddish tinge to upper back and arms, greyish white below. Black stripe from forehead to rump. White stripe on cheeks and thighs. Scaly, sparsely furred tail. **Threats:** Bushfires, land clearing, car strikes.

TAMMAR WALLABY *Macropus eugenii*

QUICK REFERENCE	
Average lifespan	14 years
Diet	Herbivore
Reproduction period	Dec–Mar
Number of offspring	1
Offspring maturity	9–24 months
Length HB ♂	590–680 mm
Length T	380–450 mm
Length HB ♀	520–630 mm
Length T	330–440 mm
Weight ♂	6–10 kg
Weight ♀	4–6 kg
Status	Least Concern

Once widespread and abundant, this species' range has severely contracted but it is still considered common in remaining areas of habitat. The Tammar is now mostly found on islands. The one found in semi-arid habitats has been observed drinking seawater.

Habitat: Dry eucalypt forest, woodland, shrubland, heath. **Behaviour:** Terrestrial, solitary, but may feed in groups, nocturnal. **Diet:** Grasses, leaves. **Breeding:** December to March, pouch life of 8–9 months. Females mature at 9 months, males at 2 years. **Features:** Dark grey-brown with white flecks. Red-tinged flanks and limbs. Pale grey to buff below. **Threats:** Habitat destruction, changing fire regimes, predation by cats and foxes.

WESTERN BRUSH WALLABY *Macropus irma*

QUICK REFERENCE	
Average lifespan	6 years
Diet	Herbivore
Reproduction period	Mar–May
Length HB	1200 mm
Length T	540–970 mm
Weight	7–9 kg
Status	Least Concern

The Western Brush Wallaby moves through open woodland with speed and agility, keeping its body low to the ground and its tail extended. Large numbers of skins were traded in the 1920s. Predation by foxes and habitat destruction has further added to the decline of this once common species.

Habitat: Open forest and woodland with low understorey of grass and shrubs, sometimes heathland. **Behaviour:** Terrestrial, solitary, active late afternoon and early morning. **Diet:** Grasses. Does not appear to need free water. **Breeding:** Possibly March to May, pouch life of 6–7 months. **Features:** Pale grey, sometimes with brown tinge. White stripe from nose to base of ear, black-rimmed ears. Paws and last half of crested tail are black. Some have bands on back and tail. **Threats:** Previously hunting. Habitat destruction, predation by foxes.

PARMA WALLABY *Macropus parma*

QUICK REFERENCE	
Diet	Herbivore
Reproduction period	Jan–Jun
Number of offspring	1
Offspring maturity	1–2 years
Length HB ♂	482–528 mm
Length T	489–544 mm
Length HB ♀	447–527 mm
Length T	405–507 mm
Weight ♂	4.1–5.9 kg
Weight ♀	3.2–4.8 kg
Status	Near Threatened

The Parma Wallaby was thought to be extinct by the 1960s and some were repatriated from New Zealand for captive breeding programs. The species occurs naturally in New South Wales from the Watagan Mountains to Gibraltar Range.

Habitat: Eucalypt forest, sometimes rainforest. **Behaviour:** Terrestrial, solitary but may feed in pairs, nocturnal. **Diet:** Grasses, herbs. **Breeding:** Possibly all year peaking from January to June, gestation about 35 days, pouch life of 30 weeks, weaned 10–14 weeks later. Females mature at 1 year; males at 2 years. **Features:** Pale grey-brown. White chest and throat. White cheek stripe to below eye. Dark stripe from forehead to mid back. May have white-tipped tail. Hops close to the ground. **Threats:** Habitat destruction. Predation by cats and foxes. Changing fire regimes, agriculture, car strike.

WHIPTAIL WALLABY *Macropus parryi*

This beautiful macropod, also called the Pretty-face Wallaby, is found in hilly country in Queensland and northern New South Wales. It lives in mobs of up to 50 where dominant males maintain control by ritualised aggression that includes pulling up clumps of grass.

QUICK REFERENCE	
Average lifespan	12 years
Diet	Herbivore
Reproduction period	All year
Number of offspring	1
Offspring maturity	2–3 years
Length HB ♂	736–1003 mm
Length T	861–1045 mm
Length HB ♀	610–879 mm
Length T	728–858 mm
Weight ♂	14–26 kg
Weight ♀	7–15 kg
Status	Least Concern

Habitat: Open eucalypt forest with grass understorey. **Behaviour:** Terrestrial, gregarious, mostly diurnal but less active in the middle of the day. **Diet:** Grasses, herbs, ferns. Rarely drinks. **Breeding:** All year with October to March peak. Gestation 34–38 days, pouch life of 37 weeks, weaned at 15 months. Females mature by 2 years, males at 2–3 years. **Features:** Light grey to brownish grey above, white below. Face and base of ears are dark brown. White cheek stripe. Light brown stripe from neck to shoulder. Long, slender tail has dark tip. **Threats:** Species is not considered under threat.

RED-NECKED WALLABY *Macropus rufogriseus*

QUICK REFERENCE	
Average lifespan	10 years
Diet	Herbivore
Reproduction period	All year
Number of offspring	1
Offspring maturity	14–24 months
Length HB ♂	770–888 mm
Length T	703–876 mm
Length HB ♀	708–837 mm
Length T	664–790 mm
Weight ♂	15–23.7 kg
Weight ♀	12–15.5 kg
Status	Least Concern

The mainland subspecies of this wallaby, *Macropus rufogriseus banksianus*, shelters amid dense shrubs and emerges late afternoon to feed in open grassy areas along the forest edges.

Habitat: Eucalypt forest, coastal heath. **Behaviour:** Terrestrial, solitary but feeds in groups, active from late afternoon but earlier on dull or cool days. **Diet:** Grasses, herbs, shrubs, seeds. **Breeding:** All year with a slight peak in summer. Gestation about 30 days, pouch life 9 months, weaned at 13 months. Females mature earlier than males. **Features:** Grizzled grey-brown to reddish brown above with red tinge to neck, pale grey to white below. Snout and paws are black. Pale stripe on upper lip. **Threats:** Species not considered under threat.

BENNETT'S WALLABY *Macropus rufogriseus rufogriseus*

QUICK REFERENCE	
Diet	Herbivore
Reproduction period	Jan–Jul
Number of offspring	1
Offspring maturity	14–24 months
Length HB ♂	712–923 mm
Length T	691–862 mm
Length HB ♀	659–741 mm
Length T	623–778 mm
Weight ♂	15–26.8 kg
Weight ♀	11–15.5 kg
Status	Least Concern

The Bass Strait islands and Tasmanian subspecies of Red-necked Wallaby is usually known as Bennett's Wallaby. It is one of the most commonly observed native animals in Tasmania.

Habitat: Forest, woodland, shrubland. **Behaviour:** Terrestrial, mostly solitary but feeds in groups, active from late afternoon but earlier on overcast or cool days. **Diet:** Grasses, herbs. **Breeding:** One season, births occur from late January to July. Gestation about 30 days, pouch life of 280 days, weaned at 12–17 months. Females mature earlier than males. **Features:** Similar to mainland Red-necked Wallaby, but has longer, darker fur and browner neck. **Threats:** Population has expanded in the last 30 years. Considered an agricultural pest and sometimes culled under licence.

ANTILOPINE WALLAROO *Macropus antilopinus*

QUICK REFERENCE	
Diet	Herbivore
Reproduction period Number of offspring	All year 1 young
Length HB ♂ Length T	830–1200 mm 745–960 mm
Length HB ♀ Length T	733–930 mm 664–813 mm
Weight ♂	18.6–51 kg
Weight ♀	14–24.5 kg
Status	Least Concern

While this wallaroo prefers flat or undulating country, it sometimes shares rocky habitats with Common and Black Wallaroos. Restricted to the tropics, the Antilopine Wallaroo typically lives in groups of up to eight, but may form mobs of 30 at a rich food source or when threatened.

Habitat: Tropical woodland and open forest with grass understorey.
Behaviour: Terrestrial, gregarious, mostly nocturnal. **Diet:** Mainly grasses, some ground plants. **Breeding:** All year, peaking at end of wet season. Gestation about 34 days, pouch life of approximately 9 months. **Features:** Fur is reddish tan above with paler underbelly and limbs. Females can be all or partly grey. Paws and tips of feet are black. No markings on face. Large black nose. **Threats:** Agriculture, changing fire regimes, climate change.

BLACK WALLAROO *Macropus bernardus*

QUICK REFERENCE	
Diet	Herbivore
Reproduction period Number of offspring Offspring maturity	Little known 1 Unknown
Length HB ♂ Length T	595–725 mm 545–640 mm
Length HB ♀ Length T	646 mm 575 mm
Weight ♂	19–22 kg
Weight ♀	13 kg
Status	Near Threatened

This is the smallest and most timid of the wallaroos, and is found in Kakadu National Park on the Arnhem Land escarpment and plateau. During the day it rests in the shade, but may be active on overcast days.

Habitat: Monsoon forest, heath, grassland, woodland with sparse grass and shrubs.
Behaviour: Terrestrial, mostly solitary, mainly nocturnal, very shy. **Diet:** Grasses, leaves, fruit and flowers of ground plants and shrubs. **Breeding:** Relatively unknown, pouch young have been observed in July and September. **Features:** Stocky build with long fur. Males are sooty brown to black, females pale grey to grey-brown. Both have dark paws, feet and tail-tips. Ears are relatively short. **Threats:** Changing fire regimes.

COMMON WALLAROO *Macropus robustus*

QUICK REFERENCE	
Diet	Herbivore
Reproduction period Number of offspring Offspring maturity	All year 1 14–24 months
Length HB Length T	1138–1986 mm 1107–1580 mm
Weight ♂	7.25–60 kg
Weight ♀	6.25–28 kg
Status	Least Concern

This large, stocky macropod can be found on escarpments and rocky slopes throughout most of Australia. West of the Great Dividing Range it is known as the Euro.

Habitat: Eucalypt forest, woodland, shrubland, grassland with rocky hills or escarpments. **Behaviour:** Terrestrial, mostly solitary, active from early evening. **Diet:** Mainly grass. Also ground plants, shrubs. **Breeding:** All year, 1 young. Gestation around 33 days, pouch life of 231–270 days. Females mature at 14 to 24 months, males at 18–20 months. **Features:** Eastern animals have coarse, shaggy, dark grey fur. Western animals have shorter reddish fur, although young males may be grey. Both types of females may be bluish grey. All have a large, black, furless nose. **Threats:** Common and widespread. Up to 20% of the population is commercially harvested in some states.

Below: Craggy, elevated territory close to shelter and cool, rocky retreats make up prime habitat.

WESTERN GREY KANGAROO *Macropus fuliginosus*

QUICK REFERENCE	
Diet	Herbivore
Reproduction period Number of offspring Offspring maturity	All year 1 14–20 months
Length HB ♂ Length T	946–2225 mm 425–1000 mm
Length HB ♀ Length T	971–1746 mm 443–815 mm
Weight ♂	18–72 kg
Weight ♀	17–39 kg
Status	Least Concern

The Western Grey Kangaroo is found in semi-arid habitats across southern Australia west of the Great Dividing Range. The male, also known as 'Stinker', has a strong odour and is particularly aggressive.

Habitat: Woodland, grassland, shrubland. **Behaviour:** Terrestrial, gregarious, active late afternoon to early morning. **Diet:** Mainly grass. Also broad-leaved ground plants, shrubs and some crops. **Breeding:** All year with summer peak. Gestation 31 days, pouch life of 42 weeks. Females sexually mature around 14 months, males at 20 months. **Features:** Light to chocolate brown flecked with grey. Paws, feet and tail-tip can be darker. Long, dark ears. Finely furred snout with hairs between upper lip and nostrils. **Threats:** Widespread and abundant. Commercially harvested under licence.

EASTERN GREY KANGAROO *Macropus giganteus*

Increased access to food and water has seen an increase in Eastern Grey numbers and an expansion of the geographic range since European settlement. Commonly seen in modified habitats such as golf courses, it lives in mobs where the male and female have separate hierarchies.

QUICK REFERENCE	
Diet	Herbivore
Reproduction period Number of offspring Offspring maturity	All year 1 18–32 months
Length HB ♂ Length T	972–2302 mm 430–1090 mm
Length HB ♀ Length T	958–1857 mm 446–842 mm
Weight ♂	19–85 kg
Weight ♀	17–42 kg
Status	Least Concern

Habitat: Forest, woodland, shrubland, grassland, agricultural and urban areas. **Behaviour:** Terrestrial, gregarious, mostly active late afternoon to early morning. **Diet:** 99% grass. Also herbs, shrubs, ferns, and crops. **Breeding:** All year peaking Spring to early Summer. Gestation of 36 days, pouch life 11 months, weaned by 18 months. Females sexually mature at 18–22 months, males at 20–32 months. **Features:** Light to dark grey above, ends of paws, feet and tail can be darker grey to black. Females usually have white chest. Finely furred snout with hairs between upper lip and nostrils. **Threats:** Widespread and abundant. Commercially harvested under licence.

RED KANGAROO *Macropus rufus*

QUICK REFERENCE	
Average lifespan	20 years
Diet	Herbivore
Reproduction period Number of offspring Offspring maturity	All year 1 2–3 years
Length HB ♂ Length T	935–1400 mm 710–1000 mm
Length HB ♀ Length T	745–1100 mm 645–900 mm
Weight ♂	22–92 kg
Weight ♀	17–39 kg
Status	Least Concern

The Red Kangaroo can be found over most of central and western Australia where annual rainfall is less than 500 millimetres. It may live in an extended family group or in mobs numbering several hundred.

Habitat: Open woodland, grassland, desert. **Behaviour:** Terrestrial, gregarious, semi-nomadic, most active from late afternoon to early morning becomes diurnal in cooler months. **Diet:** Grasses, broad-leaved ground plants, shrubs. **Breeding:** All year. Gestation of 33 days, pouch life of 34 weeks, weaned at 12 months. Mature at 2 to 3 years. **Features:** Short dense fur. Eastern males usually rusty red and females blue-grey. In western regions, both sexes are red. Whitish belly, chest and limbs. Squarish snout with distinctive black and white patches around the nose. Broad white cheek stripe. **Threats:** Widespread and abundant. Commercially harvested under licence.

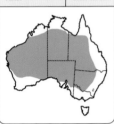

Males are powerful mammals, perfectly capable of disembowelling an attacker, human or otherwise.

NAILTAIL WALLABIES

SUBORDER: MACROPODIFORMES
SUPERFAMILY: MACROPODOIDEA
FAMILY: MACROPODIDAE

These shy, attractive wallabies with their slender faces and distinctive markings were named after the small, horny spur on the ends of their tails. The function of the 3–6 millimetre spur is not clear. One theory suggests it is used to aid the wallaby in making sharp turns when travelling a high speed by acting as a pivot point.

Of the three species that once thrived in Australia's semi-arid shrubland and grassy woodland, only the Northern Nailtail Wallaby remains common. The Crescent Nailtail is extinct and the Bridled Nailtail is Endangered. Being selective browsers and grazers, nailtail wallabies have not been able to compete with the indiscriminate appetites of cattle, sheep, feral goats and rabbits.

Nailtail wallabies rest alone during the day in a scraped-out depression at the base of a dense shrub or clump of grass. They emerge just before dusk to feed in small groups in more open areas. When disturbed, a nailtail wallaby will drop flat on the ground or crawl quietly back into the scrub.

Bridled Nailtail Wallaby

GREG HARM

The purpose of the 'nail' has mystified scientists, but this photograph of Bridled Nailtail Wallabies, taken in 2007, appears to show it being used as a weapon.

FACTS

- Nailtail wallabies were called 'organ-grinders' because their forearms make circular motions when they hop.

- When hopping quickly, a nailtail wallaby's tail curves upward.

- There was once a bounty on Bridled Nailtail wallabies because farmers considered them pests.

- Nailtail wallabies will scrape aside leaf litter to expose tender plant shoots.

LOCATION TIPS

▶ Idalia NP, Qld

▶ Barkly Tableland, NT

▶ East Kimberley, WA

BRIDLED NAILTAIL WALLABY *Onychogalea fraenata*

QUICK REFERENCE	
Average lifespan	6 years
Diet	Herbivore
Reproduction period Number of offspring Offspring maturity	All year 1 9–14 months
Length HB ♂ Length T	510–700 mm 380–540 mm
Length HB ♀ Length T	430–540 mm 360–440 mm
Weight ♂	5–8 kg
Weight ♀	4–6 kg
Status	Endangered

The Bridled Nailtail Wallaby was thought to be extinct for over 30 years until 1973 when one was spotted by a fencing contractor after he read a magazine article about extinct animals. Today the total population is between 200–300 individuals. Several captive populations exist on land trust properties in NSW and Queensland.

Habitat: Semi-arid grassy woodland, shrubland, and brigalow scrub. **Behaviour:** Terrestrial, mainly solitary, mostly nocturnal. **Diet:** Grasses, soft ground plants, shrubs. **Breeding:** All year with a spring–summer peak, 1 young. Females mature at 9 months; males at 14 months but may not breed until 2 years. **Features:** Grey-brown above, paler flanks and underside. White 'bridle' stripe from back of neck to underarm. Dark stripe from nose to eye; pale cheek stripe to below eye. Long, slender ears. Horny nail at tail tip. **Threats:** Competition with introduced herbivores. Predation by foxes, dogs, Dingos and cats. Drought, disease, habitat change.

NORTHERN NAILTAIL WALLABY *Onychogalea unguifera*

QUICK REFERENCE	
Diet	Herbivore
Reproduction period Number of offspring Offspring maturity	All year 1 11–15 months
Length HB ♂ Length T	540–690 mm 600–730 mm
Length HB ♀ Length T	490–600 mm 600–650 mm
Weight ♂	6–9 kg
Weight ♀	4.5–7 kg
Status	Least Concern

This nailtail wallaby's range extends from inland grass plains to coastal floodplains. It may travel several kilometres when feeding at night, but remains close to cover. It will make a repeated grunting or growling sound if disturbed.

Habitat: Open woodland, shrubland, tussock grassland. **Behaviour:** Terrestrial, mainly solitary, nocturnal. **Diet:** Small ground plants, succulents, fruit, grass shoots. **Breeding:** All year, 1 young. Females mature around 11 months; males at 12–15 months. **Features:** Sandy fur with dark stripe from mid back to tail. May have pale cheek and hip stripes. Long slender ears. Tail has dark tufted tip ending in horny nail. **Threats:** Not currently under threat. Possibly agriculture, fox predation and changing fire regimes.

ROCK-WALLABIES

SUBORDER: MACROPODIFORMES
SUPERFAMILY: MACROPODOIDEA
FAMILY: MACROPODIDAE

Yellow-footed
Rock-wallaby

Rock-wallabies may not be able to leap tall
buildings in a single bound, but they make
scaling a cliff face seem effortless. While
most of these macropods are no more than half
a metre tall, their speed and grace are awe-inspiring.

These accomplished rock hoppers are equipped with
powerful spring-loaded hind legs and thick, textured soles for
maximum traction, as well as flexible, muscular tails for stability and
steering control.

The rocky outcrops, gorges and escarpments of Australia's ancient
mountains and eroded plateaus are the favoured haunts of rock-
wallabies. They shelter in crevices and caves, and browse among the rocks
or descend to graze on the edges of open grassy areas. Grasses make up
most of their diet, but they also feed on leaves and fruit, particularly figs.
A specialised stomach helps them digest this fibrous plant food.

FACTS

- There are 16 species in the genus Petrogale, all sharing one common ancestor.

- Female rock-wallabies tend to be a third smaller than males.

- Aborigines used pit traps to catch rock-wallabies and the elders controlled distribution of the meat.

- Rock-wallabies live for up to 8 years in the wild.

- The Purple-necked Rock-wallaby secretes a water-soluble pigment that stains the fur on its face and neck.

- Feral goats compete with rock-wallabies for food and shelter.

- The Nabarlek is the only macropod to have self-replacing molar teeth.

- In 1908, a Sydney fur trader sold 92,500 Brush-tailed Rock-wallaby skins.

- The Yellow-footed Rock-wallabies were hunted for sport in the Flinders Ranges until 1912.

A female Allied Rock-wallaby with young in pouch rests near a cave entrance.

Power-boosted hind legs propel a Mareeba Rock-wallaby's extraordinary leap across a granite crevice.

Behaviour

Rock-wallabies live in colonies and the number of individuals in each colony depends on the availability of food and shelter. In some species, social interactions are limited to mating encounters and shared feeding areas.

Colonial life for a Yellow-footed Rock-wallaby is a more rigid affair. Each group within a large Yellow-foot colony consists of a dominant male, several females and juveniles, and a few subservient males. The leader has exclusive breeding rights and maintains his dominance by hissing, stamping, chasing and occasional physical violence.

Female rock-wallabies can breed throughout the year, but most young are produced when conditions are favourable. As with other macropods, the female carries an embryo-in-waiting, which is born a few weeks before the incumbent joey permanently vacates her pouch. The newly weaned juvenile learns the finer points of rock-hopping at its mother's heels, but is left in a cave or crevice while she looks for food.

When feeding and basking, rock-wallabies will stand up to investigate noises, ready to make a bounding retreat if alarmed. Their size, agility and camouflage colours offer some protection from predators that invade their rocky domains. However, they are defenceless on open ground.

Above left: Grooming and sunbathing are regular daytime activities for Black-footed Rock-wallabies. **Above right:** Juvenile rock-wallabies are left in the safety of a cave or crevice when their mother searches for food.

Black-footed Rock-wallabies blend in well with their semi-arid, rocky habitat.

IAN MORRIS

Time and Change

Fossils reveal rock-wallabies once migrated long distances between suitable habitats. Now that much of the land between rocky outcrops is cleared and fenced for agriculture and grazing, their wandering days are over.

Mareeba Rock-wallaby

When separate colonies of the same species of rock-wallaby cannot cross open spaces safely, there is little opportunity to interbreed, so nature works with the genetic material that is available. The members of each colony develop features to suit conditions in their particular habitat. Eventually the wallabies of separate groups become distinct species — there are so many physical differences that breeding across groups will not produce viable offspring, even when given the chance.

Yellow-footed Rock-wallabies can be found in open woodland as well as rocky habitat.

153

ALLIED ROCK-WALLABY *Petrogale assimilis*

QUICK REFERENCE	
Diet	Herbivore
Reproduction period	All year
Number of offspring	1
Offspring maturity	19–24 months
Length HB ♂	470–590 mm
Length T	409–545 mm
Length HB ♀	445–550 mm
Length T	445–550 mm
Weight ♂	4.7 kg
Weight ♀	4.3 kg
Status	Least Concern

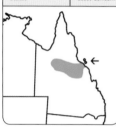

This Queensland rock-wallaby's distribution spreads west from Home Hill to Croydon and Hughenden near the southern boundary of the wet tropics. The species is also found on Palm and Magnetic Islands. Pair bonding between the sexes is maintained by grooming and sharing of feeding and daytime resting sites.

Habitat: Open eucalypt forest and woodland. **Behaviour:** Terrestrial, gregarious, mostly nocturnal. **Diet:** Grasses, leaves, fruit, seeds. **Breeding:** All year, 1 young. Females mature at 19 months, males at 24 months. **Features:** Dark brown to grey-brown above, buff coloured belly, forearms, hind legs and tail base. Pale cheek stripe and sometimes dark stripe on forehead. Dark feet, brushy tail-tip. **Threats:** Predation by cats, eagles, pythons. Agriculture, habitat fragmentation.

SHORT-EARED ROCK-WALLABY *Petrogale brachyotis*

QUICK REFERENCE	
Diet	Herbivore
Reproduction period	All year
Number of offspring	1
Length HB ♂	435–550 mm
Length T	387–550 mm
Length HB ♀	405–485 mm
Length T	320–520 mm
Weight ♂	3.2–5.6 kg
Weight ♀	2.2–4.7 kg
Status	Least Concern

The Short-eared Rock-wallaby usually lives near permanent water and relies on monsoon rains to renew its food supplies. It is found from the Kimberley around to the Gulf of Carpentaria in areas where rainfall exceeds 700 millimetres per year. Little is known about this secretive animal. Often the only signs of its presence are lots of small droppings on the rocks.

Habitat: Tropical woodland, rainforest and adjacent grasslands. **Behaviour:** Terrestrial, gregarious, nocturnal. **Diet:** Grasses, leaves, fruit and seeds. **Breeding:** Possibly all year, 1 young. **Features:** Short, fine fur varies from uniform light grey to dark grey or brown above. Dark stripe from forehead to between shoulders. May have white or dark neck stripe, or pale side and hip stripes. Short ears are uniform colour with white margins. **Threats:** Predation by cats, dogs, pythons, eagles and Dingos. Changed fire regimes, mining and agriculture.

MONJON *Petrogale burbidgei*

QUICK REFERENCE	
Diet	Herbivore
Reproduction period	Aug–Oct
Number of offspring	1 young
Length HB	306–353 mm
Length T	264–290 mm
Weight	0.9–1.4 kg
Status	Near Threatened

Discovered in 1976, the Monjon, also known as the Warabi, is the smallest of the rock-wallabies. It is found in rugged sandstone country along parts of the Kimberley coastline in Western Australia and on the nearby islands of the Bonaparte Archipelago.

Habitat: Open woodland and vine scrub. **Behaviour:** Terrestrial, gregarious, mostly nocturnal. **Diet:** Dry leaves, possibly fruit and flowers. **Breeding:** Little is known. 1 young, observed in August and October. **Features:** Olive marbled with fawn and black, fawn underneath with yellow-tinged flanks. Indistinct pale stripe from snout to base of ear. Pale midline stripe on head and neck. Olive-grey tail with bushy tip. Short ears. Black foot pads. **Threats:** Predation by cats, Dingos and birds of prey. Changing fire regimes, drought.

NABARLEK *Petrogale concinna*

QUICK REFERENCE	
Diet	Herbivore
Reproduction period	All year
Number of offspring	1
Offspring maturity	2 years
Length HB	290–350 mm
Length T	220–310 mm
Weight	1.05–1.7 kg
Status	Endangered

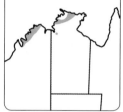

This small rock-wallaby inhabits sandstone outcrops on the coastal plains of northern Australia. It is the only macropod to have an unlimited number of molar teeth — these erupt and move forward in the jaw as teeth are worn down and lost due to the abrasive silica-rich plants it eats.

Habitat: Open woodland, vine scrub, monsoon rainforest, grassland. **Behaviour:** Terrestrial, gregarious, mostly nocturnal, very fast and agile. **Diet:** Grasses, sedges, ferns. **Breeding:** All year with a peak in the wet season, 1 young. Mature by 2 years. **Features:** Fur is rufous, marbled with grey, black above, sometimes with a darker shoulder stripe, and greyish white below. Delicate, pointed muzzle. Tail has dark and brushy tip. **Threats:** Habitat modification due to changed fire regime. Possibly predation by cats.

UNADORNED ROCK-WALLABY *Petrogale inornata*

QUICK REFERENCE	
Diet	Herbivore
Reproduction period	All year
Number of offspring	1
Offspring maturity	18 months
Length HB ♂	507–570 mm
Length T	490–640 mm
Length HB ♀	454–560 mm
Length T	430–560 mm
Weight ♂	3.4–5.6 kg
Weight ♀	3.1–5 kg
Status	Least Concern

This Queensland species makes its home in coastal areas from Home Hill to Rockhampton and on Whitsunday Island. The Unadorned Rock-wallaby is commonly seen in campsites, parks and gardens and has even been sighted on dam walls, roofs of buildings and cars. It shares its range with the less common Proserpine Rock-wallaby.

Habitat: Vine thickets, coastal shrub, eucalypt forest and woodlands. **Behaviour:** Terrestrial, gregarious. **Diet:** Grasses, leaves of shrubs and trees. **Breeding:** All year. 1 young. Mature at 18 months. **Features:** Muted grey-brown above, sandy belly and limbs. Sometimes with faint stripe on cheek and middle of back. Tail dark and brushy at tip (sometimes white-tipped). **Threats:** Habitat destruction and fragmentation. Species is locally common.

BLACK-FOOTED ROCK-WALLABY *Petrogale lateralis*

QUICK REFERENCE	
Average lifespan	12 years
Diet	Herbivore
Reproduction period	All year
Number of offspring	1
Offspring maturity	1 year
Length HB ♂	501–521 mm
Length T	490–613 mm
Length HB ♀	450–470 mm
Length T	445–590 mm
Weight ♂	4.1–5.2 kg
Weight ♀	2.8–4.4 kg
Status	Near Threatened

This wallaby's common name is confusing for wildlife watchers because it is the bottom of its feet that are black. Males and females in a colony have separate pecking orders. This genetically diverse species includes five different races. The Macdonnell Ranges race is described below.

Habitat: Rocky outcrops with deep fissures and caves. **Behaviour:** Terrestrial, gregarious, mostly nocturnal. **Diet:** Grasses and some leaves, seeds and fruits. **Breeding:** All year. 1 young. Mature at 12 months. **Features:** Dark grey-brown above, light-coloured cheek stripe, dark stripe from between ears to beyond shoulders, white side stripe, dark grey to brown tail. **Threats:** Predation mainly by foxes and cats. Competition with rabbits, goats, and sheep. Agriculture, changing fire regimes, introduced grasses.

MAREEBA ROCK-WALLABY *Petrogale mareeba*

This cryptic rock-wallaby obtained its status as a species in 1992. It is found among granite and basalt outcrops on the Atherton Tableland and is commonly seen at Granite Gorge.

Habitat: Open forest, grassy woodland, vine thickets. **Behaviour:** Terrestrial, gregarious, mostly nocturnal. **Diet:** Grasses and leaves. **Breeding:** All year, 1 young. **Features:** Usually grey-brown above, but may be dark brown to almost black, depending on habitat. Paler underside, forearms, hind legs and tail base. May have pale cheek and forehead stripes. Tail darkens towards the bushy end, which may have a grey-white tip. **Threats:** Habitat fragmentation, agriculture. Predation by Dingos and dogs.

QUICK REFERENCE	
Diet	Herbivore
Reproduction period	All year
Number of offspring	1 young
Length HB ♂	425–548 mm
Length T	420–530 mm
Length HB ♀	425–500 mm
Length T	415–467 mm
Weight ♂	4.5 kg
Weight ♀	3.8 kg
Status	Least Concern

BRUSH-TAILED ROCK-WALLABY *Petrogale penicillata*

Originally widespread and abundant, populations of Brush-tailed Rock-wallabies are now scattered along the Great Dividing Range from southern Queensland to The Grampians in Victoria. It prefers the north face of rocky outcrops where it can bask.

Habitat: Eucalypt forest, rainforest, rocky outcrops, woodlands. **Behaviour:** Terrestrial, gregarious, nocturnal. **Diet:** Grasses, leaves, fruit, seeds, flowers, bark, fungi. **Breeding:** All year, autumn peak. 1 young. Females mature at 18 months, males at 24 months. **Features:** Coarse, shaggy fur is brown above with reddish neck, shoulders and rump. Underside is paler, sometimes with white chest blaze. May have pale grey side stripe with darker stripe below. White cheek stripe and black stripe from forehead to back of head. Feet and last part of bushy tail are dark brown to black. Ears slightly yellow inside, black outside. **Threats:** Previously hunting. Predation by dogs, foxes and cats. Competition with goats, rabbits and wild horses. Habitat destruction and fragmentation.

QUICK REFERENCE	
Diet	Herbivore
Reproduction period	All year
Number of offspring	1
Offspring maturity	18–24 months
Length HB ♂	529–586 mm
Length T	510–700 mm
Length HB ♀	510–570 mm
Length T	500–630 mm
Weight ♂	5.5–10.9 kg
Weight ♀	4.9–8.2 kg
Status	Near Threatened

PROSERPINE ROCK-WALLABY *Petrogale persephone*

QUICK REFERENCE	
Diet	Herbivore
Reproduction period	All year
Number of offspring	1
Offspring maturity	20–24 months
Length HB ♂	492–633 mm
Length T	564–709 mm
Length HB ♀	526–603 mm
Length T	515–660 mm
Weight ♂	4.3–10.2 kg
Weight ♀	3.5–8.1 kg
Status	Endangered

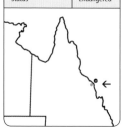

This relatively large rock-wallaby species is found in Queensland around Proserpine, Airlie Beach and on some islands of the Whitsundays. It has been confused with a tree-kangaroo as it sometimes climbs sloping trunks of trees. Males can weigh 60% more than females.

Habitat: Coastal forest and vine thickets with nearby open grassy woodland.
Behaviour: Terrestrial, gregarious, nocturnal. **Diet:** Grasses, leaves, fruit, flowers.
Breeding: All year, 1 young. Females mature at 20 months, males at 24 months.
Features: Dark with purplish tinge on back, cream or yellowish underneath. Dark stripe from forehead to shoulders. Ears black on the back and reddish at the base. Dark paws and tail. Tail paler underneath and may have white tip. **Threats:** Predation by eagles and dogs. Small population size, habitat destruction, car strikes, disease.

PURPLE-NECKED ROCK-WALLABY *Petrogale purpureicollis*

QUICK REFERENCE	
Diet	Herbivore
Reproduction period	All year
Number of offspring	1
Offspring maturity	9–11 months
Length HB	47–60 cm
Length T	55–70 cm
Weight	3.7–6.6 kg
Status	Least Concern

ATAGLANCE.COM.AU

This rock-wallaby's unusual colouration varies from pink to purple and burgundy brown, is water-soluble, occurs seasonally and fades upon death. The pigment is secreted from glands through the animal's skin, like the Red Kangaroo's cinnabarinic acid. Perhaps used for scent-marking, attracting potential mates, advertising reproductive status, displaying dominance and deterring diseases and parasites.

Habitat: Boulders, cliffs, gorges, rocky outcrops amongst dry Eucalyptus, Acacia woodlands and spinifex grasslands with access to permanent water.
Behaviour: Terrestrial, mostly nocturnal, small colonies of up to 20. **Diet:** Herbs, grasses. **Features:** Light brown body with light underside. Tail is pale with dark tip. Light pink to vivid reddish purple face, cheeks, eyes and neck depending on season. Dark brown stripe down the back. **Threats:** foxes, cats, goats, drought.

ROTHSCHILD'S ROCK-WALLABY *Petrogale rothschildi*

One of the largest rock-wallabies, Rothschild's is now found only in remote areas of central Western Australia in the Hamersley Range and on offshore feral-free islands in the Dampier Archipelago. This rock-wallaby used to be found on islands closer to the coast but was wiped out by foxes and cats. It is similar to the Black-footed Rock-wallaby and smaller than its mainland counterparts.

....

Habitat: Granite outcrops. **Behaviour:** Terrestrial, gregarious, mostly nocturnal. **Diet:** Herbs, grasses in spinifex and shrublands. **Breeding:** Unknown. Possibly similar to Black-footed Rock-wallaby. **Features:** Golden brown. Ears and upper part of head and face are dark brown, switching dramatically to light grey on the bottom half. Black stripe runs down its back. A purple sheen is occasionally observed on the back of the Rothschild's neck and shoulders. **Threats:** foxes, cats, Pilbara Olive Python, fires, mining.

....

ATAGLANCE.COM.AU

QUICK REFERENCE	
Diet	Herbivore
Reproduction period	Unknown
Number of offspring	1
Length HB	47–60 cm
Length T	55–70 cm
Weight	3.7–6.6 kg
Status	Least Concern

YELLOW-FOOTED ROCK-WALLABY *Petrogale xanthopus*

This is the largest and perhaps the most beautiful of the rock-wallabies. It is found in semi-arid habitats. It is best known from the Flinders Ranges, South Australia, but a small population lives in Idalia National Park south-west of Blackall, Queensland.

....

Habitat: Open woodland, rocky outcrops. **Behaviour:** Terrestrial, gregarious, mostly nocturnal. **Diet:** Grasses, leaves. **Breeding:** All year, peaking after good rainfall. 1 young. Mature at 18 months. **Features:** Fawn-grey above, white below. Rich brown stripe from crown to mid back. White stripe on cheek, side and thigh. Brown stripe on shoulder and upper thigh. Ears, arms, legs and tail are orange-yellow. Tail has dark bands. **Threats:** Previously hunting. Habitat destruction. Predation by eagles, foxes and cats. Competition with goats, rabbits, sheep and cattle.

....

QUICK REFERENCE	
Average lifespan	10 years
Diet	Herbivore
Reproduction period	All year
Number of offspring	1
Offspring maturity	18 months
Length HB	480–650 mm
Length T	565–700 mm
Weight	6–12 kg
Status	Vunerable

PADEMELONS

SUBORDER: MACROPODIFORMES
SUPERFAMILY: MACROPODOIDEA
FAMILY: MACROPODIDAE

LOCATION TIPS

▶ Maiala NP, Qld

▶ Mt Field NP, Tas.

▶ Washpool NP, NSW

▶ Wilsons Promontory NP, Vic.

Pademelons are the resident macropods of Australia's wet eastern forests. Their low-slung, compact bodies are ideal for travelling through thick undergrowth. They move quickly with short, bouncy hops while holding arms in and extending the tail straight behind the body. When resting, a pademelon swings its short, thick tail between its legs, sits on the base of the tail and leans back against a tree or rock.

Red-legged Pademelons

Pademelons shelter and forage in the forest, and do most of their eating from late afternoon to early morning. They use a network of runways when moving to and from their feeding grounds, and may travel several kilometres in a night.

They are normally timid creatures, rarely straying far from the edges of the forest. When frightened, a pademelon will thump its hind feet to warn its feeding companions, and then bolt for safety. Pademelons will, however, accept human company when fed regularly and may approach visitors at picnic and camping grounds.

TASMANIAN PADEMELON *Thylogale billardierii*

QUICK REFERENCE	
Average lifespan	6 years
Diet	Herbivore
Reproduction period	All year
Number of offspring	1
Offspring maturity	14 months
Length HB ♂	630 mm
Length T	417 mm
Length HB ♀	560 mm
Length T	320 mm
Weight ♂	3.8–12 kg
Weight ♀	2.4–10 kg
Status	Least Concern

Tasmanian Pademelons used to exist on the mainland but fell victim to the fur and leather trade. They were also a food item favoured by Aborigines and Europeans.

Habitat: Rainforest, wet eucalypt forest, tea-tree scrub, damp or well-vegetated areas of open woodland. **Behaviour:** Terrestrial, mainly solitary, mostly nocturnal. **Diet:** Grasses, herbs, leaves. **Breeding:** All year with a peak in autumn, 1 young. Mature at 14–15 months. **Features:** Thick fur is dark brown to grey-brown above, reddish-tinged buff underneath and inside ears. Short face. Short, thick tail is about two thirds of head and body length. Female has 4 teats. **Threats:** Only partially protected, hunting outside of parks and reserves is allowed.

RED-LEGGED PADEMELON *Thylogale stigmatica*

QUICK REFERENCE	
Diet	Herbivore
Reproduction period	All year
Number of offspring	1
Offspring maturity	11–15 months
Length HB ♂	470–536 mm
Length T	372–473 mm
Length HB ♀	386–520 mm
Length T	301–445 mm
Weight ♂	3.7–6.8 kg
Weight ♀	2.5–4.2 kg
Status	Least Concern

This pademelon's distribution extends farther north than does that of the Red-necked Pademelon. The female calls her wayward young with a soft 'tsk' sound; when rejecting a suitor, she issues a harsh rasp. The adult pademelon thumps the ground with its hind feet to signal an alarm.

Habitat: Rainforest, wet eucalypt forest, monsoon vine forest. **Behaviour:** Terrestrial, mainly solitary, rests early afternoon and around midnight. **Diet:** Leaves, fruit, seed, grasses. **Breeding:** All year, 1 young. Females mature at 11 months; males at 15 months. **Features:** Soft, thick fur is grey-brown above, cream to pale grey below. Cheeks, arms and legs are red-tinged. Rainforest dwellers have darker fur. Female has 4 teats. **Threats:** Habitat destruction. Predation by Dingos, pythons, quolls, dogs, cats and Red Foxes.

RED-NECKED PADEMELON *Thylogale thetis*

QUICK REFERENCE	
Diet	Herbivore
Reproduction period	All year
Number of offspring	1
Offspring maturity	17 months
Length HB ♂	300–620 mm
Length T	270–510 mm
Length HB ♀	290–500 mm
Length T	270–370 mm
Weight ♂	2.5–9.1 kg
Weight ♀	1.8–4.3 kg
Status	Near Threatened

This small macropod inhabits forest edges and uses well-defined runways to travel between the shelter of the forest and their open feeding grounds. It is sometimes considered a pest when agricultural land abuts the forest.

Habitat: Rainforest, wet eucalypt forest. **Behaviour:** Terrestrial, mainly solitary, timid, most active late afternoon to early morning. **Diet:** Grasses, shrubs. **Breeding:** All year, peaking in Autumn and Spring. 1 young. Females mature around 17 months. **Features:** Thick soft fur is brownish grey above with red tinge on neck and shoulders. Belly, chest and chin are pale. Female has 4 teats. **Threats:** Habitat destruction. Predation by dogs, cats and foxes.

QUOKKA

SUBORDER: MACROPODIFORMES
SUPERFAMILY: MACROPODOIDEA
FAMILY: MACROPODIDAE

In 1696, Dutch navigator Willem de Vlamingh mistakenly identified the Quokka as a large rat and named its island home Rottnest (rat nest). Until the 1960s it was also common in the wetter parts of south-west Western Australia. It is now found in isolated populations south of Perth.

The Quokka is a habitat specialist. It prefers to live in young vegetation which has been burnt within the last 10–12 years. On Rottnest Island, groups of up to 150 congregate around freshwater soaks during dry summers. Isolated mainland populations are making a comeback in swampy areas where introduced predators are controlled.

Quokkas live in groups dominated by the oldest males, which aggressively defend their resting places but are quite content to eat and drink with the rankless females and juveniles. Quokkas browse on leaves and will climb low bushes to reach food.

Their survival depends on fresh drinking water, and Quokkas will delay breeding if conditions are too hot and dry. After a joey vacates the pouch at about 26 weeks of age, it continues to suckle while learning to forage with its mother.

QUOKKA *Setonix brachyurus*

QUICK REFERENCE	
Average lifespan	10 years
Diet	Herbivore
Reproduction period Number of offspring Offspring maturity	All year 1 18 months
Length HB ♂ Length T	430–540 mm 250–310 mm
Length HB ♀ Length T	390–500 mm 235–285 mm
Weight ♂	2.7–4.2 kg
Weight ♀	1.6–3.5 kg
Status	Vulnerable

The Quokka is the only species in its genus. It looks like other small wallabies except for having a comparatively short, thick tail. However, features of its teeth and skull place it in a separate genus from other wallabies.

Habitat: Coastal shrubland, eucalypt forest and woodland with shrubby understorey.
Behaviour: Terrestrial, gregarious, active day and night; well-developed social structure.
Diet: Grasses, leaves and stems; often malnourished by summer's end. **Breeding:** January–March on Rottnest Island, all year on mainland; 1 young. Mature at 18 months. **Features:** Robust, compact body. Coarse, thick fur is grey-brown tinged with red. Ears are small and round. Naked nose. Short, thick tail is sparsely furred and has visible scales. Bristly hairs on toes. Female has 4 teats. **Threats:** Predation by Dingos, cats and foxes. Habitat destruction and changed fire regimes. Disease, car strike, climate change.

SWAMP WALLABY

SUBORDER: MACROPODIFORMES
SUPERFAMILY: MACROPODOIDEA
FAMILY: MACROPODIDAE

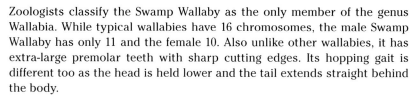

Zoologists classify the Swamp Wallaby as the only member of the genus Wallabia. While typical wallabies have 16 chromosomes, the male Swamp Wallaby has only 11 and the female 10. Also unlike other wallabies, it has extra-large premolar teeth with sharp cutting edges. Its hopping gait is different too as the head is held lower and the tail extends straight behind the body.

More of a browser than a grazer, the Swamp Wallaby prefers habitats with a dense understorey. It is more diurnal than most macropods. It rests and forages amongst the undergrowth during the day, and moves out to more open feeding grounds at night.

Breeding is much the same as for other macropods, except that the female mates a second time before giving birth so that pregnancies overlap. A joey vacates its mother's pouch by nine months of age to make way for the embryo-in-waiting, but continues to suckle for another six months.

FACTS

- Swamp Wallabies can eat plants such as hemlock which are toxic to other species.
- The nicknames 'Stinky' and 'Stinker' refer to the unsavoury smell given off by its meat when cooked.
- The Swamp Wallaby is notoriously shy. It emits a throaty, defensive growl if threatened.

LOCATION TIPS

- ▶ Great Sandy NP, Qld
- ▶ Royal NP, NSW
- ▶ Grampians NP, Vic.

SWAMP WALLABY *Wallabia bicolor*

QUICK REFERENCE	
Average lifespan	15 years
Diet	Herbivore
Reproduction period	All year
Number of offspring	1
Offspring maturity	18 months
Length HB ♂	723–847 mm
Length T	690–862 mm
Length HB ♀	665–750 mm
Length T	640–728 mm
Weight ♂	12.3–20.5 kg
Weight ♀	10.3–15.4 kg
Status	Least Concern

The Swamp Wallaby exploits a variety of habitats, but is the largest macropod found in dense coastal heath. It can be distinguished from other wallabies by its dark colour. Some island populations have developed a golden colour form which may actually be a separate sub-species.

Habitat: Forest, woodland, brigalow scrub, coastal heath. **Behaviour:** Terrestrial, solitary, mostly nocturnal. **Diet:** Grasses, ferns, shrubs, fungi. **Breeding:** All year, 1 young. Mature at 15–18 months. **Features:** Coarse fur is dark brown to charcoal above, tinged yellow to red-orange below. Dark face with pale yellow or light brown cheek stripe. Dark paws. Dark tail sometimes has white tip. **Threats:** Predation by dogs, Dingos and eagles. The Swamp Wallaby survived the fur trade because it has very coarse fur.

MARSUPIAL MOLES

ORDER: NOTORYCTEMORPHIA

STANLEY BREEDEN

FACTS

- A marsupial mole's ears are just small holes surrounded by dense hair.

- The Northern Marsupial Mole (Kakarratul) is smaller than the southern (Itjaritjari) species and is cinnamon in colour.

- Marsupial moles travel 100–200 mm below the surface, but may suddenly 'dive' 2.5 m.

- In captivity, they often feed above ground.

- Some males have a rudimentary pouch.

- Marsupial mole fossils 15–20 million years old have been found in north-west Queensland.

FAMILY: NOTORYCTIDAE

Australia has two marsupial mole species which have features similar to the placental moles of other continents even though they are not related. Both species are relics of an ancient lineage, having separated from other marsupials an incredible 64 million years ago. Marsupial moles are unusual Australian mammals that have had scientists puzzled over how to classify them since 1888. It was finally decided they were different enough from other marsupial groups to warrant their own Order called **Notoryctemorphia**.

These blind, desert-dwelling carnivores spend most of their time tunnelling underground in search of insect larvae. Their bodies are well suited to a burrowing lifestyle, with two large spade-like front claws and a horny shield to protect the snout. Fine fur, a short, tapered tail and lack of external ears streamline the body. A marsupial mole seems to swim through the sand and, as it moves forward, the tunnel fills behind it. It digs horizontal tunnels 10–20 centimetres below the surface, and has been known to sink vertical shafts exceeding depths of two metres. It sleeps standing up with its back arched against the tunnel roof so it does not suffocate. Sinuous tracks of parallel grooves are the only signs of its brief above-ground forays that may occur after rain.

Marsupial moles vary in colour from a pale silvery grey to white through to pink and even a deep golden brown. Generally, the Northern Marsupial Mole (Kakarratul) is a golden-orange in colour, while the Southern Marsupial Mole (Itjaritjar) is paler.

KAKARRATUL *Notoryctes caurinus*

The Kakarratul (previously known as the Northern Marsupial Mole) is smaller than the Itjaritjari *(below)*. It lives in the Gibson, Little Sandy, and Great Sandy Deserts of Western Australia, on the coast between Broome and Karratha and possibly the Tanami Desert. Very few specimens (approx. 20) have ever been collected. Tracks are turtle-like but lack tail marks such as those of the Itjaritjari.

QUICK REFERENCE	
Diet	Insectivore/ Carnivore
No Reproductive information available	
Length HB	86–93 mm
Length T	16–18 mm
Weight	30–50 g
Status	Endangered

Habitat: It lives in underground burrow systems in sand dune country and in sandy soils along river flats and is thought to surface after rains. **Behaviour:** It has an unusually low metabolism and the ability to vary its body temperature as needed – possibly in order to adapt to its underground life. **Diet:** Insects and small reptiles. **Breeding:** Unknown. **Features:** Body is covered in orange or golden white silky fur. Tiny eyes are sightless and tiny ears are covered with fur; skull and snout protected by bony shield are smaller and narrower than that of the Itjaritjari. Spade-like front claws are used to 'swim' under the sand. Teeth differ as well – no anterior premolars and cheek teeth are smaller. **Threats:** Foxes, cats, dingos, fire, cattle, camels.

ITJARITJARI *Notoryctes typhlops*

STANLEY BREEDEN/LOCHMAN TRANSPARENCIES

QUICK REFERENCE	
Diet	Carnivore
No Reproductive information available	
Length HB	69–115 mm
Length T	13–24 mm
Weight	40–70 g
Status	Endangered

Marsupial moles burrow in sand dunes, interdune flats and river flats. Aboriginal people of central Australia, who call the mole *Itjaritjari*, (previously known as the Southern Marsupial Mole) traded their pelts to settlers and camel drivers.

Habitat: Sandy deserts with spinifex or mulga. **Behaviour:** Terrestrial, solitary. **Diet:** Insects; small reptiles. **Breeding:** Unknown. **Features:** Soft, silky fur varies from yellowish white to deep gold. Pad of leathery skin on snout. Short, scaly, knobbed tail. 5 toes on each foot, 2 on front feet modified for digging. Female has 2 teats and backward-opening pouch. **Threats:** Predation by Feral cats, foxes and Dingos; it was also a food source for Indigenous Australians.

PLACENTAL MAMMALS

There is a greater number and a wider variety of eutherian, or placental, mammals in the world than there are marsupials and monotremes. They successfully exploit the Earth's terrestrial resources as well as its marine habitats. While their method of reproduction is no more efficient than a marsupial's, having a more complex brain structure is a distinct advantage in the competition for survival.

There are nine living orders of Australian eutherian mammals. Bats were the first terrestrial placental mammals to migrate to Australia, arriving some 55 million years ago just prior to the final break up of Gondwana. They were followed by the first rodents that crossed the narrowing gap between Australia and South-East Asia about four to five million years ago. Bats and rodents now represent about 46% of all native mammal species in Australia.

Primitive marine mammals that originated in the northern hemisphere began appearing in Australia's coastal seas about 28 million years ago. Among their descendants that now breed here, or visit regularly, are several species of seals, dolphins, whales and the Dugong.

Spectacled Flying-fox,
Pteropus conspicillatus

Rising sea levels delayed the arrival of other placental mammals until the human species discovered sea travel. Their successful colonisation of Australia was assisted by the other placental mammals they brought with them. Although many of these introduced species are widespread and well established, they are not considered native mammals.

Above: Dingo, *Canis familiaris dingo*. **Opposite:** Australian Sea-lion, *Neophoca cinerea*.

BATS

ORDER: CHIROPTERA

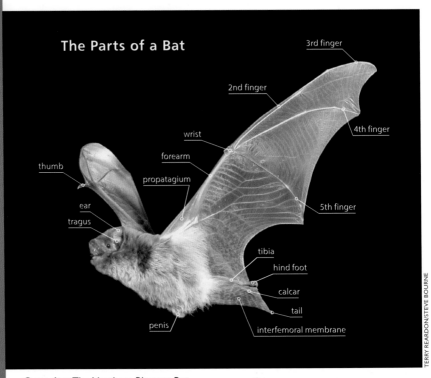

Bats are a very successful group of mammals. They are the only mammals that are able to truly fly, thanks to thin sheets of skin supported by modified arms and extremely long fingers. These winged placental mammals belong to the order Chiroptera, a Latin term meaning 'winged hand', and are all thought to have evolved from a primitive, shrew-like ancestor. Australian bats are usually divided into two groups: Megabats (large fruit and nectar eating bats) and Microbats (small insect eating bats).

Ghost Bat

Almost 90 species of bats across nine families live in Australia. They represent about 20% of its native mammalian fauna. In keeping with their tropical origins, most Australian bats are found in warm humid environments and many species are also found in Papua New Guinea and parts of Asia. Bat diversity decreases as you travel southwards. Where two-thirds of Australia's bat species occur on Cape York in Queensland, only eight species are found in Tasmania.

FACTS

- There are around 75 species of microbats and 12 species of megabats in Australia.

- The largest microbat (the Ghost Bat) is up to two times larger than the smallest megabat (the Eastern Blossom Bat).

- There are no vampire bats in Australia, they are only found in Central and South America.

- Microbats have small eyes and poor vision and they all use echolocation to navigate. Megabats have large eyes and excellent vision and do not use echolocation.

- Bats turn 'right way up' and hang by their thumbs to pass urine and faeces.

- Young bats are called pups.

- A female bat's nipples are in her armpits.

- Bats hang by their feet because they cannot stand upright. Their bones are so light (an adaptation for flying) they cannot support the bat's body weight.

- A bat's wing membrane feels like the skin on your eyelids, it is highly elastic and able to heal quickly if it is torn.

The Parts of a Bat

3rd finger

2nd finger

4th finger

wrist

forearm

thumb

propatagium

ear

tragus

5th finger

tibia

hind foot

calcar

tail

penis

interfemoral membrane

TERRY REARDON/STEVE BOURNE

Opposite: The Northern Blossom Bat

Grey-headed Flying-fox

FACTS

- Australia's 12 species of megabats include flying-foxes, blossom bats and tube-nosed bats.

- Megabats play an important role in tree pollination and seed dispersal.

- Male flying-foxes scent their necks to attract females. Each species has a characteristic odour.

- Megabats have excellent vision and do not use echolocation to navigate or find food.

- A Black Flying-fox travelling at 40 km/h beats its wings about 120 times per minute.

- A blossom bat collects nectar with its bristly tongue and eats pollen that it grooms from its fur.

MEGABATS

FAMILY: PTEROPODIDAE

Megabats can grow to just over one kilogram with a wingspan of up to 1.6 metres. They eat fruit, flowers or nectar and find their food by sight, smell and the noise of other bats feeding. They have claws on their first and second fingers unlike microbats, which only have claws on the first finger or thumb. The tail is short or nonexistent. They hang upside down to rest and wrap their wings around their body like a cloak. While most megabats are large, blossom bats are around 60 millimetres in length.

Learning to Fly

A flying-fox cannot fly when it is born so it is carried by its mother for the first month or so. It clings to her with its claws and curved milk teeth and feeds on demand from a nipple located in each armpit. When a young one is strong enough to roost, it is left in a crèche at the camp during the night. By two months of age it can fly but does not join the nightly fly-out for another month.

Social Structure

Flying-foxes are intelligent, gregarious animals. Daytime roosts or camps are where they court, mate, raise their young, squabble over territories and occasionally sleep. Beneath the chaotic noise of a large camp lies a complex social structure. There may be border guards, food scouts, breeding pairs, separate groups of youths and even nursery trees. Some camps are used for a few weeks; others may be occupied for several months. When local food supplies dwindle, the bats move to another camp. During the breeding season, hundreds of thousands of bats that consist of up to three different species may congregate at a single camp, usually located on the edge of a watercourse.

Flying-fox camp in town park, Singleton, NSW, showing a mother carrying its young.

Grey-headed Flying-fox camp in Yarra Bend Park, Vic.

FINDING MEGABATS

- Flying-fox camps are located easily by the noise and smell, and by spectacular mass fly-outs at dusk.

- At night listen for the chatter and flapping wings of individuals in fig, palm, mango and other fruiting trees.

- Flying-foxes can be carriers of viruses harmful to humans and should not be handled.

LOCATION TIPS

▶ Brisbane, Qld

▶ Daintree NP, Qld

▶ Kakadu NP, NT

▶ Ballina, NSW

▶ Melbourne, Vic.

NORTHERN BLOSSOM BAT *Macroglossus minimus*

Even smaller than the Eastern Blossom Bat, this fruit bat is found along the top end of Australia from Kimberley across Cape York down the eastern coast to Tully. It is an important pollinator of native plants. This bat's very fast metabolism makes it burn energy at high rates so it goes into torpor for several hours each day.

Habitat: Rainforests, mangrove forests, paperbark swamps and eucalypt woodlands neighbouring these habitats. **Behaviour:** Roosts alone or in small groups of two or three. **Diet:** Nectar, pollen, fruit (figs). **Breeding:** Possibly all year in far north; females can have at least two, if not three litters a year. **Features:** Fur is light reddish-brown on back and lighter underneath. Eyes are large and bright, muzzle is long and narrow and tongue is very long and covered with papillae that act like a nectar mop. Front incisors are either small or missing. Male has a V-shaped pink gland on its chest. A strip of bare skin extends along inside of leg. **Threats:** Unknown.

QUICK REFERENCE	
Diet	Frugivore/ Nectarivore
Reproduction period	All year in the far north
Number of offspring	1
Offspring maturity	6 months
Length HB	59–64 mm
Length T	Tiny stub
Weight ♂	14 g
Weight ♀	12 g
Status	Least Concern

EASTERN BLOSSOM BAT *Syconycteris australis*

QUICK REFERENCE	
Diet	Nectarivore/ Frugivore
Reproduction period Number of offspring	All year 1
Length HB Length T	60 mm 0 mm
Weight ♂	16–22 g
Weight ♀	16–26 g
Status	Least Concern

LES HALL

Also known as the Queensland Blossom Bat, this tiny species is the size of a mouse. The Eastern Blossom Bat roosts alone in dense vegetation and usually fly three to five metres above the ground. It may be confused with the similar Northern Blossom Bat where their ranges overlap in North Queensland.

Habitat: Rainforest, eucalypt forest, heathland and paperbark swamp. **Behaviour:** Roosts alone; sometimes feeds in large groups. Arboreal, nocturnal. **Diet:** Mainly nectar and pollen, also fruit and leaves. **Breeding:** In NSW, 1 young is born October to November and a second February to April. Breeds all year in the north. **Features:** Long, soft fur is fawn to reddish brown and extends to ankles. Paler, sometimes white flecked below. No tail. Large first claw on wing. **Threats:** Food availability.

EASTERN TUBE-NOSED BAT *Nyctimene robinsoni*

QUICK REFERENCE	
Diet	Frugivore/ Nectarivore
Reproduction period Number of offspring	Oct–Dec 1
Length HB Length T	85–110 mm 20–25 mm
Weight	36–56 g
Status	Least Concern

This well-camouflaged bat looks like a dead leaf when roosting. It often flies along forest pathways close to the ground and has a high-pitched whistling call. The function of the tubular nostrils is not known.

Habitat: Rainforest, woodland and heath. **Behaviour:** Mostly roosts alone, sometimes feeds in small groups. Nocturnal, arboreal. **Diet:** Fruit, blossoms. **Breeding:** Females give birth to 1 young, usually October–December. **Features:** Fur is grey to light brown with dark stripe down back. Brown wings with light green to yellow spots. Prominent tubular nostrils. Bulging brown eyes, bright eyeshine. Short tail. **Threats:** Sometimes feeds low to the ground and is predated by cats. Entanglement in barbed wire fences.

BLACK FLYING-FOX *Pteropus alecto*

This common flying-fox roosts high in the canopy and is a noisy feeder. It has lost much forest habitat and is now well-adapted to living in urban areas. Its camp may hold hundreds of thousands and is usually situated near major food sources.

QUICK REFERENCE	
Diet	Frugivore/ Nectarivore
Reproduction period	Jan–Feb/ Mar–Apr
Number of offspring	1
Length	240–280 mm
Weight	500–950 g
Status	Least Concern

Habitat: Rainforest, eucalypt forest, mangroves, paperbark swamps, urban areas. **Behaviour:** Gregarious, nocturnal, arboreal. Sometimes roosts in mixed colonies with other species. **Diet:** Prefers native fruits and nectar. Also eats cultivated fruit. **Breeding:** Mating occurs March to April on the east coast and January to February in the Northern Territory. Gestation 6 months. 1 young. **Features:** Short black fur often tipped with white. Reddish collar on back of neck. Brown eye-rings may be present. Leg fur extends to knees. Wingspan can be greater than 1 m. **Threats:** Habitat destruction. Mass mortalities in heatwaves, car strike, electrocution.

SPECTACLED FLYING-FOX *Pteropus conspicillatus*

The population of the threatened Spectacled Flying-fox has declined 78% between 1985 and 2000. It is an important long-distance dispersal agent for the seeds of rainforest trees and also a significant pollinator.

QUICK REFERENCE	
Diet	Frugivore
Reproduction period	Apr–May
Number of offspring	1
Offspring maturity	2–4 years
Length HB	220–240 mm
Weight ♂	500–1000 g
Weight ♀	450–800 g
Status	Vulnerable

Habitat: Tropical rainforest; nearby mangroves. **Behaviour:** Gregarious, nocturnal, arboreal. **Diet:** Rainforest fruits and flowers. Also cultivated fruit. **Breeding:** Mating occurs April to May. 1 young born from October to December. Juveniles nursed for 5 months. Females mature at 2 years and males at 3 to 4 years. **Features:** Dark brown to black, sometimes grey flecked. Straw-coloured fur surrounds eyes and extends to snout. Yellow neck ruff; silvery in some bats. Legs furred to knees. **Threats:** Habitat destruction, persecution, tick paralysis, mass mortality in heatwaves, cyclones, electrocution, entanglement in barbed wire fences and fruit netting.

GREY-HEADED FLYING-FOX *Pteropus poliocephalus*

QUICK REFERENCE	
Average lifespan	18 years
Diet	Nectarivore/ Frugivore
Reproduction period	Mar–Apr
Number of offspring	1
Offspring maturity	2–3 years
Length HB	230–289 mm
Weight ♂	300–1100 g
Status	Vulnerable

Australia's only endemic flying-fox. Large summer breeding camps of the threatened Grey-headed Flying-foxes are shared with Little Red and Black Flying-foxes, the latter of which it sometimes interbreeds with. Movement between colonies is so extensive it is thought they act as one single population.

Habitat: Rainforest, eucalypt forest, woodland, swamps, urban areas. **Behaviour:** Gregarious, nocturnal, arboreal. **Diet:** Nectar and pollen supplemented by native and introduced fruit. **Breeding:** Mating in early Autumn. Gestation 6 months. 1 young usually born in October; some as late as February. Mature at 2 to 3 years. **Features:** Head and belly pale grey, back is silver grey or dark grey. Yellow/orange mantle surrounds neck. Leg fur extends to ankles. Wingspan can exceed 1 m. **Threats:** Habitat destruction and fragmentation, persecution, competition, disease, electrocution, barbed wire, heat waves.

LITTLE RED FLYING-FOX *Pteropus scapulatus*

QUICK REFERENCE	
Diet	Nectarivore
Reproduction period	Nov–Jan
Number of offspring	1
Length HB	195–235 mm
Weight ♂	350–604 g
Weight ♀	310–560 g
Status	Least Concern

The Little Red is the most widespread species of flying-fox and is found in all States except Tasmania. This nomad forms large temporary camps that can have more than one million individuals.

Habitat: Forest, woodland, swamps, vine thickets, mangroves. **Behaviour:** Nocturnal, gregarious, arboreal. **Diet:** Nectar and pollen, mainly from Eucalypts. Occasionally fruit, sap, leaves, bark and insects. **Breeding:** Mating occurs November to January. One young is born each year between April and May. **Features:** Reddish brown with light brown to yellow on neck, shoulders and around eyes. Upper surface of leg is furless. Reddish brown wings, translucent in flight. Wingspan is less than 1 m. **Threats:** Habitat destruction and fragmentation, changing fire regimes, predation by birds of prey and reptiles including crocodiles.

MICROBATS

FAMILIES: RHINONYCTERIDAE, MEGADERMATIDAE, RHINOLOPHIDAE, HIPPOSIDERIDAE, EMBALLONURIDAE, MOLOSSIDAE, MINIOPTERIDAE & VESPERTILIONIDAE

Microbats (suborder Microchiroptera) have only one claw on the leading edge of each wing and usually rest with their wings folded against the side of the body. Though not blind, most have small eyes. They live alone or in groups and use a variety of hidden sites such as caves, mines and tree hollows as daytime roosts. Many species hibernate in winter. Microbats are nocturnal predators that hunt mainly insects and navigate by sight and echolocation.

High Frequency Transmitters

Each type of microbat has its own set of echolocation signals that suits its habitat and the way it catches food. A bat's larynx generates sound pulses ranging from 5 to 200 kHz. These are sent out through the mouth and nostrils. Pulses that bounce back off surrounding objects are picked up by the bat's large ears. These sound echoes can tell a bat the size and location of its prey, how fast it is moving and in what direction.

Hibernation

Microbats need a lot of energy to fly and to replace body heat lost through their large wing surfaces. During winter they have trouble finding enough insects to meet these high energy requirements. While some species migrate, others hibernate until conditions improve. When a bat shuts down operations, its body temperature drops to 2–3 °C above that of its surroundings and it survives on stored body fat. The last of these reserves is used when the bat awakens and has to exercise its wings before being able to fly. Consequently, disturbance during hibernation can have disastrous effects on a colony of microbats.

FACTS

- Some microbats use their hind feet to catch fish and aquatic insects from the water's surface.

- The carnivorous Ghost Bat, with a wingspan of up to 600 mm, is one of the world's largest microbats.

- During their annual migration, bent-wing bats may fly more than 1,000 km.

- Many microbats have elaborate ear and nose structures for transmitting and receiving ultrasonic frequencies.

- A microbat can eat up to 50% of its own body weight in insects each night.

- Microbats roost in caves, tree hollows, rock crevices, culverts, abandoned mines, buildings, tunnels, under bark, and even in curled leaves.

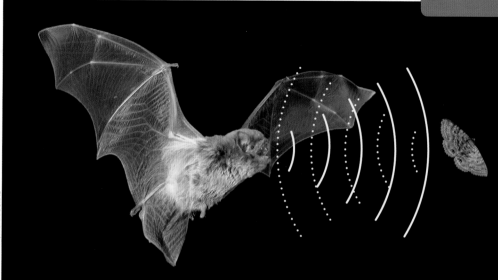

TERRY REARDON/STEVE BOURNE

Shown here are the echolocation calls produced by bats as they search for insects in the field.

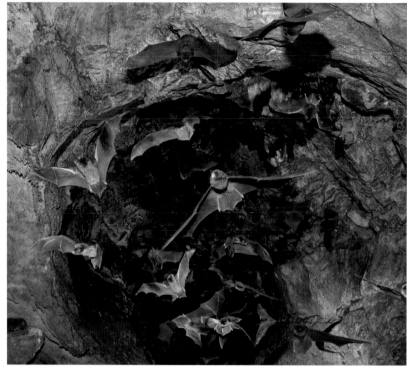

A rush of wings as Common Bent-wing Bats leave Church Cave, Wee Jasper, NSW.

GHOST BAT *Macroderma gigas*

QUICK REFERENCE	
Diet	Carnivore
Reproduction period	Jul–Aug
Number of offspring	1
Length HB	100–130 mm
Weight	140–165 g
Status	Vulnerable

Australia's largest microbat and only strictly carnivorous bat. It eats a variety of
insects and small vertebrates, which are mostly caught on the ground then taken
up to feeding perches. The Ghost bat roosts in caves, crevices and old mines.

Habitat: Rainforest, arid areas, woodlands, mangroves. **Behaviour:** Gregarious, nocturnal,
sensitive to disturbance. **Diet:** Insects, frogs, reptiles, birds and small mammals.
Breeding: Mating occurs in July and August. Gestation is 3 months. Single young born
September to November. **Features:** Soft fur is light to dark grey above, pale grey to white
below. Long ears joined at centre of forehead. Simple nose leaf. Large eyes. No tail.
Threats: Habitat destruction and fragmentation, small population size, disturbance from cave
tourism and mining, competition with cats and foxes, entanglement on barbed wire fences.

EASTERN HORSESHOE BAT *Rhinolophus megaphyllus*

Distinguished by its complex, horseshoe-shaped noseleaf, this bat species is very sensitive. Mothers may abandon their young if people enter maternal caves during the breeding season. When foraging it flies low and close to foliage then consumes its prey in special feeding roosts.

Habitat: Forages in rainforest, open forest, and woodland. Roosts in warm, humid caves, mines and buildings.
Behaviour: Nocturnal, gregarious. Sensitive to disturbance. Hibernates during winter in the South.
Diet: A range of insects and spiders. Prefers moths. **Breeding:** Mates in late Autumn and Winter. 1 young is born in November or December. Females mature at 2–3 years and males at 2 years. **Features:** Greyish brown back, lighter belly. Horseshoe-shaped fleshy area around nose. Large ears. Slow, fluttery flight. **Threats:** Habitat destruction, roost disturbance, mining.

QUICK REFERENCE	
Diet	Insectivore
Reproduction period	May–Jul
Number of offspring	1
Offspring maturity	2–3 years
Length HB	42–58 mm
Length T	38–43 mm
Weight	7–13 g
Status	Least Concern

LARGE-EARED HORSESHOE BAT *Rhinolophus robertsi*

The Large-eared Horseshoe Bat sports very large ears and a distinctive yellow nose-leaf that partially covers its tiny eyes. The horseshoe — large horseshoe shaped fleshy area around the nose — is long and wide. The size of this species, larger in the north, depends on the latitude on which it is found.

Habitat: Rainforest, riparian forest and woodland between Townsville up to the Iron Range on Cape York and in savanna woodland out west to Chillagoe where they are found in cave systems. **Behaviour:** Known to roost alone or in small groups but are often found sharing caves with other microbat species including Eastern Horseshoe and Eastern Bentwing Bats. **Diet:** Insectivore. **Features:** Long greyish-brown fur above with lighter coloured fur below. **Threats:** Cane toads, cats, loss of caves and old mines, land clearing.

QUICK REFERENCE	
Average lifespan	7 years
Diet	Insectivore
Reproduction period	Oct–Dec
Number of offspring	1
Length HB	54–60 mm
Length T	31–34 mm
Weight	10.1–16.2 g
Status	Endangered

LES HALL

ORANGE LEAF-NOSED BAT *Rhinonicteris aurantia*

QUICK REFERENCE	
Diet	Insectivore
Reproduction period	July
Number of offspring	1
Offspring maturity	7–18 months
Length HB	45–55 mm
Length T	23–29 mm
Weight	7–11 g
Status	Least Concern

This brightly coloured bat roosts in warm, humid caves in groups of 20 to several thousand. It emerges at dusk, flying low to the ground in a characteristic zigzag pattern. The Pilbara population may be a separate sub-species.

Habitat: Roosts in moist caves, forages in woodland, shrubland and grassland. **Behaviour:** Nocturnal, gregarious. **Diet:** Moths, beetles and other insects. **Breeding:** Mating occurs in July. Single pup born in December. Females mature at 7 months and males mature at 18 months. **Features:** Bright orange fur, sometimes with brown or yellow tinges. Dark brown wings and reddish limbs. Pointed ears. Lower part of noseleaf is broad with centre gap; upper part has scalloped edge. Deep-set nostrils are separated by high ridge. **Threats:** Car strike, predation by Ghost Bats, mining and cave disturbance.

DUSKY LEAF-NOSED BAT *Hipposideros ater*

QUICK REFERENCE	
Diet	Insectivore
Reproduction period	May–Jun
Number of offspring	1
Length HB	35–45 mm
Length T	17–28 mm
Weight	4.5–10 g
Status	Least Concern

The smallest Australian member of the leaf-nosed bat family, this species resembles a large moth when in flight. It prefers to roost in very dark, warm and humid sites including caves, mines and tree hollows and cohabitates with other species, including the Ghost Bat which is a known predator.

Habitat: Rainforests, mangroves, woodland, vine thicket. **Behaviour:** Nocturnal, gregarious. **Diet:** Mainly moths, also other insects. **Breeding:** A single pup is born in October or November after a gestation of 5 months. **Features:** Grey to ginger-grey back with pale belly. Nose is simple and slightly square in shape. Round ears with minor point. Flies slow and low to the ground. **Threats:** Cave disturbance, mining, destruction of feeding habitat.

FAWN LEAF-NOSED BAT *Hipposideros cervinus*

LES HALL

QUICK REFERENCE	
Diet	Insectivore
Reproduction period Number of offspring	Nov–Dec 1
Length HB Length T	50–55 mm 21–31 mm
Weight	6–9 g
Status	Least Concern

This small cave dweller is widely spread throughout South-east Asia. In Australia the Fawn Leaf-nosed Bat is found on Cape York north of Coen to the Torres Strait islands.

Habitat: Forages in rainforests, open eucalypt and gallery forests along waterways as well as open parkland and around buildings. **Behaviour:** Roosts in warm humid caves and abandoned mines in groups of 20–100 but up to 900. **Diet**: They perch hunt insects from 1–6 m above the ground but will also flutter low to the ground. **Breeding:** Females form maternity colonies in the same caves in which they roost. Young are born Nov–Dec. **Features:** Colour can vary from grey to greyish-brown and reddish-orange. Ears are wide and triangular. Lower half of the small nose-leaf — distinctively wider than the upper half — narrows underneath the nostrils to expose leaflets. Males have a small forehead gland which produces an odourless fluid of unknown function. **Threats:** Cats, mine disturbance, habitat destruction.

DIADEM LEAF-NOSED BAT *Hipposideros diadema*

This species uses a variety of daytime roosts including caves, mines, sheds and tree hollows. It hangs from a branch waiting to ambush insects then returns to the ambush site to eat. It can catch a number of insects all at once and will store them in cheek pouches to consume later.

Habitat: Rainforest, eucalypt forest. **Behaviour:** Nocturnal, gregarious, secretive. **Diet:** Beetles, moths, ants, spiders and bugs. **Breeding:** Females form maternity groups towards the end of the year; single young is born in early summer. **Features:** Usually grey to yellowish-brown with pale blotches on shoulders and belly. Dark wings and reddish limbs. Upper part of noseleaf has scalloped edge. Tiny eyes. Pointed ears with horizontal ridges and furred base. **Threats:** Habitat destruction, disturbance of roosting sites, agriculture, limestone mining.

QUICK REFERENCE	
Diet	Insectivore
Length HB Length T	75–95 mm 32–45 mm
Weight	30–57 g
Status	Least Concern

ARNHEM LEAF-NOSED BAT *Hipposideros inornatus*

QUICK REFERENCE	
Diet	Insectivore
Number of offspring	1
Length HB Length T	66–77 mm 32–46 mm
Weight	22–35 g
Status	Endangered

IAN MORRIS

Previously regarded as a subspecies of the Diadem Leaf-nosed Bat (*H. diadema*), this large leaf-nosed bat is found in sandstone caves and old mines on the Kakadu escarpment in Arnhem Land on the Top End of the Northern Territory. It has the most limited distribution of any Australian bat. Young grasps false pubic teat with its teeth and faces backwards when mother flies.

Habitat: Monsoon and eucalypt forest, woodland and open heath on plateau.
Behaviour: Secretive. Lower echolocation call frequency than all other leaf-nosed bats. **Diet:** Insects including beetles, moths, ants, cockroaches. **Features:** The fur is brown to light grey with darker tips and paler underneath. Occasional specimens with orange fur are seen in a colony. **Threats:** Cats.

SEMON'S LEAF-NOSED BAT *Hipposideros semoni*

QUICK REFERENCE	
Diet	Insectivore
Reproduction period Number of offspring	Nov 1
Length HB Length T	40–50 mm 21–26 mm
Weight	6–10 g
Status	Endangered

BRUCE TAUBERT

A small brown leaf-nosed bat with long narrowly pointed ears found from Townsville to the Cape York Peninsula. Distinguished from the Northern Leaf-nosed Bat by the longer central wart, it is only found only in coastal northern Queensland.

Habitat: Tropical rainforest, monsoon forest, wet sclerophyll and open savanna woodlands. **Behaviour:** Roost in caves and tree hollows. Male and female echolocation calls have different frequencies. **Diet:** Moths, spiders and beetles. **Features:** The fur colour is brown above and slightly lighter on the belly. The wing membrane near the body is covered with whitish brown hair. The nose-leaf has a club shaped protuberance (6–8 mm long) projecting vertically from the centre of the lower portion of the nose-leaf. There is a small wart on the centre of the upper nose-leaf. The upper nose-leaf is divided into four depressions. There are two supplementary leaflets under each side of the lower nose-leaf. **Threats:** Roost disturbance, introduction of herbivores, fire.

NORTHERN LEAF-NOSED BAT *Hipposideros stenotis*

This species is only found in the Kimberley, the Top End of the Northern Territory and far north-west Queensland. This bat roosts in the twilight area of sandstone caves and old mines.

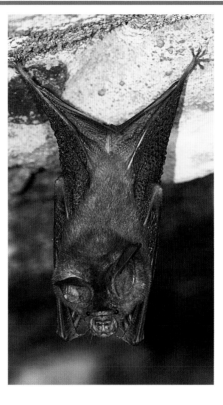

Habitat: Monsoon thickets, tall open forests, floodplains, open grasslands, spinifex near rocky escarpments and outcrops. **Behaviour:** Only roosts in sandstone caves. **Diet:** Moths, beetles, ants, cockroaches, lacewings and ants. **Features:** The long fine white-based fur of this species is grey-brown above and slightly paler on the belly. The long sharply pointed ears are haired for one third of their length. The nose-leaf is complex and covers most of the muzzle. It is similar in appearance to Semon's Leaf-nosed bat but the wart in the centre of the nose-leaf is smaller and it has a smaller wart on the top edge of the upper leaflet. **Threats:** Loss of habitats, wildfire.

QUICK REFERENCE	
Diet	Insectivore
Reproduction period Number of offspring	Oct–Jan 1
Length HB Length T	40–45 mm 20–28 mm
Weight	4.5–8 g
Status	Least Concern

YELLOW-BELLIED SHEATH-TAILED BAT *Saccolaimus flaviventris*

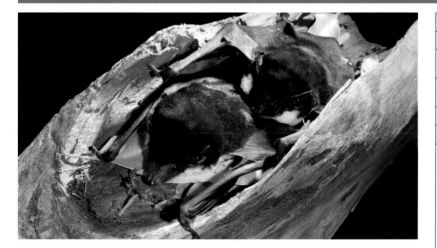

QUICK REFERENCE	
Diet	Insectivore
Reproduction period Number of offspring	Dec–Mar 1
Length HB Length T	72–92 mm 20–35 mm
Weight	30–60 g
Status	Not Evaluated

This very handsome bat is easily identified by its fur colour and sheath-tail. It roosts in small colonies in tree hollows over a wide area of mainland Australia.

Habitat: Wide range including wet and dry sclerophyll forests, open woodland, mallee, grasslands, acacia shrublands and deserts. **Behaviour:** Colonies roost in tree hollows. It is a high and fast flyer. **Diet:** Beetles, flying ants, grasshoppers, crickets, wasps. Feeds high in the canopy or low to the ground in open areas. **Features:** Back fur is jet black and the belly fur is pure white, cream or yellow. The muzzle is hairless and pointed. Males have a large throat pouch. **Threats:** Tree clearing, bushfires, barbed-wire fences.

COASTAL SHEATH-TAILED BAT *Taphozous australis*

QUICK REFERENCE	
Diet	Insectivore
Reproduction period Number of offspring	Sept–Nov 1
Length HB Length T	80–90 mm 20–25 mm
Weight	30–50 g
Status	Near Threatened

LES HALL

A medium-sized bat found in caves and rock cracks along the Queensland coast from Shoalwater Bay to the Torres Strait Islands. It can be found in the same area as the Common Sheath-tailed bat but is smaller in size.

Habitat: Abandoned mines, sea caves, boulder piles, rock fissures, old war bunkers, shallow caves, in open eucalypt forests, grasslands, heathlands, mangroves, paperbark swamps along the coast. **Behaviour:** Roost on near-vertical rock surfaces and scurry into crevices when disturbed. Colonies of 2–25 and up to 100. Forage above the canopy. **Diet:** Beetles and other insects. **Features:** Fur colour is greyish-brown on the back, slightly paler under, with older individuals having a ginger tinge to their fur. Males have a throat pouch, but females only have a vestigial ridge there. Wing pouch near the wrist. **Threats:** Sand mining, disturbance of roosting sites.

COMMON SHEATH-TAILED BAT *Taphozous georgianus*

QUICK REFERENCE	
Average lifespan	4 years
Diet	Insectivore
Reproduction period Number of offspring Offspring maturity	Aug–Sept 1 9–21 months
Length HB Length T	75–89 mm 21–32 mm
Weight	19–51 g
Status	Least Concern

The Common Sheath-tail roosts near the entrances of caves, in crevices and old mines. It clings to the rock wall rather than hanging from the roof and individuals keep some distance between them in the roost. It flies high and fast using a zigzag or grid pattern when hunting, and feeds in flight.

Habitat: A variety of rocky habitats in northern Australia. **Behaviour:** Nocturnal, gregarious, territorial when roosting. **Diet:** Flying insects. **Breeding:** Mating occurs in spring. Single, well-developed young, born in December. Females mature at 9 months and males at 21 months. **Features:** Dark brown back, lighter below. Yellow-brown hairs underside of tail. Tail protrudes above sliding membrane. Long narrow wings. Nostrils at end of pointed snout. Ridged ears. **Threats:** No major threats known.

HILL'S SHEATH-TAILED BAT *Taphozous hilli*

This endemic bat roosts in caves and cracks in rocky escarpments in the dry inland of Northern Territory and Western Australia.

Habitat: Eucalypt woodlands, open plains, spinifex grasslands and acacia shrublands. **Behaviour:** Live in groups of 2–10 in twilight zones of open caves, rock splits, abandoned mines, crevices and boulder piles. **Diet:** Insects. **Features:** The fur is dark brown above and slightly lighter on the rump. Belly fur has an orange tinge tipped with olive brown. The wings are a greyish brown. The males have a small throat pouch which contains glandular material. **Threats:** Cats, loss of habitat (old mines).

QUICK REFERENCE	
Diet	Insectivore
Reproduction period	Nov–Apr
Number of offspring	1
Length HB	63–75 mm
Length T	26–35 mm
Weight	20–25 g
Status	Least Concern

TROUGHTON'S SHEATH-TAILED BAT *Taphozous troughtoni*

This endemic species is found roosting in caves and old mines in the far north west of Queensland near Mount Isa. It may be found in the same area as the Common Sheath-tailed Bat but can be distinguished by its much larger size and weight.

Habitat: Sclerophyll forests, spinifex hummock grasslands, Mulga shrublands, open woodlands. **Behaviour:** Roosts of fewer than 20, occasionally up to 100 in cave twilight zones, abandoned mines, rocky outcrop cracks and crevices. **Diet:** Feeds primarily on beetles. **Breeding:** Mating occurs late Aug to early Sept. Gestation is 3 months. **Features:** It is olive brown to dark brown above, with greyish guard hairs, and the fur is lighter below. The forearm and tail membrane are lightly furred and the face is mainly bare. A radio-metacarpal wing pouch is present but there are no throat pouches in either sex. **Threats:** Loss of habitat (old mines and caves).

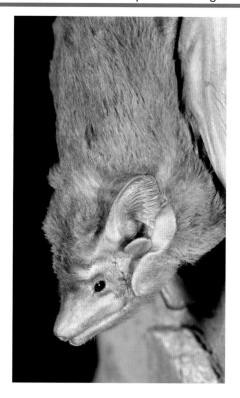

QUICK REFERENCE	
Diet	Insectivore
Reproduction period	Nov–Dec
Number of offspring	1
Offspring maturity	3 months
Length HB	80–84 mm
Length T	30–39 mm
Weight	30–35 g
Status	Least Concern

WHITE-STRIPED FREE-TAILED BAT *Austronomous australis*

QUICK REFERENCE	
Diet	Insectivore
Reproduction period Number of offspring	Dec–Jan 1
Length HB	85–100 mm
Length T	40–55 mm
Weight ♂	32–48 g
Weight ♀	26–35 g
Status	Not Evaluated

The largest of the Australian free-tailed bats, the White-Striped is a seasonal migrator found in most of Australia except the Top End. The frequency range of its echolocation call is the lowest of any Australian bat.

Habitat: Forests, woodlands, shrublands, open agricultural landscapes, urban areas, grasslands, deserts and scattered stands of trees. **Behaviour:** Tree dweller. Roosts in tree hollows of old eucalypts with multiple entrances, alone or in groups of up to 25. Fast flyer. **Diet:** Moths beetles, grasshoppers, ants. **Breeding:** Copulation, ovulation and fertilisation occur in late August. Young born Dec–Jan, weaned by May. **Features:** Large, very distinctive bat with dark brown to black velvety fur on the back and belly. Named for the two stripes of white fur underneath. Prominent throat pouch in both sexes with tuft of hairs used for scent marking. **Threats:** Loss of tree hollows, land clearing, wildfire.

GREAT NORTHERN FREE-TAILED BAT *Chaerephon jobensis*

QUICK REFERENCE	
Diet	Insectivore
Reproduction period Number of offspring	Nov–Dec 1
Length HB Length T	80–90 mm 35–45 mm
Weight	20–30 g
Status	Least Concern

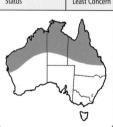

GLENN HOYE

This bat is found in northern Australia from Pilbara through Kimberley across the top to north Queensland. It is the only representative of the *Chaerephon* genus in Australia.

Habitat: All habitats up to the edge of the rainforests. **Behaviour:** High flyer roosts in tree hollows in groups of 10–15. Also found in caves and buildings and under bridges and jetties in colonies of up to 300. Call is a chirrup audible to human ears. **Diet:** Cockroaches, moths, beetles, crickets, ants, lacewings, mosquitoes, sawflies and earwigs. **Features:** The fur on the back is short and velvety, usually very dark brown in colour but can also be reddish brown. Belly fur is a pale version of the back fur. There is no throat pouch in either sex, as opposed to the larger White-striped Freetail Bat. **Threats:** Loss of tree hollows, roost disturbance, wildfire.

NORTHERN FREE-TAILED BAT *Mormopterus lumsdenae*

QUICK REFERENCE	
Diet	Insectivore
Reproduction period Number of offspring	Nov–Dec 1
Length HB Length T	59–68 mm 33–38 mm
Weight	12–18 g
Status	Least Concern

Found only in the tropics and subtropics and widely distributed across northern Australia from WA to Queensland, this is the largest member of the Mormopterus genus (based on weight).

Habitat: Rainforest, eucalypt woodlands, river flood plains, tall open forests, savannah woodlands, grasslands and shrublands. **Behaviour:** Roosts in tree hollows and under roofs. They forage above the canopy and on the ground. **Diet:** Moths, beetles and also lacewings, flies, grasshoppers and ants. **Breeding:** Females give birth to one young during summer wet season. **Features:** Fur on the back of this robust bat is short and dark grey to brown above and lighter grey underneath. Skin on the ears and face is brown to dark grey, as are the wing membranes. Ears are triangular and rounded at the tip.

EAST-COAST FREE-TAILED BAT *Mormopterus norfolkensis*

QUICK REFERENCE	
Diet	Insectivore
Length HB Length T	50–55 mm 32–45 mm
Weight	8–13 g
Status	Vulnerable

Also known as the Eastern Mastiff bat, or Norfolk Island Mastiff bat, this species is not actually found on Norfolk Island. It roosts mainly in tree hollows and is known to share its roost with other microbat species.

Habitat: Open forest, woodland, mangroves and occasionally rainforest.
Behaviour: Nocturnal, may be solitary or gregarious. **Diet:** Flying insects including bugs and beetles. **Breeding:** Young are born in late November or early December. **Features:** Dark brown to reddish brown fur on back, paler below. Tail projects from tail-membrane by 3–4 cm. Wrinkled snout lacking noseleaf. Long, narrow wings. **Threats:** Habitat destruction (particularly removal of hollow trees), use of pesticides. Possibly changing fire regimes.

LITTLE BENT-WINGED BAT *Miniopterus australis*

QUICK REFERENCE	
Diet	Insectivore
Reproduction period Number of offspring	Jul–Aug 1
Length HB Length T	45–55 mm 42–48 mm
Weight	5–10 g
Status	Least Concern

This bat is known to form colonies of hundreds of thousands of individuals, some of the largest in Australian cave-dwelling bats. At Mt Etna pythons, frogs and Ghost Bats wait at the cave's entrance around dusk to catch an easy meal as the Little Bent-wings fly out.

Habitat: Rainforest, swamp, wet and dry sclerophyll forest, vine thicket.
Behaviour: Nocturnal, gregarious. **Diet:** Moths, wasps, ants, mosquitoes and other small insects. **Breeding:** Mating occurs late winter. One young is born in December.
Features: Chocolate brown fur on back, paler underneath. Fur is long and thick. Tip of wing folds back under wing when at rest. Short muzzle. Short, rounded roughly triangular ears.
Threats: Disturbance of maternity caves, mining, habitat destruction.

SOUTHERN BENT-WINGED BAT *Miniopterus orianae bassanii*

QUICK REFERENCE	
Average lifespan	22 years
Diet	Insectivore
Number of offspring	1
Length HB Length T	52–58 mm 52–58 mm
Weight	13–19 g
Status	Critically Endangered

The fast flying Southern Bent-winged inhabits limestone and sandstone caves and man-made structures in the far south-east corner of South Australia over the border into south-west Victoria.

Habitat: Woodlands bordering large natural wetlands, river basins and agricultural areas.
Behaviour: Flies high where there are trees and low in open areas. Fast flyer. Roosts during the day in limestone and sandstone caves and lava tubes. They enter torpor during winter months when food is limited. **Diet:** Primarily moths. **Breeding:** They congregate in nursery caves by October for Oct–Dec births depending on location. **Features:** Greyish-brown to dark brown fur on back, lighter underneath. Short snout and domed head. Short slightly rounded triangular ears. **Threats:** Cave disturbance.

EASTERN BENT-WINGED BAT *Miniopterus orianae oceanensis*

QUICK REFERENCE	
Diet	Insectivore
Reproduction period Number of offspring	Dec–Jan 1
Length HB Length T	58–65 mm 52–58 mm
Weight	10–17 g
Status	Not Evaluated

This species has been found in substantial numbers — up to 100,000 — clinging to the walls and ceilings of caves and abandoned mines scattered up and down the east coast of Australia from south-central Victoria to the tip of Cape York, mostly east of the Great Dividing Range.

Habitat: Rainforests, sclerophyll forests, monsoon forest, open woodland, melaleuca forest, open grasslands. **Behaviour:** Roosts in limestone caves, abandoned mines, culverts, lava tubes, concrete bunkers. Forest dwellers fly high above the canopy; grassland bats fly within a few metres of the ground. **Diet:** Moths, cockroaches, beetles. **Breeding:** Populations centre on a maternity cave each year. Mating occurs following weaning and sperm is stored over the winter. **Features:** Dark reddish-brown to black fur on back, paler underneath. Forehead rises sharply from short stubby snout into a domed head. Short triangular ears. **Threats:** Loss of habitat, changed agricultural patterns.

NORTHERN BENT-WINGED BAT *Miniopterus orianae orianae*

This dome-headed microbat is found in caves and abandoned mines as well as in WWII bunkers, culverts, stormwater drains, under bridges and in buildings from Kimberley through the Top End. It consumes 3–4 g of insects each night.

QUICK REFERENCE	
Diet	Insectivore
Reproduction period Number of offspring	December 1
Length HB Length T	47–63 mm 43–58 mm
Weight	9–16 g
Status	Not Evaluated

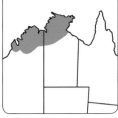

Habitat: Rainforest, wet and dry sclerophyll, tropical woodland, monsoon thickets, riparian corridors. **Behaviour:** Flies high in forest habitats and low in grasslands and open woodlands. **Diet:** Grasshoppers, leaf-hoppers, beetles, flies, spiders, mosquitoes, midges. **Breeding:** Large numbers of males and females — into the thousands — form maternity roosts during the wet season. **Features:** Dark brown fur on back, lighter underneath. Slightly larger than Eastern Bentwing. Short snout and domed head. **Threats:** Ghost bats.

GOLDEN-TIPPED BAT *Phoniscus papuensis*

QUICK REFERENCE	
Diet	Insectivore
Reproduction period	Nov–Jan
Number of offspring	1
Length HB	50–60 mm
Length T	36–43 mm
Weight	5–9.3 g
Status	Least Concern

This bat's wing structure allows it to hover to facilitate plucking spiders from their webs. Long needle-like upper canines — dagger-like for catching spiders — fit into pockets in the lower lip.

Habitat: Rainforest with well-developed eucalypt or Brushbox overstorey, tall open forests, wet and dry sclerophyll, casuarina dominated riparian forest, coastal melaleuca forests. **Behaviour:** Individuals and maternal colonies of 5–20 females and young often roost in abandoned domed-shaped bird nests as well as under epiphytic mosses and tree hollows. Roosts are changed every four days. **Diet:** Primarily orb-weaving spiders, some moths, beetles, flies and balls of spider web. **Breeding:** Females give birth to one young between Nov–Jan. **Features:** Distinctive bat with dark brown, woolly fur with bright golden yellow tips that extends along the wing bones, tail and legs. Long erect ears and tragus. Short pointed muzzle, nose extends beyond the lower jaw. **Threats:** Mining, invasive species, agriculture, aquaculture.

FLUTE-NOSED BAT *Murina florium*

QUICK REFERENCE	
Diet	Insectivore
Reproduction period	Oct–Nov
Length HB	47–57 mm
Length T	31–37 mm
Weight	6–11 g
Status	Least Concern

LES HALL

Discovered relatively recently, this elusive and unusual bat is distinguished by its sideways pointing tubular nostrils that look like small tubes.

Habitat: High and lowland tropical rainforests, tall open forests of flooded gums and gallery forests. **Behaviour:** Roosts are located in understorey tree ferns, dead epiphytes, palm fronds, leaf clusters and abandoned bird nests 1–8 m from the ground. Changed every four days, roosts are sometimes used multiple times. A high-pitched whistle is emitted while foraging in sub-canopy and canopy, avoiding open areas. **Diet:** Beetles and spiders with the occasional fly. **Breeding:** Unknown. **Features:** The woolly fur is greyish brown or reddish brown on the back, paler on the belly. The fur gets thinner when it extends over the upper tail membrane and the wing membrane is attached to the outer toe, as opposed to the ankle in most other bats. **Threats:** Habitat loss and fragmentation.

LARGE-FOOTED MYOTIS *Myotis macropus*

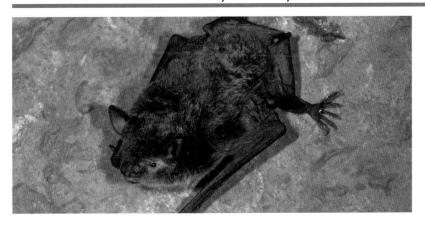

QUICK REFERENCE	
Diet	Insectivore/ Carnivore
Reproduction period Number of offspring	Various 1
Length HB Length T	52–56 mm 36–40 mm
Weight	7–12 g
Status	Least Concern

The Large-footed Myotis roosts in groups in caves, mines, tunnels, buildings and trees. Its large feet, long toes and sharp claws help it forage when it flies low over ponds, lakes and streams, dipping down to catch aquatic insects and small fish from the water's surface.

Habitat: Forested areas close to bodies of water. **Behaviour:** Nocturnal, gregarious. Territorial within roost. **Diet:** Predominantly freshwater invertebrates. Occasionally small fish, frogs and flying insects. **Breeding:** In the south, breed once a year, twice in central parts, thrice in tropics. **Features:** Grey-brown back; paler below. Older individuals are ginger. Large feet, long ankles, and flattened toes with curved claws. Tail enclosed in membrane. Nose overhangs bottom lip. **Threats:** Roost site disturbance, declining water quality.

NORTHERN PIPISTRELLE *Pipistrellus westralis*

BRUCE TAUBERT

QUICK REFERENCE	
Diet	Insectivore
Reproduction period Number of offspring	Possibly all year 1
Length HB Length T	34–42 mm 29–37 mm
Weight	2.7–3.3 g
Status	Not Evaluated

This tiny bat, endemic to Australia, is one of the smallest mammals found on the continent, with some individuals weighing as little as 2.7 g. It lives primarily in the mangroves in parts of Kimberley, coastal NT and the western part of the Gulf of Carpentaria.

Habitat: Probably tree hollows restricted to mangroves in WA but also found in melaleuca swamps, pandanus, fresh water mangroves and in dense pindan thickets. **Behaviour:** They forage along waterways **Diet:** Flying insects including moths, ants as well as cockroaches and spiders. **Features:** The fur on the back is very dark brown tipped with light brown, and light brown with light coloured tips underneath. The ear shape is similar to the Forest Pipistrelle, broadly triangular, but has a less rounded tip. The wing membrane attaches to the outer toe.

WESTERN FALSE PIPISTRELLE *Falsistrellus mackenziei*

QUICK REFERENCE	
Diet	Insectivore
Reproduction period Number of offspring	Nov–Dec 1
Length HB Length T	55–67 mm 40–53 mm
Weight	17–26 g
Status	Near Threatened

JIRI LOCHMAN/LOCHMAN TRANSPARENCIES

Endemic to Australia, this falsistrelle inhabits south-western Australia up to Perth and out to the edge of the wheat belt.

Habitat: In or next to stands of old growth sclerophyll forests dominated by karri, jarrah, marri and tuart and trees associated with the coastal plains. **Behaviour:** These gregarious bats roost most of the year by sex in tree hollows, logs, branches and stumps in groups of 5–30. **Diet:** Flying insects. **Features:** Both of the falsistrelles have dark brown to reddish brown fur on the back with a cinnamon coloured belly. The triangular ears with rounded tips stand erect well out of the fur and are distinguished by a notch on the outer margin. **Threats:** Logging and clearing of old growth forests, wildfires.

EASTERN FALSE PIPISTRELLE *Falsistrellus tasmaniensis*

QUICK REFERENCE	
Diet	Insectivore
Length HB Length T	55–70 mm 40–52 mm
Weight	17–28 g
Status	Least Concern

LES HALL

Also known as the Eastern Falsistrelle, this species roosts mainly in eucalyptus hollows and occasionally in buildings and under loose bark of trees. Males and females probably roost separately. It flies in or near the canopy hunting flying insects, preferring to forage in open forest or using cleared trails.

Habitat: Open forest. Prefers tall, mature, wet forest at high-altitude. **Behaviour:** Nocturnal. Hibernates in winter. Little else known. **Diet:** Predominantly beetles, also bugs and moths. **Breeding:** Females are pregnant late spring to early summer. **Features:** Dark, reddish brown back with paler grey belly. Long ears set back on head. Sparsely haired nose. Lacks noseleaf. **Threats:** Habitat destruction (particularly removal of hollow trees), use of pesticides, logging.

NORTHERN LONG-EARED BAT *Nyctophilus arnhemensis*

An isolated population of this forest dwelling bat is found in Pilbara, WA and other populations stretch from Kimberley through the Top End to the western Gulf of Carpentaria.

QUICK REFERENCE	
Diet	Insectivore
Number of offspring	1
Length HB Length T	40–59 mm 35–41 mm
Weight	5–8 g
Status	Least Concern

Habitat: Prefer wet habitats from monsoon forests to riverine melaleuca forests but also found in dry open woodland and tall open forests.
Behaviour: Roosts under soft peeling melaleuca bark, in tree hollows and at the base of Pandanus trees and in foliage. Aerial hunters capable of gleaning prey off leaf surfaces.
Diet: Beetles, cicadas. **Features:** The fur is a rusty brown colour on the back, and lighter underneath. The fleshy ridge behind the muzzle is very indistinct but has a very shallow groove. **Threats:** Loss of tree hollows, wildfires.

EASTERN LONG-EARED BAT *Nyctophilus bifax*

Also known as the Northern Long-eared Bat, this species roosts in tree hollows, buildings, under loose tree bark or in dense foliage. It requires a variety of roost sites in a small area. When foraging it focuses on the edge of the canopy using its manoeuvrability to catch prey.

QUICK REFERENCE	
Diet	Insectivore
Reproduction period Number of offspring	May 2
Length HB Length T	45–55 mm 34–46 mm
Weight ♂	7–12 g
Weight ♀	7–13 g
Status	Least Concern

Habitat: Rainforest, tall open forest and woodland near water courses.
Behaviour: Nocturnal. Little else is known. **Diet:** Insects including moths, ants and beetles. **Breeding:** Mating occurs in May and 2 pups are born in October. **Features:** Fur is tan brown on back and grey-brown on belly. Large, broad head and muzzle. Low, hairless ridge behind noseleaf. Large, ridged ears. Broad wings. **Threats:** Habitat destruction (particularly removal of hollow trees).

LESSER LONG-EARED BAT *Nyctophilus geoffroyi*

QUICK REFERENCE	
Diet	Insectivore
Reproduction period	April–May
Number of offspring	Twins born late Oct–Nov
Offspring maturity	7–15 months
Length HB	40–50 mm
Length T	31–35 mm
Weight	6–12 g
Status	Least Concern

LES HALL

This very common and beautiful endemic bat is immediately recognised by the Y-shaped groove behind the ridge around the nostrils.

Habitat: Primarily monsoon and riverine melaleuca forests but also found in open woodland, tall open forest, alpine areas and deserts. **Behaviour:** Roosts alone or in small groups in crevices, under peeling melaleuca bark, tree hollows, base of Pandanus leaves, in foliage and mud nests. Shifts roosts often. Highly sophisticated echolocation. **Diet:** Moths, cockroaches, beetles, flies, beetles etc. caught on the fly and gleaned from surfaces. **Breeding:** Maternity colonies include up to 15 females and often a single adult male. Offspring are usually twins. **Features:** Variable fur colour, ranging from dark to light or grey brown, and much lighter in colour underneath. Desert bats are the palest of all in colour and can have a white belly. Very long ears are joined together above the forehead. **Threats:** Loss of tree roosts and land clearing.

GOULD'S LONG-EARED BAT *Nyctophilus gouldi*

QUICK REFERENCE	
Diet	Insectivore
Number of offspring	1–2 young
Offspring maturity	7–15 months
Length HB	55–65 mm
Length T	45–55 mm
Weight	9–13 g
Status	Least Concern

LES HALL

This microbat roosts in tree hollows, rock crevices, unused bird nests and buildings. It hunts low to the ground and stops echolocating just before catching its prey to avoid detection. The West-Australian population is likely to be a separate species.

Habitat: Forest and woodland with a dense understory. **Behaviour:** Nocturnal. Males are mainly solitary, females are gregarious. Hibernates in winter. **Diet:** Flying and non-flying insects. **Breeding:** 1 or 2 pups are born in late spring or early summer. Females mature at 7–9 months and males at 12–15 months. **Features:** Dark brown to dark grey on back with a light grey belly. Very long ears which fold down when resting. Broad wings. **Threats:** Habitat destruction (particularly removal of hollow trees), predation by cats.

PYGMY LONG-EARED BAT *Nyctophilus walkeri*

LES HALL

QUICK REFERENCE	
Diet	Insectivore
Reproduction period	Twins born Oct–Nov
Number of offspring	2
Length HB Length T	38–44 mm 26–36 mm
Weight	3.3–7 g
Status	Least Concern

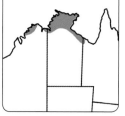

The smallest of the long-eared bats is found only in the Top End and just across to the eastern Kimberley.

Habitat: Melaleuca and pandanus swamps, monsoon forest and rocky gorges with palms, also savanna woodland and tall open forest with pandanus and melaleuca.
Behaviour: Known to roost in pandanus and Livistona palms. Also roost in branch fissures and under dried bark. Tree hollows serve as maternity roosts. **Diet:** Moths, beetles, cockroaches, termites, spiders, leaf-hoppers and lacewings. **Breeding:** Females give birth to twins Oct–Nov. **Features:** Pale orange-brown fur on back and a cream coloured belly. Membranes are dark brown. Small distinct muzzle has a distinctive central groove.
Threats: Loss of habitat and fires.

LARGE-EARED PIED BAT *Chalinolobus dwyeri*

This endemic bat is found from Shoalwater Bay, across the Blackdown Tableland in central-eastern Queensland and down to Ulladulla in southern NSW. Distribution is poorly understood.

Habitat: Dry sclerophyll forests and woodlands, cypress pine woodlands, rainforest fringes, tall open forests, sandstone outcrops, and subalpine woodland. **Behaviour:** Roost in rock overhangs, mine tunnels, caves and martin mud nests in groups of 3–40. **Diet:** Insects; specifics are unknown. **Breeding:** Twins are common. **Features:** Glossy black fur on the back, with light brown fur underneath. White stripes can be seen on either side of the body where the wing is attached, and they meet in the pubic region, forming a 'V'. The ears are very large and when held together will meet above the head.
Threats: Land clearing, wildfire.

GLENN HOYE

QUICK REFERENCE	
Diet	Insectivore
Reproduction period Number of offspring	Nov–Dec 1–2
Length HB Length T	47–56 mm 42–50 mm
Weight	6.8–12 g
Status	Vulnerable

GOULD'S WATTLED BAT *Chalinolobus gouldii*

QUICK REFERENCE	
Diet	Insectivore
Reproduction period	Sept (north); Oct (central); Nov (south)
Number of offspring	1–2
Offspring maturity ♀	1 year
Length HB	46–75 mm
Length T	31–51 mm
Weight	7–18 g
Status	Least Concern

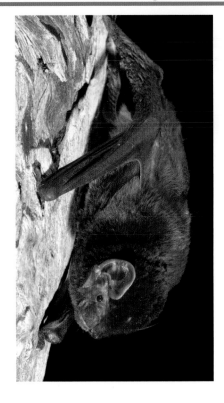

This very adaptable bat is found in a wide variety of habitats all over Australia (including Tasmania).

Habitat: Virtually all Australian habitats. **Behaviour:** Roost in tree hollows and hollow limbs of mature living trees, also found in buildings, tree stumps, roll of canvas, tractor exhaust pipes, in leaves. Emerging early, right after sunset, makes them vulnerable to predation. **Diet:** Moths, ants, cockroaches, stoneflies, crickets, beetles, caterpillars, flies, cicadas. **Breeding:** Mating occurs May–June. **Features:** The fur on the back is a dark brown but grades to black on the shoulders and head. The back edge of the ear is continuous with a large lobe (wattle) at the corner of the mouth. **Threats:** Cats, loss of tree hollows, wildfire.

CHOCOLATE WATTLED BAT *Chalinolobus morio*

QUICK REFERENCE	
Diet	Insectivore
Reproduction period	Oct–Nov
Number of offspring	1–2
Length HB	50–61 mm
Length T	45–50 mm
Weight	8–11 g
Status	Least Concern

GLENN HOYE

Endemic to Australia, this bat occupies a wide variety of habitats extending across Australia from coastal North Queensland inland around to coastal and inland WA and south WA. Several isolated inland populations occur in all states.

Habitat: Limestone caves on the Nullarbor and in south-west WA; tree hollows in forests, woodlands, mallee, open plains. **Behaviour:** Opportunistic foragers roost in tree hollows, exfoliating bark, houses, fairy martin nests. Female colonies of 6–70 have been found. Males usually roost alone. Mixed sex colonies of up to 400 have been recorded. Roosts can be changed daily. **Diet:** moths, beetles but also flies, ants, lacewings and wasps. **Features:** South-eastern Australian bats are a uniform brown, the colour of milk chocolate, on the back and belly, but some central and western individuals may be lighter brown underneath. Ears are short, and the lobe at the corner of the mouth is small, but the next one along on the lower lip is easily seen. **Threats:** Loss of tree roosts, wildfire.

HOARY WATTLED BAT *Chalinolobus nigrogriseus*

This widespread species of microbat is usually the first to appear at dusk. It catches insects in the air, on the ground and on tree trunks. The Hoary Wattled Bat has a twisting and turning flight. It roosts in tree hollows, buildings and rock crevices.

Habitat: Forest, woodland, mangroves, sand dunes, shrubland and urban areas.
Behaviour: Nocturnal. Little else is known. **Diet:** Insects including flies, moths, beetles, mosquitoes and cicadas. **Breeding:** Single young born between September and November.
Features: Blackish grey above with white-tipped hairs giving a 'frosted' appearance. Short head with rounded forehead. Tail enclosed by membrane.
Threats: Habitat destruction, agriculture, roost disturbance.

QUICK REFERENCE	
Diet	Insectivore
Reproduction period Number of offspring	Sept–Nov 1
Length HB Length T	45–55 mm 35–42 mm
Weight	7.5–10 g
Status	Least Concern

TERRY REARDON

LITTLE PIED BAT *Chalinolobus picatus*

GLENN HOYE

QUICK REFERENCE	
Diet	Insectivore
Reproduction period Number of offspring	Nov 1–2
Length HB Length T	42–50 mm 35 mm
Weight	3–8 g
Status	Near Threatened

This handsome bat is found in south central and western Queensland and extends into western NSW and across the border into South Australia and Victoria.

Habitat: Dry forest woodland and mallee. **Behaviour:** Roosts in dead tree hollows, caves, abandoned mines and building. **Diet:** Primarily moths. **Features:** Glossy black fur on the back which extends onto the tail membrane, light grey fur underneath. As with the Large Pied Bat, there are two white stripes of fur along each side of the body, converging to form a 'V'. The ears are quite short and will not meet when pressed over the head.
Threats: Tree clearing, loss of old mines.

GREATER BROAD-NOSED BAT *Scoteanax rueppellii*

QUICK REFERENCE	
Diet	Insectivore and possible Carnivore
Reproduction period Number of offspring	Dec–Jan 1–2
Length HB Length T	80–95 mm 40–55 mm
Weight	25–35 g
Status	Least Concern

This heavily built and belligerent endemic bat is known to eat other bats in captivity and it is believed that this is probably the case in the wild as well.

Habitat: Woodland, moist and dry eucalypts, tall forest in deep gullies and ranges and along human-made corridors. **Behaviour:** Roosts in tree hollows, cracks and fissures in trunks and dead branches, under dead bark, building roofs. High slow flyer hunts on the fly. **Diet:** Beetles, grasshoppers, moths, large flies and perhaps other bat species. **Breeding:** Females from maternity colonies in tree hollows. **Features:** Dark reddish brown fur on the back, slightly paler on the belly. The slender ear is triangular. Often confused with the Eastern Falsistrelle, it can be distinguished by its triangular tragus that is less than half the length of the ear and a different shape. It has only two upper incisors, whereas the Falsistrelle has four. **Threats:** Loss of tree hollows, land clearing, wildfires.

LITTLE BROAD-NOSED BAT *Scotorepens greyii*

QUICK REFERENCE	
Diet	Insectivore
Number of offspring	2
Length HB Length T	45–55 mm 25–40 mm
Weight	8–12 g
Status	Least Concern

LES HALL

Endemic to Australia, this species is widespread and abundant across most mainland states. It forages near water and has been seen hunting moths its own size. Small groups of up to 20 individuals roost in tree hollows, abandoned buildings and even hollow fence posts.

Habitat: Grassland, woodland, desert, monsoon forest, and swamps. **Behaviour:** Nocturnal, gregarious, feisty. **Diet:** Mosquitoes, moths, beetles, bugs and other flying insects. **Breeding:** Mating takes place before winter. Twins are born in December. **Features:** Chestnut to grey-brown fur on back, paler underneath. Muzzle is broad and square when viewed from above. Erect, broadly curved ears. **Threats:** Habitat destruction (particularly removal of hollow trees), logging, agriculture.

A colony of Little Bent-winged Bats clustered on the wall of an abandoned mine.

EASTERN BROAD-NOSED BAT *Scotorepens orion*

QUICK REFERENCE	
Diet	Insectivore
Reproduction period	May
Number of offspring	2
Length HB	43–54 mm
Length T	27–38 mm
Weight ♂	7–12 g
Weight ♀	7–13 g
Status	Least Concern

Found in lower numbers and in a smaller range than its cousin, the Little Broad-nosed bat, the Eastern Broad-nosed bat roosts mainly in tree hollows and occasionally buildings. One known roost in a hollow Eucalypt was seven metres above the ground.

Habitat: Tall wet forest, rainforest and open forest. **Behaviour:** Nocturnal, gregarious, little else is known. **Diet:** Insects. **Breeding:** Mating results in sperm being stored by the female with fertilisation occurring in spring. 1 young is born late spring or early summer. **Features:** Warm brown fur on back, drab brown underneath. Robust build. Broad muzzle. **Threats:** Habitat destruction (particularly removal of hollow trees), logging, agriculture.

INLAND FOREST BAT *Vespadelus baverstocki*

QUICK REFERENCE	
Diet	Insectivore
Reproduction period	Nov–Dec
Number of offspring	1
Offspring maturity	4 months
Length HB	36–43 mm
Length T	26–34 mm
Weight	3–6 g
Status	Least Concern

BRUCE TAUBERT

This very tiny endemic bat is widely distributed in arid and semi-arid inland areas of all the states except Tasmania.

Habitat: Woodlands, mallee, chenopod shrublands, stony deserts, creeks, open and closed woodlands, plains and hilly terrain. **Behaviour:** Roosts mostly in very small tree hollows and abandoned buildings. **Diet:** Unknown. **Breeding:** Females carry their single young for only one week after giving birth in December. **Features:** Has two colour forms – one is light fawn brown fur on the back with a creamy white belly and other is a brownish grey on the back with a whitish belly. The facial skin is pink in colour, and the wing membranes are grey. The tragus is sometimes white in colour. **Threats:** Cats, loss of tree hollows, land clearing.

NORTHERN CAVE BAT *Vespadelus caurinus*

LINDY LUMSDEN

QUICK REFERENCE	
Diet	Insectivore
Reproduction period	Most of the year
Number of offspring	1
Length HB	32–40 mm
Length T	30–35 mm
Weight	3–5 g
Status	Least Concern

This tiny bat is found in the rugged terrain of Kimberley and across the Top End to just across the Queensland border.

Habitat: Rocky hills and escarpments in woodlands, open and monsoon forests. **Behaviour:** Roosts in caves and sometimes buildings. **Diet:** Moths, caddis flies. **Breeding:** May produce two or more litters a year. **Features:** Brown fur on back and belly. Skin on face, wings and forearms is dark, almost black. **Threats:** Loss of caves and mines, land clearing, wildfire.

FINLAYSON'S CAVE BAT *Vespadelus finlaysoni*

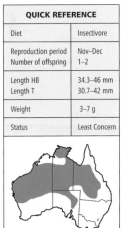

QUICK REFERENCE	
Diet	Insectivore
Reproduction period	Nov–Dec
Number of offspring	1–2
Length HB	34.3–46 mm
Length T	30.7–42 mm
Weight	3–7 g
Status	Least Concern

This endemic bat is widely distributed throughout arid and semi-arid inland regions of Australia.

Habitat: Grasslands, spinifex grasslands, savannah woodlands, open forest, mulga — all near hilly terrain or rocky outcrops. **Behaviour:** Roosts in caves and rock crevices as well as abandoned mines. Females roost in large numbers while males roost in small groups. Young can roost separately from adults. **Diet:** Unknown. **Breeding:** Mating times vary. **Features:** Very dark brown to black fur with a reddish tinge on the back, paler underneath; dark skin on the face and wing membranes. **Threats:** Cats, loss of old mines.

EASTERN FOREST BAT *Vespadelus pumilus*

QUICK REFERENCE	
Diet	Insectivore
Reproduction period	Oct
Number of offspring	1–2
Length HB	35–44 mm
Length T	27–34 mm
Weight	3.5–6 g
Status	Least Concern

LES HALL

Isolated populations of this little brown endemic bat occur east of the Great Divide from the Atherton Tablelands to Kirrama, Kroombit Tops to just north of Sydney.

Habitat: Moist forests. **Behaviour:** Roost in both large dead and live tree hollows — sizes of which vary greatly. Maternity roosts usually close to creeks. **Diet:** Moths, beetles, flies, wasps, ants. **Breeding:** Females give birth to twins in Oct. **Features:** Fur on the back is the colour of dark chocolate, and the belly is light brown. The fur is quite long and fluffy and extends on to the tail membrane. The skin on the nose and ears is dark brown, and the membranes are black. **Threats:** Loss of tree hollows, land clearing, wildfires.

SOUTHERN FOREST BAT *Vespadelus regulus*

QUICK REFERENCE	
Diet	Insectivore
Reproduction period	Nov–Jan
Number of offspring	1
Length HB	36–46 mm
Length T	28–39 mm
Weight	3.6–7 g
Status	Least Concern

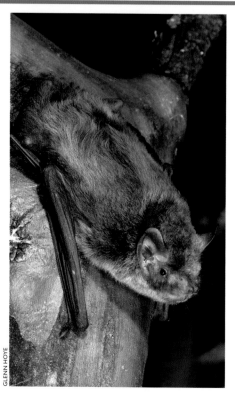

GLENN HOYE

This small endemic forest bat is found from the Queensland border along the Great Dividing Range through NSW to Victoria and south SA along the coast to southern WA.

Habitat: Wet and dry sclerophyll, low shrub woodland, mixed temperate woodland, mallee. **Behaviour:** Colonies of up to 100 are found in tree hollows. Males roost separately from females except during breeding season. Often roost in Adelaide houses. **Diet:** Moths, beetles, termites, flies. **Breeding:** Mating in April. **Features:** The fur on the back is a reddish brown and very light brown underneath. The wing membranes and ears are dark grey, almost black. **Threats:** Loss of tree hollows, land clearing and wildfire.

EASTERN CAVE BAT *Vespadelus troughtoni*

GLENN HOYE

QUICK REFERENCE	
Diet	Insectivore
Reproduction period Number of offspring	Nov 1–2
Length HB Length T	37–43 mm 31–38 mm
Weight	4–7 g
Status	Least Concern

This uncommon bat is found from Cape Melville in North Queensland to northern NSW. A few records have been recorded further inland.

Habitat: Tropical mixed woodlands wet and dry sclerophyll close to sandstone or volcanic escarpments along the Great Dividing Range. Also in dry sclerophyll along the coast and GDR. **Behaviour:** Roost in sandstone overhead caves, crevices, boulder piles, mines and occasionally buildings mostly near well-lit areas. Also in Fairy Martin nests, under bridges and in culverts. They roost packed close together in small (single sex) to large (mixed sex) groups. **Diet:** Have been observed hawking mosquitoes. **Breeding:** May produce two litters a year. Colonies contain equal number of males and females. **Features:** Fur on the back is light brown and reddish tipped behind the ears and on the head, paler on the belly. **Threats:** Loss of caves, old mines and wildfire.

LITTLE FOREST BAT *Vespadelus vulturnus*

QUICK REFERENCE	
Diet	Insectivore
Reproduction period Number of offspring Offspring maturity ♂ Offspring maturity ♀	Nov–Dec 1–2 2nd year 1st year
Length HB Length T	34–48 mm 27–35 mm
Weight	2.5–5.5 g
Status	Least Concern

This endemic tiny bat — one of Australia's smallest — lives in southern central Queensland down through eastern and central NSW to Victoria and over the border into south-eastern South Australia.

Habitat: Wet and dry sclerophyll forests, river red gums forests. Montane and dry woodland, blackwood swamp, Brigalow and semi-evergreen vine thicket. **Behaviour:** Roosts in dead tree hollows and dead branches on live trees, in roof cavities and hollows in dead timber. Segregated colonies vary in size from one to 120. **Diet:** Flying insects and the occasional spider. **Breeding:** Females store sperm in the uterus. Males store sperm to remain reproductively active through winter. **Features:** Light brown or brownish grey fur on the back, almost creamy or white underneath. Ears and membranes pale grey, tragus is almost white. **Threats:** Cats, loss of tree roosts, land clearing, wildfire.

NATIVE RATS & MICE

ORDER: RODENTIA

Spinifex Hopping-mouse

FACTS

- There are more than 60 species of native rodents and 5 species of introduced rodents in Australia.

- The Water Rat is one of the few animals able to eat parts of the poisonous Cane Toad without ill effect.

- The Long-tailed Mouse of Tasmania's Antarctic Beech forests mates for life.

- Pebble-mound mice carry 5 g stones in their mouths and carefully arrange them around burrow entrances with their front paws.

- The Giant White-tailed Rat from north Queensland's tropical forests has been known to open tin cans with its incisor teeth.

FAMILY: MURIDAE

Rodents are thought to be the most successful placental mammal group worldwide with 40% of all living mammals (some two thousand species) belonging to the order Rodentia. They are the only group of terrestrial mammals that are found living on every continent except for Antarctica. All Australian rodents belong to the family Muridae which evolved in South-East Asia around 15 million years ago when it was widely separated from Australia by water.

Australia's first rodents arrived between four and five million years ago. Mouse-like placental mammals were carried here from South-East Asia by the sea's floating debris. Once here, they made the most of what their new home had to offer. They spread out, diversified and became uniquely Australian. Two more waves of rodents reached Australian shores during the last two million years and have since become naturalised. There are now more than sixty species of Australian rats and mice. They range in size from six grams to 750 grams, represent about one quarter of all our native mammal species and can be found in almost every terrestrial habitat as well as several aquatic habitats.

Spinifex Hopping-mouse with young.

Diet

All Australian Rodents are omnivores but most prefer to eat plants, grains and fruit. Their diet is supplemented by insects when other food is scarce. Two species, the Water Rat and Water Mouse, are mainly carnivores but also eat insects and some plant matter.

Water Rat

The group's success is thought to be due to their specialised dentition. A rodent has an upper and lower pair of curved, chisel-edged incisor teeth that grow continuously and are self-sharpening, with a covering of very hard enamel. Gnawing on tough plants keeps these incisors to a manageable length. Next to the incisors is a gap called the Diastema, then three pairs of upper and lower molars. Most rodents lack canine and premolar teeth.

Like other herbivores, a rodent has a specialised gut system to break down cellulose and absorb nutrients. Some desert species are very good at reabsorbing water in the lower part of their gut to reduce water stress. This water conservation measure, along with very efficient kidneys, allows them to live on a moist diet without needing access to free water.

Young Barking Owl feeding on a rodent.

Feast and Famine

Rodents are an important source of food for carnivorous animals. When, following good rains, Australia's dry countryside is carpeted with new plant growth, well-fed rodents breed quickly, often and in large numbers. These population explosions attract a host of predators that also feed up and breed quickly. As the land dries and rodent numbers drop, most of the carnivores face starvation or migration. A nucleus of predators and prey will survive the dry period that follows, ready to feast and multiply during the next wet season.

Threats and Conservation

Native rodent species and populations have declined since Europeans arrived in Australia, with at least nine species becoming extinct. A further five species of rodents are endangered and twelve species are listed as vulnerable. There are many reasons for this decline including extensive predation by introduced cats and foxes, habitat destruction, changing weather patterns and fire regimes and competition with introduced herbivores such as rabbits and sheep. Native rodents are also mistakenly identified as introduced pests and killed.

Less commonly, some rodents that were previously thought to be extinct have been rediscovered some time later. One example is the New Holland Mouse, which was lost for over 120 years and rediscovered near Sydney in 1967.

JOHNCARNEMOLLA/DREAMSTIME

Above: The introduced sheep compete for food.
Below: Plains mouse with young.

Fire, one of the many threats to native rodent populations.

Finding Rodents

Look for tracks with obvious claw marks left by the four-clawed front toes and five-clawed hind toes. Check for relatively small, cylindrical scats pointed at one or both ends on runways and at burrow entrances. Some species leave excavated debris at entrances. Try spotlighting tree-rats in the canopies of tropical forests and woodlands.

LOCATION TIPS

▶ Found all over Australia in habitats where suitable food and shelter are available. Rodents are particularly numerous and diverse in the arid centre of Australia.

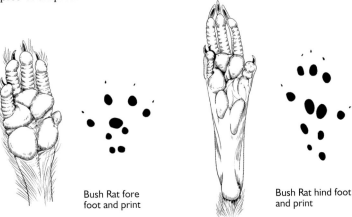

Bush Rat fore foot and print

Bush Rat hind foot and print

WATER RAT *Hydromys chrysogaster*

One of Australia's largest rodents, the Water Rat is amphibious. It shelters ashore in burrows or hollow logs and hunts on land and under water. Food is consumed at feeding sites on land. When it swims in water it can be mistaken for a Platypus.

Habitat: Near permanent bodies of fresh or brackish water; sometimes on the seashore. **Behaviour:** Amphibious, active day and night. Territorial. **Diet:** Aquatic insects, crustaceans, mussels, fish, frogs, lizards, waterbirds, small mammals. **Breeding:** All year with a spring–summer peak. Gestation 34 days, 3–4 young, up to 5 litters a year. Females mature at 4 to 8 months. **Features:** Sleek, thick, waterproof fur is black to grey or brown above, white to orange below. Flattened head, long nose and many whiskers. Long, thick tail with white tip. Small ears. Broad, partially webbed hind feet. **Threats:** Habitat destruction, predation by cats and foxes, salinity. Previously hunted for fur.

QUICK REFERENCE	
Diet	Carnivore
Reproduction period	All year
Number of offspring	3–4
Offspring maturity	4–8 months
Length HB ♂	231–345 mm
Length T	227–320 mm
Length HB ♀	245–370 mm
Length T	242–325 mm
Weight ♂	400–1275 g
Weight ♀	340–992 g
Status	Least Concern

WATER MOUSE *Xeromys myoides*

QUEENSLAND MUSEUM/BRUCE COWELL

QUICK REFERENCE	
Diet	Carnivore
Reproduction period	All year
Number of offspring	2–4
Length HB ♂	72–126 mm
Length T	62–94 mm
Length HB ♀	74–124 mm
Length T	63–99 mm
Weight	32–64 g
Status	Vulnerable

This species is also called False Water Rat due to its partially aquatic habit and lack of webbing on its feet. It builds nests above the high-tide mark for breeding and protection from predators. It forages on intertidal land during incoming and outgoing tides and leaves the remains of its meals in small middens.

Habitat: Mangroves, freshwater swamps, tidal flats, saline grasslands. **Behaviour:** Nocturnal, terrestrial, gregarious. **Diet:** Freshwater invertebrates, including crustaceans, flatworms and molluscs. **Breeding:** Possibly all year, 2 to 4 young. **Features:** Short, dense, silky fur is slate-grey above, sometimes spotted or flecked, and pure white below. Fur is water resistant. Hind feet not webbed. All feet covered by fine white hair. Small eyes. Round, short ears. Tail is thin, with fine hairs, lightly ringed and lacks white tip. Pungent odour. **Threats:** Small, fragmented populations. Habitat destruction, agriculture, overgrazing, water pollution, mining.

CENTRAL SHORT-TAILED MOUSE *Leggadina forresti*

QUICK REFERENCE	
Diet	Omnivore
Reproduction period	Dependent on rainfall
Number of offspring	3–4
Length HB Length T	70–199 mm 50–70 mm
Weight	13–20 g
Status	Least Concern

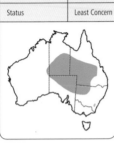

This mouse inhabits Australia's extremely harsh inland environments from where WA borders on NT and South Australia to southern inland Queensland and north-west NSW.

Habitat: Grasslands, tussock, sparse chenopod shrublands with loam, clay gibber soils. **Behaviour:** Nocturnal, solitary. Builds grass nests in shallow burrows. Can move up to one kilometre a night. **Diet:** Seeds, green vegetation and arthropods. **Breeding:** Females have 3–4 young per litter after rainfall. **Features:** Short thick grey-brown fur above, white below. Blunt nose, short rounded ears. Tail is distinctly shorter than head and body. **Threats:** Cats, foxes, sheep (grazing).

NORTHERN SHORT-TAILED MOUSE *Leggadina lakedownensis*

QUICK REFERENCE	
Diet	Omnivore
Reproduction period Number of offspring	All year 4
Length HB (mainland) Length HB (islands)	50–85 mm 67–92 mm
Length T (mainland) Length T (islands)	39–69 mm 71–81 mm
Weight (mainland) Weight (islands)	15–20 g 24–32 g
Status	Least Concern

This endemic north Australian mouse is found on Cape York, in the Tropical Savannah across the northern part of Australia and Pilbara as well as on Thevenard and Serrurier Islands off WA. Impressive population fluctuations in Kakadu do not appear to be linked to environmental factors.

Habitat: Spinifex and tussock grasslands to samphire and sedgelands, acacia shrublands, eucalypt and melaleuca woodlands with most habitats being seasonally inundated on clay soils. **Behaviour:** Nocturnal, solitary. **Diet:** Invertebrates and plant material. **Breeding:** One or two litters of up to 4 young. **Features:** Short thick grey-brown fur above, white below. Similar to the Central Short-tailed Mouse but for the forward-pointing upper incisors. **Threats:** Cats, foxes, grazing.

BROAD-TOOTHED RAT *Mastacomys fuscus*

HANS & JUDY BESTE/LOCHMAN TRANSPARENCIES

QUICK REFERENCE	
Diet	Herbivore
Reproduction period	Oct–Feb (Tas); Dec–Mar (Snowy Mtns)
Number of offspring	1–4
Length HB Length T	142–175 mm 100–130 mm
Weight	97–145 g
Status	Vulnerable

This heavy-set rat occurs in cool high rainfall areas of NSW and northern Victoria, of southern Victoria and the north-west coast Tasmania.

Habitat: Boulders, shrubs or grass tussocks in alpine and subalpine heathlands, wet sedgelands and wet sclerophyll forests. **Behaviour:** Primarily nocturnal. Builds runways under dense vegetation. Will congregate with up to four others — male and/or female — during winter. **Diet:** Grass, leaves, seeds, fungi, and bark. **Breeding:** Two litters per season. **Features:** Long, fine, thick brown fur with yellow-tips below. Dark feet, short dark tail with small bristles. **Threats:** Cats, foxes, habitat loss, climate change.

COMMON ROCK-RAT *Zyzomys argurus*

IAN MORRIS

QUICK REFERENCE	
Average lifespan	1–2 years
Diet	Omnivore
Reproduction period Number of offspring Offspring maturity	All year 1–4 5–6 months
Length HB Length T	85–122 mm Up to 125 mm
Weight	26–55 g
Status	Least Concern

This is the most widespread of the five species of rock-rats and also occupies a wider range of habitats. An earlier name for these species was 'thick-tailed rats', which refers to the animals' most distinctive feature used to store fat for times of food shortage. If the delicate skin on the tail is torn away, the tail withers.

Habitat: Rocky outcrops, which provide shelter for nesting, within open forest or woodland with a grassy understorey. **Behaviour:** Terrestrial, mostly nocturnal. **Diet:** Leaves, stems, seeds, fungi, insects. **Breeding:** All year. Gestation of 35 days, 1–4 young, mature at 5–6 months. Young are left in the nest, not carried with the mother. **Features:** Delicate build. Light brown above, white below. The sparsely furred tail has a thick base. The tail is often damaged or missing. **Threats:** No threats are listed for this species.

BRUSH-TAILED RABBIT-RAT *Conilurus penicillatus*

QUICK REFERENCE	
Average lifespan	6 years
Diet	Granivore
Reproduction period	Mar–Oct
Number of offspring	2
Offspring maturity	11 weeks
Length HB	135–227 mm
Length T	102–235 mm
Weight ♂	116–242 g
Weight ♀	102–202 g
Status	Vulnerable

IAN MORRIS

Also known as the Brush-tailed Tree-rat, this large and vocal rodent lives in northern Australia in family groups that shelter in logs, tree hollows and amongst Pandanus fronds. It is sometimes found in bulky grass nests at the base of trees.

Habitat: Open eucalypt forest, woodland with grass understorey, coastal stands of Casuarina and Pandanus. **Behaviour:** Semi-arboreal, gregarious, mostly nocturnal. **Diet:** Mainly grass seeds, also leaves, stems and insects. **Breeding:** March to October. Gestation 36 days. 1–4 young per litter. Several litters per season. Weaned at 3–7 weeks. **Features:** Robust build. Grey-brown above with rufous neck patch. Cream to white below, sometimes with grey chest patch. Long tail ends in black or white brush. White feet. Large ears. **Threats:** Habitat destruction, altered fire regimes, grazing, mining and predation by feral cats.

GRASSLAND MELOMYS *Melomys burtoni*

QUICK REFERENCE	
Diet	Omnivore
Reproduction period	All year
Number of offspring	2–5
Length HB ♂	90–160 mm
Length T	90–175 mm
Length HB ♀	95–145 mm
Length T	100–170 mm
Weight ♂	26–124 g
Weight ♀	26–97 g
Status	Least Concern

IAN MORRIS

This common rodent was once classified as eight separate species. This is reflected by its many common names including Scale-tailed Rat, Little Melomys, Banana Rat and Tree Rat. It is an agile climber and builds spherical nests above the ground which are usually 20–30 centimetres in diameter with two entrances.

Habitat: Coastal grassland, forests, woodland, vine thickets, swamps, mangroves, cane-fields. **Behaviour:** Nocturnal. Terrestrial and arboreal. **Diet:** Seeds, fruit, plant stems, insects. **Breeding:** All year in WA and NT; autumn and winter in Qld. 2–5 young, weaned at 3 weeks. **Features:** Varies from dark grey through grey-brown to reddish brown above, paler below. Sometimes pale orange on sides. Broad hindfeet. Mosaic pattern of scales on sparsely furred, semi-prehensile tail. **Threats:** Common and widespread. Considered a pest in sugar cane growing areas.

CAPE YORK MELOMYS *Melomys capensis*

JIRI LOCHMAN/LOCHMAN TRANSPARENCIES

QUICK REFERENCE	
Diet	Herbivore
Reproduction period Number of offspring Offspring maturity ♀	All year 2 80 days
Length HB ♂ Length T	120–162 mm 129–172 mm
Length HB ♀ Length T	119–152 mm 133–171 mm
Weight ♂	45–116 g
Weight ♀	45–96 g
Status	Not Evaluated

This lovely big-eyed melomys lives in the rainforests and neighbouring ecosystems on Cape York and offshore islands. It is not shy about entering human habitats and is often mistaken for a rat.

Habitat: Rainforests, monsoon forest, wet sclerophyll, eucalypt woodland.
Behaviour: Nocturnal, both arboreal and terrestrial, semi-prehensile tail helps it climb around trees and vines. **Diet:** Leaves, fruits, shoots and seeds. **Breeding:** Nests in tree hollow nests lined with dry leaves. Females has 4 teats but usually only gives birth to 2 young. They produce several litters a year. **Features:** Light to orange-brown above, cream to white underneath. Fawn feet. Almost naked tail is brown to black. **Threats:** Cats.

FAWN-FOOTED MELOMYS *Melomys cervinipes*

QUICK REFERENCE	
Diet	Omnivore
Reproduction period Number of offspring	All year 1–3
Length HB Length T	100–160 mm 105–180 mm
Weight	45–120 g
Status	Least Concern

This species is found in a variety of habitats and shows a preference for living in disturbed areas such as roadsides and forest edges. It has a large home range for a rodent (three to four hectares) and makes nests from leaves and grass in hollows, logs, burrows, and dense vegetation.

Habitat: Rainforest, vine thicket, woodlands, mangroves and bottle tree scrub.
Behaviour: Nocturnal, partly arboreal. **Diet:** Seeds, fruit, fungi, leaves and occasionally insects. **Breeding:** All year peaking from September to March. Gestation 38 days. 1–3 young. Several litters per year. **Features:** Colour is variable. Usually reddish or orange-brown on back with pale white to grey belly. Long, fawn hind foot. Hairless tail is brown to black sometimes with white tip, longer than head and body length with small mosaic-like scales.
Threats: Species is abundant. Predators include Dingoes, quolls, owls, pythons and cats.

BLACK-FOOTED TREE-RAT *Mesembriomys gouldii*

QUICK REFERENCE	
Diet	Omnivore
Reproduction period Number of offspring	All year 1–3
Length HB ♂ Length T	251–308 mm 334–412 mm
Length HB ♀ Length T	251–290 mm 320–392 mm
Weight ♂	650–830 g
Weight ♀	580–882 g
Status	Near Threatened

STANLEY BREEDEN/LOCHMAN TRANSPARENCIES

One of the largest rodents in Australia, it's suggested this species is our equivalent to a squirrel. Sadly, it has declined significantly in the last ten years. It shelters in tree hollows, pandanus palms and sometimes building roofs during the day, emerging to forage over a wide area at night.

Habitat: Open forest and woodlands with dense understorey. **Behaviour:** Nocturnal; mainly solitary. Arboreal and terrestrial. **Diet:** Hard fruits, flowers, seeds, invertebrates, and grass. **Breeding:** All year peaking in August and September. Gestation is 43–44 days. 1–3 young; weaned at 4 weeks. **Features:** Solid build. Long, shaggy fur is grizzled grey with black above and paler below. Ears are large and black. Long, furred tail with white brush at the tip. **Threats:** Habitat destruction, predation by cats, changing fire regimes, agriculture.

BUSH RAT *Rattus fuscipes*

QUICK REFERENCE	
Diet	Omnivore
Reproduction period Number of offspring Offspring maturity	All year 5 4 months
Length HB Length T	111–214 mm 105–195 mm
Weight	40–225 g
Status	Least Concern

KEN STEPNELL

The Bush Rat prefers habitats with dense undergrowth and is susceptible to bushfires and logging activities. It shelters during the day in short tunnels dug under logs and rocks. There are four distinct subspecies of Bush Rat which are variable in appearance.

Habitat: Rainforest, eucalypt forest, woodland, coastal heath. **Behaviour:** Terrestrial, mostly solitary, nocturnal. **Diet:** Insects, grass, leaves, fruit, seeds, fungi. **Breeding:** All year, 5 young per litter, several litters per year. The young are weaned at 4–5 weeks and are mature at 4 months. **Features:** Soft, thick fur is variable in colour; usually grey-brown to reddish brown above, paler below. Brown, grey or black tail with rings of scales. Tail is shorter than head–body length. Rounded ears. Hind feet are usually darker than front feet. **Threats:** Habitat destruction, logging, altered fire regimes, cats, foxes.

SWAMP RAT *Rattus lutreolus*

JIRI LOCHMAN/LOCHMAN TRANSPARENCIES

QUICK REFERENCE	
Diet	Omnivore
Reproduction period Number of offspring Offspring maturity	All year 3–5 3 months
Length HB Length T	112–197 mm 56–147 mm
Weight	50–200 g
Status	Least Concern

The Swamp Rat is able to swim for short periods to cross bodies of water or escape floods. It nests in underground burrows or in tussock grasses at ground level, and moves about in the tunnels it digs through dense vegetation. It can out-compete other native rodent species in moist habitats.

Habitat: Swamps; dense vegetation near waterways. **Behaviour:** Active day and night. Terrestrial, territorial, cryptic. **Diet:** Mainly reeds, grasses, and seeds; also fruit and arthropods. **Breeding:** All year peaking spring to autumn. 3–5 young per litter; several litters per year. Weaned at 3 weeks; mature from 3 months. **Features:** Stocky build. Blackish-brown fur on back, paler belly and chin. Small ears. Tail is dark grey, two thirds the length of head and body, scaly, and sparsely haired. **Threats:** Habitat destruction, fire, predation by cats, dogs and foxes.

CANEFIELD RAT *Rattus sordidus*

HANS & JUDY BESTE/LOCHMAN TRANSPARENCIES

QUICK REFERENCE	
Diet	Omnivore
Reproduction period Number of offspring	All year 6
Length HB Length T	100–210 mm 100–162 mm
Weight	50–260 g
Status	Least Concern

This fairly large rat is found in a variety of habitats on the Darling Downs and from Mackay to the tip of Cape York. It is considered an economic pest in sugarcane fields.

Habitat: Primarily tropical grasslands, also open forests, grassy open patches within dense rainforests. **Behaviour:** Terrestrial. Digs burrows for large colonies and runways through thick vegetation. **Diet:** Stems and seeds of grasses and broad-leafed herbs, insects. **Breeding:** Females usually pregnant from late spring to early winter. **Features:** Fur is long, coarse, golden brown; long guard hairs on the rump. Ears are light grey. **Threats:** Cats.

PALE FIELD-RAT *Rattus tunneyi*

QUICK REFERENCE	
Diet	Herbivore
Reproduction period	Jan–Aug/ Aug–Oct
Number of offspring	2–11
Offspring maturity	5 weeks
Length HB	118–194 mm
Length T	78–151 mm
Weight	46–165 g
Status	Least Concern

IAN MORRIS

This attractive rodent favours creek banks in grassy habitats with sandy soil. It makes shallow burrows with numerous entrances that are marked by small piles of soil and droppings. It also shelters in termite mounds. Prior to European settlement, it is likely this species lived over much of the continent.

Habitat: Grassy woodland, grassland, cane fields. **Behaviour:** Terrestrial, mostly solitary, nocturnal. **Diet:** Grass seeds, roots, and stems. **Breeding:** Spring in the east, January to August in NT and WA. Gestation of 21–22 days, 2–11 young. Weaned at 3 weeks, mature at 5 weeks. **Features:** Shiny coat is brown or yellow-brown above, grey or cream below. Scaly tail is shorter than head and body. Large, bulging eyes. Large ears. Female has 10 teats. **Threats:** Habitat damage caused by introduced mammals such as rabbits, sheep, cattle and goats. The introduced species *Rattus rattus* also eliminates this species.

LONG-HAIRED RAT *Rattus villosissimus*

QUICK REFERENCE	
Diet	Omnivore
Reproduction period	All year
Number of offspring	Up to 12
Length HB ♂	150–220 mm
Length T	125–180 mm
Length HB ♀	120–205 mm
Length T	100–175 mm
Weight ♂	65–289 g
Weight ♀	54–200 g
Status	Least Concern

HANS & JUDY BESTE/LOCHMAN TRANSPARENCIES

Nicknamed 'Plague Rat', the endemic Long-haired Rat is famous for its population explosions — following rains — covering areas of up to 130,000 km² in northern WA, NT, Queensland, South Australia and possibly North-west NSW. One of the most fertile rodents in Australia capable of producing up to 12 young every three weeks.

Habitat: Most habitats but retreats to moist areas during dry periods. **Behaviour:** Terrestrial, mostly nocturnal. Very social and vocal during plagues. Builds extensive and complex burrow systems in which it spends up to 80% of its time. **Diet:** Stems, leaves, with occasional carnivorous and cannibalistic tendencies. **Breeding:** Opportunistic. Can produce up to 12 young every three weeks. **Features:** Long shaggy fur, light greyish-brown above and pale grey or cream below. Small ears. **Threats:** Cats

KIMBERLEY ROCK-RAT   *Zyzomys woodwardi*

JIRI LOCHMAN/LOCHMAN TRANSPARENCIES

QUICK REFERENCE	
Diet	Herbivore
Reproduction period	All year
Length HB Length T	121–166 mm 111–130 mm
Weight	80–190 g
Status	Least Concern

This large rock-rat lives in rugged hard-to-reach areas of north and north-western Kimberley and its offshore islands, and close to the NT border near Kununurra.

Habitat: Boulder piles and rock screes in rainforest patches and open sandstone country. **Behaviour:** Mostly nocturnal. **Diet:** Rainforest tree and grass seeds. **Breeding:** May occur throughout the year. **Features:** Cinnamon-brown fur sprinkled with brown hairs above, white below. Moderately furred fragile tail is thick at base and tapers smoothly. **Threats:** Loss of habitat, change in fire regimes, cats.

GIANT WHITE-TAILED RAT   *Uromys caudimaculatus*

JIRI LOCHMAN/LOCHMAN TRANSPARENCIES

QUICK REFERENCE	
Diet	Omnivore
Reproduction period Number of offspring	Sept–Feb 2–3
Length HB ♂ Length T	305–382 mm 340–362 mm
Length HB ♀ Length T	275–357 mm 323–357 mm
Weight ♂	500–890 g
Weight ♀	500–800 g
Status	Least Concern

One of Australia's largest native rodents, The Giant White-tailed Rat inhabits a wide range of habitats in north Queensland, from just south of Townsville to the tip of Cape York.

Habitat: In higher altitude rainforests and closed sclerophyll forests as well as wetter open forests and woodlands. Melaleuca forests, mangroves and swamps at lower altitudes. **Behaviour:** Agile climber. Strong jaws can chew through tin cans and thick electrical cables. Very vocal emitting honking calls and high-frequency ultrasonic alarm inaudible to humans. Forages in trees as well as on ground. **Diet:** Fruit, nuts, fungi, insects, small reptiles, amphibians, crustaceans and bird eggs. **Breeding:** Gestation is 36 days. Young independent at 3 months. **Features:** Greyish-brown above with a white belly and pale paws. Long naked tail is greyish-black from base to the last third, where it is white. **Threats:** Cats.

SPINIFEX HOPPING-MOUSE *Notomys alexis*

QUICK REFERENCE	
Diet	Omnivore
Reproduction period	All year
Number of offspring	1–6
Offspring maturity	2 months
Length HB	95–112 mm
Length T	131–150 mm
Weight	27–45 g
Status	Least Concern

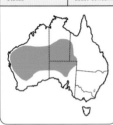

This unusual rodent is found in the arid and semi-arid regions of central and western Australia. It shelters from the desert heat in metre-deep burrow systems with several vertical entrances, which maintain a constant temperature and high humidity. The population increases very quickly after good rain, sinking back to a lower level as conditions dry and food diminishes.

Habitat: Woodland, grassland and desert with spinifex hummocks usually on sandy soils. **Behaviour:** Terrestrial, gregarious, nocturnal. **Diet:** Seeds, roots, leaf shoots, fungi, flowers, insects. **Breeding:** All year. Normal gestation of 32 days. 1–6 young (commonly 3 or 4). Mature at 2 months. **Features:** Light brown above, grey-white below. Long, tufted tail. Long hind feet and legs, upright stance. Large, rounded, sparsely furred ears. Bare chest patch. **Threats:** Predation by feral cats, foxes.

FAWN HOPPING-MOUSE *Notomys cervinus*

QUICK REFERENCE	
Diet	Herbivore/Insectivore
Reproduction period	Whenever suitable
Number of offspring	1–5
Length HB	95–120 mm
Length T	105–160 mm
Weight	30–50 g
Status	Vulnerable

HANS & JUDY BESTE/LOCHMAN TRANSPARENCIES

The population of the endemic Fawn Hopping-Mouse is now restricted to the Lake Eyre Basin in north-east South Australia and Queensland's south-west Channel Country.

Habitat: Gibber plains, stony alluvial flats. **Behaviour:** Nocturnal. Digs simple burrows in clay depressions and gibber plain sandy areas. **Diet:** Seeds, green plants and insects. **Features:** Pinkish-fawn to pale yellowish-grey above and white below. Large ears, bulging eyes, short muzzle, long hind feet, long tufted tail. No throat pouch. **Threats:** Climate change, grazing.

DUSKY HOPPING-MOUSE *Notomys fuscus*

QUEENSLAND MUSEUM

QUICK REFERENCE	
Average lifespan	3 years
Diet	Omnivore
Reproduction period Number of offspring Offspring maturity	All year 1–5 2 months
Length HB Length T	76–115 mm 115–155 mm
Weight	26–55 g
Status	Vulnerable

This small mouse is threatened in the three states in which it is found — Queensland, NSW and South Australia. Populations boomed following good wet seasons from 2005–2008, making it possible for the species to be regularly detected in north-western NSW after an absence of 150 years.

Habitat: Arid desert dune fields with Nitre Bush and Sandhill Canegrass.
Behaviour: Digs deep burrow systems with vertical shafts in dunes and hummocks.
Diet: Seeds, stems, flowers, green shoots, insects, small lizards. **Breeding:** Opportunistic, depends on conditions. **Features:** Orange to fawn fur above and white underneath. Both sexes have a well-developed throat pouch. Large ears. **Threats:** Habitat degradation, competition from rabbits and other introduced herbivores, foxes.

MITCHELL'S HOPPING-MOUSE *Notomys mitchellii*

JIRI LOCHMAN/LOCHMAN TRANSPARENCIES

QUICK REFERENCE	
Diet	Omnivore
Reproduction period	July–Nov
Length HB Length T	100–125 mm 140–155 mm
Weight	40–60 g
Status	Least Concern

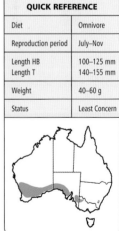

The long-legged, long-eared Mitchell's Hopping-Mouse lives in the southern areas of WA, South Australia and Victoria where winters are cool and wet and summers are warm and dry.

Habitat: Sandy soils and dune fields of the mallee/eucalypt woodlands.
Behaviour: Gregarious. Burrows during the day. Builds nest chambers 1 m below surface.
Diet: Plant roots, green leaf and seeds. **Breeding:** Populations fluctuate significantly depending on rainfall. **Features:** Fawn to dark greyish-brown above with orange tinted flanks and pale grey to shiny white below. Dark tufts of hair at the end of brownish-grey tail with pale grey underside. **Threats:** Habitat loss and fragmentation, grazing.

ASH-GREY MOUSE *Pseudomys albocinereus*

QUICK REFERENCE	
Diet	Omnivore
Reproduction period	All year
Number of offspring	3–5
Offspring maturity	3 months
Length HB	63–95 mm
Length T	95–105 mm
Weight	14–40 g
Status	Least Concern

JIRI LOCHMAN/LOCHMAN TRANSPARENCIES

This Mouse is found in semi-arid habitats of Western Australia from Cape Arid National Park to three islands in Shark Bay. The island populations are a separate sub-species. Family groups live in complex burrow systems up to 600 mm deep and three to four metres in length. For most of the year the Ash-grey Mouse does not need to drink water; it gets sufficient moisture from its food.

Habitat: Heath and shrubland on sandy soils. **Behaviour:** Terrestrial, gregarious, nocturnal. **Diet:** Seeds, plant material, small arthropods. **Breeding:** Spring in western parts of range; opportunistic in eastern parts. 38 days gestation. 2–6 young are mature the following August. **Features:** Long, soft fur is silver-grey tinged with fawn above, white below. Pink paws. Large rounded ears. **Threats:** Habitat destruction, predation by cats and foxes.

SILKY MOUSE *Pseudomys apodemoides*

QUICK REFERENCE	
Average lifespan	3 years
Diet	Omnivore
Reproduction period	All year
Number of offspring	2–5
Length HB	65–80 mm
Length T	90–110 mm
Weight	16–22 g
Status	Least Concern

MICHAEL WILLIAMS/LOCHMAN TRANSPARENCIES

The distribution of this endemic master burrow builder is restricted to the far south-east corner of South Australia and just over the Victorian border.

Habitat: Dry mallee heathlands. **Behaviour:** Nocturnal. Builds extensive burrows up to 3 m deep recognised by the soil heaps and pop-holes. Often built at the base of Banskia trees which provide food and moisture. **Diet:** Seeds, berries, nectar, cockroaches. **Breeding:** Up to 5 litters a year produced under favourable conditions. **Features:** Brown flecked silver-grey fur above and white below. Large ears and bulging eyes. Fine white hairs on pink tail that often features 10–15 grey-brown bands. **Threats:** Cats, foxes, fire.

PLAINS MOUSE *Pseudomys australis*

KEN STEPNELL

QUICK REFERENCE	
Diet	Omnivore
Reproduction period Number of offspring Offspring maturity	All year 1–7 55–70 days
Length HB Length T	90–145 mm 85–125 mm
Weight	30–65 g
Status	Vulnerable

The Plains Mouse is restricted to the Lake Eyre basin and the Nullarbor Plain. It lives in underground colonies connected by surface runways. Also known as the Plains Rat or Eastern Mouse, this rodent lacks sweat glands and produces concentrated urine, helping it to survive without drinking.

Habitat: Arid gibber plains and clay pans. **Behaviour:** Terrestrial, gregarious, nocturnal, placid. **Diet:** Seeds, plant material, invertebrates, fungi. **Breeding:** All year, usually after heavy rain. Gestation 30–31 days. 1–7 young (normally 3 or 4); weaned at 17–28 days. **Features:** Thick, soft fur silvery grey above and white or cream below. Large ears. Tail is grey on top, light below similar length to head and body and lighter towards the tip. **Threats:** Overgrazing by rabbits, sheep and cattle. Predation by Dingos, foxes and birds of prey.

WESTERN PEBBLE-MOUSE *Pseudomys chapmani*

JIRI LOCHMAN/LOCHMAN TRANSPARENCIES

QUICK REFERENCE	
Reproduction period Number of offspring	All year 4
Length HB Length T	52–67 mm 73–79 mm
Weight	10–15 g
Status	Least Concern

The Western Pebble-mouse lives in small family groups in burrows underneath mounds of pebbles. Mounds may be up to nine square metres containing thousands of pebbles and are used by successive generations. Individuals carry pebbles weighing up to five grams in their mouth then arrange them using their front limbs.

Habitat: Rocky hummock grassland, shrubland and Acacia scrub. **Behaviour:** Nocturnal, terrestrial, gregarious. **Diet:** Not documented. **Breeding:** All year. 4 young per litter. Several litters per year. **Features:** Buff brown on head back and sides, white throat and belly. Long head, large ears. Tail longer than head and body. **Threats:** Predation by cats and foxes, mining.

DELICATE MOUSE *Pseudomys delicatulus*

QUICK REFERENCE	
Diet	Herbivore
Reproduction period	All year
Number of offspring	3–4
Offspring maturity	6 g
Length HB	55–75 mm
Length T	55–80 mm
Weight	6–15 g
Status	Least Concern

QUEENSLAND MUSEUM/JEFF WRIGHT

This small rodent prefers the open, sparsely vegetated habitats found across tropical northern Australia. Populations are mobile and have been known to increase after grass fires. During the day the Delicate Mouse shelters from the sun's heat in shallow burrows, termite mounds and hollow logs.

Habitat: Open grassland and woodland on sandy soils; coastal dunes.
Behaviour: Terrestrial, nocturnal. **Diet:** Mostly native grass seeds. **Breeding:** All year in favourable conditions. Gestation of 28–31 days, usually 3–4 young per litter, 1 gram at birth. Several litters per year. Weaned by 1 month old and mature from weight of 6 grams.
Features: Orange brown fur on back with black guard hairs. White or cream belly and cheeks. Nose and feet are pale pink. Long, slender tail. **Threats:** Predation by cats and foxes.

DESERT MOUSE *Pseudomys desertor*

QUICK REFERENCE	
Diet	Herbivore
Reproduction period	All year
Number of offspring	3
Length HB	70–105 mm
Length T	67–103 mm
Weight	11–35 g
Status	Least Concern

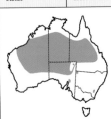

JIRI LOCHMAN/LOCHMAN TRANSPARENCIES

This small endemic mouse is found across most of Australia in arid and semi-arid regions and into tropical savannas with low rainfall.

Habitat: Open eucalypt, acacia and riparian woodlands, heath, samphire, shrublands, spinifex grasslands, cane grass dunes with dense grass, sedge or shrub groundcover.
Behaviour: Terrestrial. **Diet:** Samphire leaves, rock fern, sedge shoots, rhizomes and grasses. **Breeding:** Highly reproductive. Populations increase after heavy rain. **Features:** Bright chestnut brown fur with long dark guard hairs causing unkempt appearance. Tail is sparsely furred brown above and lighter below. White upper lip. Large eyes have pale orange ring. **Threats:** Introduced grasses, changing fire regimes, grazing.

EASTERN CHESTNUT MOUSE *Pseudomys gracilicaudatus*

QUICK REFERENCE	
Diet	Omnivore
Reproduction period Number of offspring	Sept–Mar 1–5
Length HB ♂ Length T	115–145 mm 82–120 mm
Length HB ♀ Length T	105–138 mm 80–114 mm
Weight ♂	55–118 g
Weight ♀	45–81 g
Status	Least Concern

QUEENSLAND MUSEUM

The Eastern Chestnut Mouse is a fire-specialist with larger populations linked specifically to regenerating vegetation, two to four years after a fire. An accelerated reproduction cycle allows it to be opportunistic. It constructs its nest from grass either above ground or in a burrow and uses runways in dense cover to move around.

Habitat: Open woodlands and forests with grassy understory; heaths and swamps.
Behaviour: Mostly nocturnal, terrestrial. **Diet:** Seeds, plant matter, fungi, and insects.
Breeding: September to March. Gestation is 27 days. 1–5 young; up to 3 litters per year.
Features: Chestnut-brown on back and flanks, greyish on belly. Stocky build. Subtle pale ring around eye. Feet pale underneath with long greyish or brown hairs on top.
Threats: Habitat destruction, changing fire regimes, predation by cats, foxes and dogs.

SANDY INLAND MOUSE *Pseudomys hermannsburgensis*

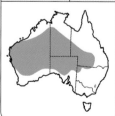

QUICK REFERENCE	
Diet	Omnivore
Reproduction period Number of offspring	All year 3–4
Length HB Length T	65–85 mm 70–90 mm
Weight	9–14.5 g
Status	Least Concern

QUEENSLAND MUSEUM/JEFF WRIGHT

The Sandy Inland Mouse appears similar to the introduced House Mouse but has larger ears, a more rounded head and lacks the characteristic musty odour of Mus musculus. It spends its day in shallow burrows, up to half a metre deep and one metre long. It sometimes uses vacant holes of Bearded Dragons or coexists with Knob-tailed Geckos.

Habitat: Arid sand dunes and grasslands; open woodlands. **Behaviour:** Nocturnal, terrestrial, gregarious. **Diet:** Seeds, plant material, roots, tubers and invertebrates.
Breeding: All year. 3–4 young. Newborns stay attached to nipples. **Features:** Grey-brown or sandy-brown above and off-white below. Superficially similar to introduced House Mouse, but with more slender build, and larger ears, eyes and tail. No odour. **Threats:** Predation by cats and foxes, competition with other herbivores, habitat destruction.

LONG-TAILED MOUSE *Pseudomys higginsi*

QUICK REFERENCE	
Diet	Omnivore
Reproduction period Number of offspring	Sept–Apr 3–4
Length HB Length T	115–150 mm 145–200 mm
Weight	50–90 g
Status	Least Concern

JIRI LOCHMAN/LOCHMAN TRANSPARENCIES

Previously present on the mainland, this species is now restricted to Tasmania including Bruny Island. It is an opportunistic omnivore that nests in hollow or rotting logs and forest-floor litter. This is the first native species to be confirmed as being eaten by a fox when they were recently introduced to Tasmania.

Habitat: Wet forests and scrub, alpine boulder fields, scree slopes. **Behaviour:** Mainly nocturnal, mostly terrestrial, territorial. **Diet:** Grass, fruit, fungi, invertebrates. **Breeding:** September to April. 1–2 litters per year, 3–4 young per litter. **Features:** Soft fur is dark grey on back and paler on belly. Slight build. Large feet. Tail is long and delicate; dark in colour above and light below. **Threats:** Introduction of foxes to Tasmania is a potential threat.

CENTRAL PEBBLE-MOUSE *Pseudomys johnsoni*

QUICK REFERENCE	
Reproduction period	May–June
Length HB Length T	58–76 mm 63–95 mm
Weight	7–20 g
Status	Least Concern

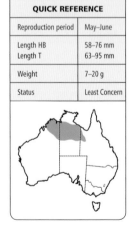

GREG BARRON/LOCHMAN TRANSPARENCIES

First described in 1985, this tiny pebble-mouse is an obsessive builder that erects cone-shaped piles of pebbles around the entrances to its burrows or carefully spreads carpets of pebbles covering an area of up to 10 m^2.
The stones it carries in its mouth can be the same weight as the mouse. Found from Kimberley through the subtropical centre of NT and over the border into the Mt Isa region of north-west Queensland.

Habitat: Plateaus with open woodland, grassy pebble-covered ridges and plains, and dense shrubby understorey. **Behaviour:** Builds complex burrows but nest comprises of a simple layer of spinifex. **Features:** Grey-brown with black guard hairs on top and white underneath. Mouth sides and feet are white.

WESTERN CHESTNUT MOUSE *Pseudomys nanus*

JIRI LOCHMAN/LOCHMAN TRANSPARENCIES

QUICK REFERENCE	
Diet	Herbivore
Reproduction period	All year except for very dry seasons
Number of offspring	3–5
Length HB ♂ Length T	85–130 mm 75–121 mm
Length HB ♀ Length T	71–116 mm 78–120 mm
Weight ♂	21–56 g
Weight ♀	17.5–56 g
Status	Least Concern

This large stout mouse from tropical north Australia is found on islands off Pilbara across Port Headland in WA across to Barkly Tableland in north-west Queensland.

Habitat: Dense tussock grasslands and eucalypt woodland on volcanic sandy and lateric soils. **Behaviour:** Primarily nocturnal. Not shy. Makes a high-pitched whistling call. Builds a grass nest. **Diet:** Native grasses and seeds. **Breeding:** Gestation 22–24 days. **Features:** Fur light orange mixed with long dark brown hairs above and cream with white based fur underneath. Light eye-ring, short ears and limbs, tail is black above and white underneath. **Threats:** Changing fire regimes, grazing, non-native grasses.

NEW HOLLAND MOUSE *Pseudomys novaehollandiae*

The total population of New Holland Mouse is estimated at fewer than ten thousand individuals and declining. Abundance is linked to regenerating vegetation, three to five years after fire. The timing of breeding is associated with food availability and quality, which is related to rainfall and fire events.

Habitat: Heathland, open woodland, sand dunes. **Behaviour:** Nocturnal, social, terrestrial. **Diet:** Seeds, leaves, fungi, invertebrates. **Breeding:** Late winter to summer, sometimes autumn. Gestation is 32 days. 2–6 young. 2–4 litters per season. Females mature at 7–13 weeks and males at 20 weeks. **Features:** Grey-brown above, greyish-white below. Similar to introduced House Mouse, with larger ears and eyes. Dusky brown tail is darker on top and 10–15% longer than head and body. No odour. **Threats:** Habitat destruction, changing fire regimes, predation by dogs, cats and foxes.

QUEENSLAND MUSEUM

QUICK REFERENCE	
Average lifespan	2 years
Diet	Omnivore
Reproduction period Number of offspring Offspring maturity	Aug–Dec 2–6 13–20 weeks
Length HB Length T	65–88 mm 81–107 mm
Weight	12–26 g
Status	Vulnerable

WESTERN MOUSE *Pseudomys occidentalis*

QUICK REFERENCE	
Diet	Omnivore
Reproduction period	Sept–Nov
Offspring maturity	1st year
Length HB	90–110 mm
Length T	120–140 mm
Weight	33–53 g
Status	Least Concern

JIRI LOCHMAN/LOCHMAN TRANSPARENCIES

This endemic mouse's distribution has been reduced to WA's south coast and southern wheatbelt in areas where the dense vegetation has remained unburned for 30–50 years.

Habitat: Dense vegetation in dry shrubland, mallee, unburned woodland with dense understorey on clay land laterite soils. **Behaviour:** Communal. Nocturnal. Shelters in burrow 20–30 cm deep during the day. **Diet:** Flowers, seeds, quandong nuts, invertebrates. **Breeding:** Young are born late spring. **Features:** Mixed light and dark grey fur with black guard hairs above and greyish-white underneath. White feet. **Threats:** Loss of habitat, changing fire regimes, cats, foxes.

EASTERN PEBBLE-MOUSE *Pseudomys patrius*

QUICK REFERENCE	
Diet	Granivore
Reproduction period	All year
Length HB	54–77 mm
Length T	55–85 mm
Weight	10–19 g
Status	Least Concern

QUEENSLAND MUSEUM/BRUCE COWELL

It was the curiosity of a geologist that assisted in the discovery of the Eastern Pebble-mouse. Generally, this species carries pebbles under half its body weight; however, it has been known to carry stones weighing more than itself. It constructs burrows under conical pebble-mounds near the base of trees or among rocks.

Habitat: Rolling ridges or hills with marble-sized pebbles in dry open woodland with a grassy understorey. **Behaviour:** Nocturnal, gregarious, terrestrial. **Diet:** Predominantly grass seeds. **Breeding:** All year peaking in late the wet season or early dry season. Females may have a series of litters in a year. **Features:** Brown fur on back, white below. Bulbous eyes. Lightly furred pink or grey tail. No odour. **Threats:** Predation by foxes, cats and dogs.

HEATH MOUSE *Pseudomys shortridgei*

JIRI LOCHMAN/LOCHMAN TRANSPARENCIES

QUICK REFERENCE	
Diet	Omnivore
Reproduction period Number of offspring	Nov–Jan 3
Length HB Length T	90–120 mm 85–100 mm
Weight	55–90 g
Status	Vulnerable

The small populations of this endemic chunky broad-faced gentle rodent are widely scattered from south-central WA to south-east South Australia and south-west Victoria.

Habitat: Dry heathland and open stringybark forest with heath understorey, mixed scrub and mallee. **Behaviour:** Terrestrial. Diurnal. Shelters in shallow burrows. **Diet:** Flowers, seeds, berries, stems, leaves, grasses, fungi. **Breeding:** Males and females stay together during 4 month breeding season during which they produce 2 litters of 3 young. **Features:** Buff and black flecked thick greyish-brown fur above and pale grey below. Blunt face, short rounded ears, hairy tail is brown above, white below with no rings. **Threats:** Cats, foxes, inappropriate fire regimes, habitat destruction and fragmentation.

TREE MOUSE *Pogonomys sp*

HANS & JUDY BESTE/LOCHMAN TRANSPARENCIES

QUICK REFERENCE	
Diet	Herbivore
Reproduction period Number of offspring	Apr–Oct 2–3
Length HB ♂ Length T	130–160 mm 160–208 mm
Length HB ♀ Length T	134–141 mm 165–197 mm
Weight ♂	52–85 g
Weight ♀	40–79 g
Status	Not Evaluated

This lovely little native mouse is so elusive it was only first recorded in 1974 when it was caught by a cat on the Atherton Tablelands. It is restricted to the rainforests of the Wet Tropics and Cape York.

Habitat: Rainforests at all elevations. **Behaviour:** Burrows in the ground during the day and forages in tree understorey and canopies. Agile climber capable of spread-eagle jumps. **Diet:** Rainforest fruits, flowers and leaves. **Breeding:** Females have 6 teats and rear 2–3 young each year. **Features:** Soft grey fur above and bright white underneath. Small rounded ears, blunt nose, black eye-ring. Very long prehensile tail curls up at the end and coils around branches for support. Loose skin between fore and hind legs serves as rudimentary gliding membrane. **Threats:** Cats.

DINGO

ORDER: CARNIVORA

DINGO

SUBORDER: CANIFORMIA
FAMILY: CANIDAE

The Dingo evolved in Asia around 6,000 years ago and is a primitive member of the Canidae family. It was most likely introduced to Australia by Asian seafarers around 4,000 years ago and is commonly regarded as a native animal because it has been here for so long. Having out-competed the Thylacine and Tasmanian Devil on the mainland, it is now the largest carnivorous land mammal in Australia.

Lifestyle

A Dingo's life begins in winter when females give birth to a litter usually of three to seven pups. After a few days of constant care, the pups are left alone in a den for much of the time while the mother rests or hunts. Within two weeks, they are being fed regurgitated meat as well as milk. When the pups are big enough, they are taken on kills and gradually introduced to the pack's territory. Aside from hunting and sleeping, Dingos spend time socialising and maintaining territorial boundaries.

Territory size depends on the abundance of food and availability of fresh water. In good habitats the average territory is about 10 km^2; however, the largest known dingo territories are 113 km^2. Habitat quality also determines the size of a pack. While forested areas suit packs of around three, packs of 12 or more may be found in undisturbed arid regions.

FACTS

- Dingos breed only once a year and usually mate for life.

- Dogs (*Canis lupus familiaris*) and Dingos (*Canis familiaris dingo*) interbreed.

- Pure Dingos can only be distinguished from wild dogs or hybrids by skull measurements and genetic testing.

- In packs, the dominant female kills the pups of other females who become nursemaids to her litter.

- More than 80% of all Dingos in south-eastern Australia are hybrids.

- Dingos mark and defend their territories and groups seldom cross boundaries.

- A fence to keep Dingos out of grazing lands stretches nearly 6,000 km from Queensland's Darling Downs to the Great Australian Bight.

- In parts of Australia, bounties of up to $100 are still offered for Dingo scalps.

- Dingos prey on fish as desert creeks and waterholes dry up.

Above: A Dingo patrols a beach on Fraser Island searching for food.
Opposite: Some Dingoes may be black, cream and tan in colour.

Behaviour

Dingos are patient, intelligent hunters with excellent vision, acute hearing and a keen sense of smell. They often hunt alone, but a pack can work together to bring down large prey such as feral Asian Water Buffalo *Bubalus bubalis*.

These opportunistic predators have wide-ranging tastes that include everything from insects to kangaroos. Peak hunting times are dawn and dusk when their favoured prey — rabbits, rodents and macropods — are on the move or distracted by the business of eating and drinking. Dingos will organise the size of the pack and adjust their strategy according to the kinds of prey they are hunting. They may cover several kilometres each night when foraging.

As Australia's apex predator, the Dingo plays a significant role in keeping ecosystems balanced. It is also important in limiting the populations of some introduced pest species such as rabbits and pigs.

Dingos and People

Upon their arrival in Australia, Dingos were adopted by Aborigines as companions, guards against malevolent night spirits, and hunting aides. In time, Dingos came to live across the entire mainland of Australia but have never made it to Tasmania. They appear in Aboriginal art, sometimes replacing older images of the Thylacine, and are the subject of numerous stories of cultural importance.

The war between graziers and Dingos began in the 1800s and continues today. Though livestock normally makes up less than 2% of a Dingo's diet, hybrids can become very aggressive and destructive, often killing simply for the thrill of the chase.

Misunderstanding the Dingo's intrinsically shy nature has also led to attacks on people. Most Dingos have a natural fear of humans and will keep their distance. In tourist areas handouts have led to Dingos becoming less fearful, to the point where they harass people to be fed.

Dingos do not bark, they howl.

Wallabies are hunted by Dingoes for food.

Finding Dingos

Check waterholes, stock watering points and other sources of fresh water at dawn and dusk. Stake out roadkill on inland roads, rubbish dumps and camping grounds for scavenging Dingos. Listen for characteristic howls and yelps at night. Look for twisted cylinders or sausage shaped scats on prominent rocks and track intersections. Never feed wild Dingos as they can lose their fear of humans and become aggressive towards people.

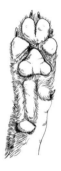

Fore foot and print

Hind foot and print

LOCATION TIPS

▶ Fraser Island, Qld

▶ Uluṟu–Kata Tjuṯa NP, NT

▶ Nadgee Nature Reserve, NSW

▶ Lake Eyre, SA

▶ Napier Range, WA

DINGO *Canis familiaris dingo*

QUICK REFERENCE	
Average lifespan	10 years
Diet	Carnivore
Reproduction period	Mar–Jun
Number of offspring	1–10
Offspring maturity	1–2 years
Length HB ♂	835–1110 mm
Length T	280–370 mm
Length HB ♀	813–1010 mm
Length T	247–350 mm
Weight ♂	12–22 kg
Weight ♀	11–17 kg
Status	Vulnerable

Dingos prefer habitats where forest or woodlands merge with heath or grassland. Use of arid habitats is determined by the availability of fresh water. Hybrids with wild dogs are difficult to distinguish from pure Dingos and are found in all populations including on Fraser Island.

Habitat: All mainland terrestrial habitats. **Behaviour:** Terrestrial, gregarious (may hunt alone), mostly nocturnal, territorial. **Diet:** Reptiles, birds, mammals, fish, insects. Occasionally fruit. **Breeding:** March to June. Gestation of 63 days, 1–10 pups, weaned at 3–4 months. Females mature at 2 years, males at 1 year. **Features:** Fur is usually ginger with white chest, paws and tail tip. About 4% are black with tan points. Completely white Dingos are rare. Naturally very lean build. Bushy tail. Upright ears. Skull is larger, snout narrower and teeth larger than in a domestic dog. **Threats:** Hybridisation with domestic dogs, human persecution.

- Seal hunting was legal in Tasmania until 1923 and in Victoria until 1949.

- A seal's blood can carry four times more oxygen than human blood.

- A female Australian Sea-lion has an 18-month breeding cycle.

- The Australian Fur-seal can dive to 200 m.

- Eared seals can stay underwater for up to 12 minutes.

- Male New Zealand Fur-seals do not feed during the breeding season, which can last over 2 months.

- The Leopard Seal preys on penguins and the young of other seals.

- Some species of earless seals sleep and mate under water.

- Female fur-seals can delay the development of their fertilised eggs.

- Seals can become bycatch in commercial fishing nets, lines and traps.

SEALS

SUBORDER: PINNIPEDIA
FAMILIES: OTARIIDAE (EARED-SEALS) & PHOCIDAE ('TRUE' SEALS)

Seals are thought to have originated in the north Atlantic region with the **Otariidae** family (called eared seals or sea-lions) appearing about 23 million years ago, getting a headstart on the **Phocidae** (called earless seals or 'true' seals) that appeared about 15 million years ago. Fossils from south-east Victoria indicate that earless seals were resident Australians about five million years ago and that their eared counterparts made it this far south three million years later.

Seals are amphibious carnivores that have held on to the fur coat, four-limbed body plan and ability to move on land inherited from their terrestrial ancestors. However, feet were exchanged for flippers and their bodies were streamlined in a successful bid to exploit the world's temperate and polar marine environments. Despite their aquatic adaptations, seals are still tied to the land, for this is where they give birth.

Top & above: Weddell Seal and young Elephant Seal, both are occasional visitors to Australian waters. **Left:** Australian Sea-lion.

Movement in Water

These air-breathing mammals may be ungainly on land, but they move through the water with surprising speed and grace thanks to a flexible skeleton, power-packed muscles and flippers. Eared seals row under water with their large front flippers. Earless seals use alternate kicks of the hind flippers to propel themselves forward.

Before diving, a seal pumps up its oxygen supply with some deep breathing and slows its heart rate. It then closes its nostrils and soft palate to prevent water from entering the lungs and gullet. A layer of fatty blubber beneath the skin and a sleek, double-layered coat of hair streamline and insulate the body.

Seals and Sea-lions are excellent and incredibly agile swimmers both on the surface and underwater.

Seals of Australian Waters

The Australian Sea-lion, New Zealand Fur-seal and Australian Fur-seal breed on the coast of the southern Australian mainland, Tasmania and offshore islands. Other species occasionally visit Tasmanian beaches. The places where seals come ashore to rest are called 'haul-out sites'.

These accomplished underwater hunters seek out prey by sight, sound and smell. Eared seals have the added advantage of rotatable whiskers that help locate small prey on the sea floor. Their seafood diet includes squid, octopus, fish, crustaceans and penguins. Some eat the pups of other species. When foraging, seals may travel vast distances and swim to great depths.

Seals were hunted in the last century for their meat, oil and fur. Today, all seals are protected in Australian waters.

Coming Ashore

Australia's southern shores and islands host substantial populations of fur-seals and sea-lions. They are more terrestrial than their earless relatives and can turn their hind limbs forward to walk in a semi-upright position. Sea-lions haul out on sandy beaches to rest and moult while fur-seals prefer rocky shores. They all favour rocky sites for mating and raising their young. The arrival of mature males at the rookeries signals the start of the breeding season. While pregnant females are staking out their birthing sites, the males aggressively challenge one another for mating territories and success is directly related to territory size.

Males may be sexually mature by the age of four, but are seldom big enough to claim a territory until eight years of age. A female gives birth to a single pup conceived during the previous season before she accepts the advances of a dominant male. She develops a strong bond with her pup through touch, smell and calls, allowing quick recognition amidst the chaos of a large colony. The pup is left in a safe crevice or nursery while its mother goes off to feed. It begins accompanying its mother on fishing expeditions at about eight months of age and is usually weaned by the start of the next breeding season.

Australian
Sea-lion

Clockwise from top left: Young Australian Fur Seals frolicking; Australian Sea-lion returning from a feeding expedition and an old bull harassing a female Sea-lion.

Watching Seals

Summer, when they gather in large breeding colonies, is the best time to see fur-seals and sea-lions. Remember, they are very territorial and aggressive at this time and should not be approached.

Seal watchers can take advantage of viewing platforms at various locations along the coast or take a boat tour to offshore haul-out and breeding sites. Visitors to Kangaroo Island can take a guided walk amongst basking sea-lions. Solitary earless seals are more likely to be seen in coastal waters or on the beach during winter.

Divers should be aware that while seals are very approachable under water, they are also a favoured food of large sharks and Killer Whales.

Earless Visitors

Earless, or 'true' seals belong to the family Phocidae. They no longer reside in Australia having been driven from its shores by the fur trade, but they occasionally venture into coastal waters. Their torpedo-shaped bodies have short front flippers and no visible ears. The shorter, backward-facing hind flippers are used for swimming but do not support the body on land, so they inch along on their bellies. Five species of earless seals are known to visit Australia:

- Crabeater Seal • Leopard Seal • Ross Seal
- Southern Elephant Seal • Weddell Seal

LOCATION TIPS

- ▶ Montague Island, NSW
- ▶ Phillip Island, Vic.
- ▶ Cape Bridgewater, Vic.
- ▶ Kangaroo Island, SA
- ▶ Eyre Peninsula, SA
- ▶ Head of Bight, SA
- ▶ Seal Island, WA
- ▶ Archipelago of the Recherche, WA
- ▶ Leeuwin–Naturaliste NP, WA
- ▶ Bridport, Tas.

BOAT TOURS

- ▶ Bruny Island, Tas.
- ▶ Phillip Island, Vic.
- ▶ Esperance, WA
- ▶ Narooma, NSW
- ▶ Stanley, Tas.

CRABEATER SEAL *Lobodon carcinophaga*

RHALLAM/DREAMSTIME

QUICK REFERENCE	
Average lifespan	14 years
Diet	Carnivore
Reproduction period Number of offspring Offspring maturity	Oct 1 2 years
Length NT	260 cm
Weight	225 kg
Status	Least Concern

The distribution of this sleek abundant seal is connected to the fluctuation of ice packs surrounding Antarctica. Individuals are occasionally spotted between Tasmania and along the southern Australian coast up to northern NSW.

Habitat: Ice floes, ocean. **Behaviour:** Forages in the ocean at night and rests, moults and breeds on ice floes. Can dive to 600 m and stay submerged for up to 24 min. **Diet:** Contrary to its name, it eats krill almost exclusively, occasionally fish and squid. Have been seen swimming in herds of up to 500. **Breeding:** Male follows female out on to floe after she gives birth. He stays with them until the pup is weaned, after which he and female mate. **Features:** Silvery brownish-grey with dark spots in winter and almost solid yellowish-white in summer. Streamlined with upturned snout. Ornate post-canine teeth.

AUSTRALIAN SEA-LION *Neophoca cinerea*

QUICK REFERENCE	
Average lifespan	12 years
Diet	Carnivore
Reproduction period Number of offspring Offspring maturity	All year 1 4–5 years
Length ♂	1.85–2.25 m
Length ♀	1.3–1.85 m
Weight ♂	180–250 kg
Weight ♀	65–100 kg
Status	Endangered

Australia's only endemic seal breeds on islands in Western Australia and South Australia, and on the mainland at Point Labatt, South Australia. The total population is estimated to be between 9,000 and 12,000 making it the rarest pinniped in the world.

Habitat: Cool temperate seas with sandy and rocky shores. **Behaviour:** Amphibious/marine, gregarious, nocturnal and diurnal. **Diet:** fish, cephalopods, crustaceans. **Breeding:** Varies across the year at different colonies. Females breed every 18 months. Gestation of 14–15 months, 1 pup per mating. Weaned at over 15–18 months. Sexually mature at 4–5 years. **Features:** Lacks thick undercoat of fur. Males are blackish to chocolate brown with distinct lighter coloured mane. Females and young are smaller and coloured silver-grey above and cream to yellow below. Blunt snout, long, white whiskers and small rolled ears. **Threats:** Entanglement in fishing nets, pollution, disease. Previously hunting.

NEW ZEALAND FUR-SEAL *Arctocephalus forsteri*

QUICK REFERENCE	
Diet	Carnivore
Reproduction period Number of offspring Offspring maturity	Nov–Jan 1 4–5 years
Length ♂	1.6–1.9 m
Length ♀	1.3–1.5 m
Weight ♂	90–160 kg
Weight ♀	35–50 kg
Status	Least Concern

This eared seal prefers protected boulder beaches with dense vegetation and tidal pools for its rookeries. Dominant males establish harems of five to 16 females. The total population is estimated at 200,000, with about half living in Australia.

Habitat: Cool temperate seas and rocky shores. **Behaviour:** Amphibious/marine, gregarious, territorial. **Diet:** Cephalopods, fish, birds. **Breeding:** November to January. Gestation of 8 months, 1 pup per season. Weaned at 10 months, sexually mature at 4 to 5 years, but males unable to hold territory until 8 years. **Features:** Dark brown to greyish brown above — looks black when wet — paler below. Dense fur underlies the coat of guard hairs. Males have a massive neck and thick mane. Newborns are black. Head profile slightly concave. Elongated, pointed snout with long whiskers and black tip. Small ears. **Threats:** Entanglement in fishing nets, pollution. Previously hunting.

AUSTRALIAN FUR-SEAL *Arctocephalus pusillus doriferus*

QUICK REFERENCE	
Average lifespan	19–21 years
Diet	Carnivore
Reproduction period Number of offspring Offspring maturity	Nov–Dec 1 3–6 years
Length ♂	1.9–2.25 m
Length ♀	1.3–1.75 m
Weight ♂	135–289 kg
Weight ♀	41–120 kg
Status	Least Concern

This is the most abundant seal in Australia with the total population estimated around 120,000 and rising (half of the pre-sealing population). Haul-out sites extend from Tasmania to southern New South Wales. Breeding colonies form at ten permanent sites in Bass Strait.

Habitat: Cool temperate seas and rocky shores. **Behaviour:** Amphibious/marine, gregarious, shy. **Diet:** Fish, cephalopods. **Breeding:** November to December. Gestation of 12 months, 1 pup per season, weaned at 9–10 months. Females mature at 3–6 years, males hold territories from 8–13 years of age. **Features:** Thick undercoat of fur beneath sleek guard hairs. Males are dark brown to brownish grey with a mane of long coarse hair. Females and young are light brown to silver grey and have a fawn to cream throat. Newborns are black. Slightly pointed snout with long whiskers. Small ears.
Threats: Entanglement in fishing nets, pollution. Previously hunting.

LEOPARD SEAL *Hydrurga leptonyx*

DMYTRO PYLYPENKO/DREAMSTIME

QUICK REFERENCE	
Average lifespan	26 years
Diet	Carnivore
Reproduction period Number of offspring Offspring maturity	Oct–Jan 1 4–4.5 years
Length ♂	2.8–3.3 m
Length ♀	2.9–3.6 m
Weight ♂	> 400 kg
Weight ♀	> 600 kg
Status	Least Concern

This very large, true seal is at the top of the southern ocean food chain. It is solitary and mainly hauls out on Antarctic pack-ice. Young Leopard Seals are occasionally seen visiting Australian waters and beaches in winter. Males and females both sing to attract mates. Mating occurs in the water soon after the previous year's young is weaned.

Habitat: Southern ocean pack ice. Occasionally Australian beaches and rocky shores. **Behaviour:** Amphibious/marine, solitary. **Diet:** Penguins, krill, fish, squid, other seals, seabirds, whale carcasses. **Breeding:** October to January. 1 pup per season, weaned at 4 weeks. Females mature at 4 years and males at 4.5 years. **Features:** Slim build with large head and distinct neck. Dark grey above, lighter below. Spots on throat and flanks. Jaws have wide gape with three-pronged molar teeth. **Threats:** Disease, climate change.

DUGONG

ORDER: SIRENIA

LOCHMAN TRANSPARENCIES

FAMILY: DUGONGIDAE

The Dugong, also known as the sea cow, belongs to the order Sirenia, and is the only herbivorous marine mammals. This rotund, whiskered mammal and its Manatee relative are thought to be the reality behind the myth of irresistible south sea nymphs – mermaids — who lured mariners to destruction on rocky coasts. Rather than enchanting sailors with seductive songs, the Dugong cruises Australia's warm coastal waters in pursuit of lush seagrass meadows.

Aside from large males that use whistling sounds to keep their herds together, the Dugong's vocal ability is limited to soft chirps. It has excellent vision and hearing. A heavy skeleton provides the necessary ballast to keep a Dugong on the sea floor while its flexible and sensitive upper lip pushes seagrass into its mouth. If leaves and new shoots are scarce, it ploughs up whole plants, leaving distinctive furrows in the silt.

Ancient Mariners

A Dugong's lifespan can exceed 70 years, making it one of the longest-lived species of marine mammal. Sexual maturity occurs between the ages of 10 and 17 years, at which stage an animal is about 2.4 metres in length and weighs around 250 kilograms.

They have a low pregnancy rate, with females breeding only once every three to seven years. Mating is a fairly violent affair in east coast waters where females are pursued and set upon by several males. In the west, the males establish small territories and it is up to the female to choose a mate. At the end of a 13–15 month pregnancy, a female moves into shallow water protected by a sandbar to give birth to her single offspring.

The calf begins feeding on seagrass within a few weeks of birth, but is not weaned for 18 or more months. It gains some protection from predators, such as sharks, by riding just above its mother's back when it is not suckling.

FACTS

- Dugongs usually stay within 5 m of the surface, although they have been seen as deep as 20 m.

- Dugongs have been known to stray as far south as Albany, WA and Tathra, NSW.

- Habitat degradation, fishing nets, boat propellers and hunting are major threats to Dugong survival.

- A Dugong's large intestine can be 25 m long.

- Large sharks, crocodiles and Killer Whales prey on Dugongs.

- A herd can number several hundred and travel up to 25 km a day.

- Dugongs are related to elephants.

- Indigenous Australians harvest about 3,000 Dugongs each year.

LOCATION TIPS

- Moreton Bay, Qld
- Hinchinbrook Channel, Qld
- Shark Bay, WA
- Van Diemen Gulf, NT

Seagrass beds are a vital food source for Dugongs.

GEOFF TAYLOR/LOCHMAN TRANSPARENCIES

WATCHING DUGONGS

- Look for Dugongs in wide, shallow bays, mangrove channels, estuaries, on the leeward side of large coastal islands and near coral reefs. Check out offshore sheltered locations in rough weather.

- Watch for Dugongs feeding inshore on the rising tide. They surface to breathe about once a minute.

- Dugongs are inquisitive and will approach divers if they have not previously been hunted.

A Dugong calf protected by its mother.

DUGONG *Dugong dugon*

GARY BELL/OCEANWIDEIMAGES.COM

QUICK REFERENCE	
Average lifespan	70 years
Diet	Herbivore
Reproduction period	All year
Number of offspring	1
Offspring maturity	6–17 years
Length (newborn)	1–3.3 m
Length (adult)	2.5–3m
Weight (newborn)	20 kg
Weight (adult)	230–420 kg
Status	Vulnerable

The Dugong is the only living herbivorous marine mammal. It lives in shallow, warm water from Shark Bay, Western Australia, around the northern coastline to Moreton Bay, Queensland and occasionally as far south as Tathra, NSW.

Habitat: Tropical and subtropical coastal waters. **Behaviour:** Marine, mainly gregarious, curious. **Diet:** Seagrass, sometimes algae and marine invertebrates. **Breeding:** Year round peaking in spring and summer. Gestation 13–15 months, 1 offspring, weaned at 18 months and sexually mature at 10–17 years. 3–7 years interval between births. **Features:** Grey to bronze above, pale below. Two nostrils on top of blunt snout, wide mouth on underside. Sensory bristles on edge and inside surface of enlarged upper lip. Clawless paddle-like front flippers, horizontal tail flukes, no hind limbs or dorsal fin. Males have two upper tusks. **Threats:** Stranding, hunting, habitat loss, pollution, disease and boat strike. Predation by sharks, crocodiles and Killer Whales.

WHALES & DOLPHINS

ORDER: CETACEA

SUBORDERS: MYSTICETI & ODONTOCETI
FAMILIES: **WHALES:** BALAENIDAE, BALAENOPTERIDAE, PHYSETERIDAE & ZEPHIIDAE
DOLPHINS: DELPHINIDAE

Whales and dolphins are members of the order Cetacea. The world's 10 species of filter-feeding baleen whales belong to the suborder Mysticeti and the 70 species of predatory toothed whales, dolphins and porpoises belong to the suborder Odontoceti.

Baleen whales are amongst the largest animals in the world. They have arched mouths and baleen plates that hang from their upper jaws like curtains. Plankton and small crustaceans such as krill and copepods are caught on these bristle-fringed plates when the whale forces water out of the sides of its mouth.

Toothed whales are a varied group of cetaceans that includes dolphins, sperm whales and the Killer Whale. They have straight jaws lined with numerous peg-like teeth. The teeth are used to grasp prey such as fish and squid, which are then swallowed whole.

A Lifetime at Sea

Cetaceans are endothermic, air-breathing mammals that spend their whole lives in the water. Their flexible, streamlined bodies are designed for speed swimming and deep diving. Powerful up-and-down strokes of the tail flukes propel the body, while the dorsal fin and side flippers assist with steering and balance. A finely tuned nervous system allows constant adjustment of the body to minimise drag. Several species are known for their spectacular breaches and aerial antics, which are thought to be a form of play, but which also help dislodge skin parasites and may also have a communication role.

Cetaceans take in air through their blowholes, which they seal off when diving. The gullet and windpipe are separate so that they do not drown when they open their mouths underwater to feed. Neither do they drown when they become unconscious: breathing is controlled by the voluntary nervous system. (However, they must be lifted to the surface before their oxygen supply is depleted.) Other aquatic adaptations include layers of insulating blubber, enormous lungs and a tolerance of high carbon dioxide levels. Soft, porous bones and collapsible ribs prevent the ribcage from being crushed by water pressure during deep dives.

FACTS

- Baleen whales have two blowholes; toothed whales have only one.

- A Killer Whale will use its head as a battering ram to break through 1 m thick ice to catch resting seals.

- A Southern Right Whale has around 500 baleen plates, each up to 2.8 metres long.

- A Bottlenose Dolphin has up to 104 teeth.

- A Sperm Whale tooth can be 25 cm long and weigh over 1 kg. Its upper teeth lie below the gum line.

- A Blue Whale can consume up to 8 tonnes of krill per day.

- An individual Southern Right Whale can be identified by the number, size, shape and position of the callosities on its head.

Humpback Whale

Indo-Pacific Bottlenose Dolphin, *Tursiops aduncus*, at Monkey Mia, WA.

Communicating with sound

Cetaceans use a variety of sounds to communicate with each other. Their calls and non-verbal but noisy surface behaviours convey information about an individual's identity, location and intentions, and are also used to indicate distress and warn of danger. High frequency whistles and vocal squeaks of various pitches are commonly used by toothed cetaceans, such as the Bottlenose Dolphin, while the baleen whales have a more extensive vocal repertoire.

The most complex vocalisations of all cetaceans are the haunting songs of migrating male Humpback Whales. From a range of groans, moans, roars, chirps and trills, two to four sounds are selected and are repeated several times to compose a phrase, which is then repeated to form a theme. A song consists of five to seven themes that are sung in a specific order, and can last from 5 to 30 minutes. All the males on a particular migration route sing the same song, even though it may change over time.

Seeing with sound

Toothed whales and dolphins use echolocation to navigate and to find food in deep or murky water. Air drawn through the blowhole is squeezed through a series of valves in the nasal sac to produce clicking sounds. The clicks are then transmitted as high frequency sound waves via fatty tissue in the forehead. The sounds that are bounced back by objects in the wave's path are picked up by the lower jaw, transferred to the middle ear and processed by the brain. This highly advanced sonar system provides three-dimensional information about the size, location and relative distance of objects. With it, a cetacean can not only single out an individual fish in a school, but can assess the school's size and direction of movement.

FACTS

- A spinner dolphin can execute 14 horizontal spins during a single leap.

- The Sperm Whale can dive to depths exceeding 2,000 m and remain submerged for more than 2 hours.

- Southern Right Whales sometimes raise their tails at right angles to the wind and sail through the water.

- In July 2005, the Australian Snubfin Dolphin *Orcaella heinsohni* was recognised as a new species.

- All cetaceans are protected in Australian waters under the Environment Protection and Biodiversity Conservation Act (EPBC Act).

Migration

Most cetaceans clock up thousands of kilometres during their lifelong search for food and mates. Baleen whales' annual migrations can exceed 16,000 km. In the southern hemisphere, Humpback and Southern Right Whales leave their cold water feeding grounds in autumn and head north to breed. After giving birth and mating, they return south and spend the summer filling up on huge quantities of krill and plankton.

From June to October, Southern Right Whales calve and nurse their young in the shallows along Australia's southern coasts, while Humpback Whales use the east and west coasts as highways to and from their tropical breeding grounds. Australia is also a summer feeding ground for Blue Whales. They are regularly seen in the Perth Canyon off the southern WA coast where they feed on krill that are nourished by a cold water upwelling from December to May.

Stranding

Mass stranding remains one of the unsolved mysteries of cetacean behaviour. One theory suggests that whales use the Earth's magnetic field to navigate. Since this field is always changing, they may become temporarily confused and mistakenly swim towards land. Species with strong social bonds, such as pilot whales and dolphins, often strand in groups. Being reluctant to desert one another, pod members may follow a sick, exhausted or disoriented member in to shore.

Solitary strandings usually involve sick or dead cetaceans that have been washed ashore. Presumably when a young animal strands, it has become separated from the herd and lost its way because it lacks navigational experience.

Migrating Humpback Whales en route from the Southern Ocean to the Great Barrier Reef to calf.

Common Bottlenose Dolphins at play.

Social interactions

Whales and dolphins are credited with a high level of intelligence that is often reflected in their sophisticated social interactions. There are several species that display a precocious ability to learn. Young Killer Whales learn from their mothers how to beach themselves and squirm back into the water before accompanying the family on raids to snatch basking seals from the shoreline. At Shark Bay, two generations of mothers in a Bottlenose Dolphin family have imparted to their offspring the protective benefits of wearing a sponge on one's sensitive snout while foraging on an abrasive sea floor.

Cetaceans also have an aptitude for coordinated behaviour that involves vocal communication. Killer Whales use a variety of squeaks and moans when working together to encircle prey or herd them into the shallows. Bottlenose Dolphins and Humpback Whales also signal their mates when corralling prey in bubble nets. One or more individuals will dive under a shoal of krill or fish and swim in a circle blowing bubbles that rise like a cylindrical curtain trapping prey in the middle. They then lunge upwards through the centre of the 'net', taking in as much food as their mouths can hold.

A cooperative approach can also be useful in threatening situations. Southern Right Whales will face into a circle and lash their tails against attacking sharks or Killer Whales. Male Sperm Whales have been known to issue warning calls and draw attention to themselves with conspicuous surface displays so that their pods can slip silently away.

FACTS

- About 70% of Humpback Whales that migrate along Australia's east coast are males.

- A newborn Southern Right Whale weighs about 1 tonne.

- A litre of whale milk contains 200 g of fat and 20 different proteins.

- Female baleen whales give birth every 2 to 3 years.

- A Blue Whale calf gains 90 kg a day while suckling.

- Pygmy Sperm Whales eject a long stream of dark-coloured, liquid faeces when threatened.

- 'Migaloo', an albino Humpback Whale, has been migrating up the east coast of Australia since 1991.

- Cetaceans are born tail first and must be lifted to the surface for their first breath.

Bottlenose
Dolphin

DUNCAN NOAKES/DREAMSTIME

FACTS

- Whaling was Australia's first primary industry.

- The dollar value of a Humpback Whale from whale watching is higher than from whaling.

- Baleen, also known as whalebone, was used in umbrellas, whips and women's corsets.

- A Blue Whale's small intestine is over 150 metres long.

- The first Australian whaling station opened in 1806 on the Derwent River in Tasmania; the last, at Albany, Western Australia, closed in 1978.

- When boiled down, a Blue Whale's body yields 75 barrels of oil.

- Whale oil was used for heating and lighting, and to make soap, lubricants, crayons, margarine and paint.

- A Humpback Whale is estimated to be worth $100,000 to the tourist industry.

Threats and conservation

Many cetaceans are poorly understood so their status may be listed as data deficient. Lack of information is just one of many threats contributing to the worldwide demise of many whale and dolphin species.

Whaling historically resulted in drastic declines of many species with over-exploitation bringing some whales to the very edge of extinction. Slow breeding rates mean that populations take many years to recover. The International Whaling Commission implemented a commercial whaling moratorium in 1986, which is still in place today. Despite this, many cetaceans are still killed by people exploiting loopholes in the moratorium, making hunting both a historic and a current threat.

Whaling in Australia ended in 1978 and today all cetaceans are protected in Australian waters under the EPBC Act. Severe penalties are imposed on anyone found injuring, interfering with or killing a whale or dolphin. Recovery plans are also in place for five whale species.

Other threats include pollution, climate change, entanglement, live capture for aquarium displays and human harvesting of cetacean prey species. In this chapter, pollution refers to both sound pollution and physical or chemical pollution of the water. Entanglement includes bycatch by commercial fisheries as well as accidental entanglement in ghost nets, rubbish, shark nets, etc.

RON & VALERIE TAYLOR

A modern whaler hauls in a recently harpooned whale.

Common Surface Behaviours

Blow: The explosive exhalation followed by inhalation of air; also the cloud of droplets that forms when a whale breathes out.

Breaching: Launching the body head first out of the water and falling back with a splash. All or part of the body may be exposed.

Fluking: Lifting the tail into the air, often before a deep dive. The flukes (fins) may be raised to show the underside or turned down.

Flipper slapping: Slapping the waving flippers against the surface of the water, often making a very loud noise.

Lobtailing: Raising the tail and slapping the flukes against the surface of the water, sometimes repeatedly.

Spyhopping: Coming vertically out of the water, head first, sometimes turning in a small circle before slipping below the surface.

Finding Whales and Dolphins

LOCATION TIPS

▶ Hervey Bay, Qld

▶ North Stradbroke
  Island, Qld

▶ Cape Byron, NSW

▶ Cape Howe, NSW

▶ Storm Bay, Tas.

▶ Freycinet NP, Tas.

▶ Wilsons Promontory,
  Vic.

▶ Warrnambool, Vic.

▶ Portland, SA

▶ Coffin Bay NP, SA

▶ Head of Bight, SA

▶ Cape Leeuwin, WA

▶ Broome, WA

▶ Shark Bay, WA

May through November is when migrating Humpback and Southern Right Whales can be seen in Queensland, New South Wales and South Australia. Whale watching is best in Victoria from November to May and in Western Australia from September to November. Take a boat tour or visit a prominent headland on a calm, clear day. A good pair of binoculars or a telephoto camera lens is useful for close-up views.

Dolphins are common all year round in coastal waters. They can be seen in shallow bays, wide river mouths and off prominent headlands. Look for them body surfing and swimming parallel to the shore just beyond the breakers. They often bow-ride with boats and have been known to swim with divers. Wild dolphins come inshore to be hand fed at Monkey Mia, WA and Moreton Island, Qld. They also feed inshore regularly at Bunbury, WA.

To identify a cetacean look for:

- body colour and relative size
- head shape
- position and shape of dorsal fin, if present
- shape and colour of flippers and tail flukes
- size, shape and frequency of blows
- surface behaviour.

Be aware that live, stranded dolphins and whales may thrash about and inadvertently injure bystanders. If you see a stranded cetacean, please phone the local Parks and Wildlife Service for assistance.

Above: A good vantage point, good weather, binoculars, a telescope or a camera with a telephoto lens are essential for watching and identifying marine mammals.

JULIE GELDARD/IPHOTOGRAPHMAGIC

Top: A majestic Humpback Whale breaching in the waters off Hervey Bay.
Above: The most frequent sightings of the Southern Right Whale are of females and
calves in warm, shallow coastal breeding grounds.

SOUTHERN RIGHT WHALE *Eubalaena australis*

QUICK REFERENCE	
Average lifespan	50 < years
Diet	Omnivore
Reproduction period Number of offspring Offspring maturity	Jul–Aug 1 5–9 years
Length HT	13–18 m
Weight	40–80 t
Status	Endangered

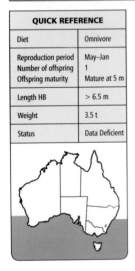

Southern Right Whales come inshore to rest and nurse their calves. Whalers regarded them as the 'right whales' to hunt because they swam slowly, floated when dead and produced large amounts of oil and baleen.

Diet: Krill, plankton. **Surface behaviour:** May breach up to 10 times in a row. Flukes raised when diving. Flipper waving and slapping, head stands, lobtailing. Sails with flukes raised at right angle to wind. Rarely strands. **Blow:** Wide V-shaped blow with 2 columns up to 5 m long. Left column taller than right. **Features:** Black, rotund body with irregular white patches on belly. Large white bumps (callosities) on lower jaw, top of head and above eyes. Distinctly arched mouth. Long, dark grey baleen. Smooth throat. No dorsal fin. Large, broad flippers with prominent ridges. The tail base is narrow and the flukes have smooth, concave edges. **Threats:** Whaling (historic and current), entanglement, pollution, climate change, krill harvesting.

PYGMY RIGHT WHALE *Caperea marginata*

QUICK REFERENCE	
Diet	Omnivore
Reproduction period Number of offspring Offspring maturity	May–Jan 1 Mature at 5 m
Length HB	> 6.5 m
Weight	3.5 t
Status	Data Deficient

This medium-sized whale is the smallest of the baleen whales and one of the least known. There have been less than 20 confirmed sightings of this species at sea including a group of 80 at southwest of Cape Leeuwin (WA). Strandings have been reported on the South and East coasts of Australia.

Diet: Krill, plankton. **Surface behaviour:** Quick, shallow surfacing. Strandings. **Blow:** Small, inconspicuous. **Features:** Dark grey above with dark eyepatch, white below. Sickle-shaped dorsal fin ⅔ way down body. Slender, streamlined shape. Head is less than ¼ of body length. Arched jawline. Small, slender flippers with rounded tips. 2 shallow throat pleats. Yellowish white baleen. **Threats:** May be naturally rare. Possibly entanglement in drift nets. This species has not been hunted.

SPERM WHALE *Physeter macrocephalus*

QUICK REFERENCE	
Average lifespan	60 < years
Diet	Carnivore
Reproduction period Number of offspring Offspring maturity	Feb–Apr 1 7–21 years
Length HT ♂	16–18 m
Length HT ♀	11–13 m
Weight ♂	45–57 t
Weight ♀	15–24 t
Status	Vulnerable

The Sperm Whale is the largest toothed cetacean. It is known for its deep dives that can exceed 2,000 m. Inside the huge head is a system of wax-filled tubes called spermaceti; this system controls buoyancy. It is the most frequent species in Tasmanian whale strandings.

Diet: Cephalopods, fish. **Surface behaviour:** Breaches often, sometimes clearing the water. Spends 5–60 minutes on surface between dives. Breathes at 12–20 second intervals. Flukes and last third of body are exposed when diving. Lobtails. Occasional mass strandings. **Blow:** Low, 2 m bushy blow angles to left. **Features:** Dark grey-brown back with 'knuckles' or ridges. May have white belly patches. Large, squarish head ⅓ of total length. Narrow, underslung lower jaw. Single blowhole on left side of head near tip. Small, paddle-shaped flippers. Triangular hump in place of dorsal fin. **Threats:** Whaling (historic), entanglement, slow breeding rate, pollution, boat strike.

DWARF MINKE WHALE *Balaenoptera acutorostrata*

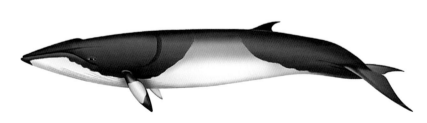

QUICK REFERENCE	
Average lifespan	60 years
Diet	Omnivore
Reproduction period Number of offspring Offspring maturity	Dec–Jun 1 Mature at 6–7 metres
Length HT	7–8 m
Weight	6 t
Status	Least Concern

Seen in Australia from March to October, the Dwarf Minke Whale is still hunted commercially. It feeds in coastal waters and sometimes enters rivers. The colouration on this species is the most complex of any baleen whale.

Diet: Krill, plankton, schooling fish. **Surface behaviour:** 45° breach with dorsal fin visible, 5–8 quick blows before diving. Flukes do not show when diving. Spyhops. May investigate boats. Strands occasionally. **Blow:** Low, vertical, diffuse cloud. Up to 2 m high. **Features:** Small, sleek, elongated body. Dark bluish grey above and white below. Sometimes has wavy line on side. Narrow triangular head with prominent central ridge. Short, yellow-grey baleen, 50–70 throat pleats. Relatively tall, curved dorsal fin beyond middle of back. Slender, pointed flippers can have white band. Tail flukes dark bluish-grey above with pale underside. **Threats:** Intensive whaling (historic and current), entanglement, pollution, climate change.

ANTARCTIC MINKE WHALE *Balaenoptera bonaerensis*

QUICK REFERENCE	
Average lifespan	May exceed 50 years
Diet	Carnivore
Reproduction period	May–June
Number of offspring	1
Offspring maturity ♂	8 years
Offspring maturity ♀	7–8 years
Length HT ♂	9.2 m
Length HT ♀	9.8 m
Weight	13 t
Status	Data Deficient

Only one species of Minke Whale was recognised until the 1990s. The southern Minkes are now recognised as a separate species from the northern ones.

Diet: Primarily krill. **Surface behaviour:** May arch tail before a long dive, but do not raise their flukes above water. Tails leave a 'rooster-tail' of spray when they break the surface. Known to be curious about vessels and will approach. Blows are low and inconspicuous. **Blow:** Hard to detect. May occur as a sequence of up to eight breaths in under a minute. **Features:** Blueish-grey back with light grey to white flanks and belly. Underside of fluke and flippers are white. Slim pointed flippers. Baleen is two-toned with dark bank delineating outer plate margin. Sharp snout. **Threats:** Reduction in sea ice due to global warming; 'scientific' pelagic whaling expeditions.

SEI WHALE *Balaenoptera borealis*

QUICK REFERENCE	
Average lifespan	65 years
Diet	Omnivore
Reproduction period	Apr–Aug
Number of offspring	1
Offspring maturity	6–8 years
Length HT ♂	12–18 m
Length HT ♀	12–21 m
Weight ♂	> 25 t
Weight ♀	> 30 t
Status	Vulnerable

The Sei Whale is the third longest of all whales and is not often seen in Australia. Too fast to be caught by early whalers, it is estimated that 24,000 Sei Whales were taken between 1960 and 1980 when Blue and Fin whale stocks were exhausted.

Diet: Krill, plankton, squid, schooling fish. **Surface behaviour:** Skim feeding occurs near surface. Sink rather than dive with no arching of back. Head rarely emerges. **Blow:** Diffuse cloud. Up to 3 m high. **Features:** Slim, elongated body. Dark grey or blue-grey back and sides. Almost white underneath. May be mottled with scars. Dorsal fin is tall, 45° and sickle-shaped. Short, narrow flippers. V-shaped head with single ridge from blowhole to tip of rostrum. Fine, dark grey baleen. **Threats:** Whaling (historic and current), pollution, entanglement, climate change, overharvesting of prey. Predation by Killer Whales.

BRYDE'S WHALE *Balaenoptera edeni*

QUICK REFERENCE	
Average lifespan	50 < years
Diet	Omnivore
Reproduction period	All year
Number of offspring	1
Offspring maturity	7–9 years
Length HT ♂	> 14.6 m
Length HT ♀	> 15.5 m
Weight	11–24 t
Status	Data Deficient

This baleen whale feeds all year round in tropical and subtropical waters. It is a high-speed, erratic swimmer that makes short dives lasting up to nine minutes. Groups of Bryde's Whales are sometimes seen lunging at schools of fish with wide open mouths, making for a spectacular show.

Diet: Small schooling fish, krill, plankton. **Surface behaviour:** Almost vertical breach with three-quarters of body visible, 4–7 blows before deep dive. Flukes rarely show when diving. May investigate boats. Strands occasionally. **Blow:** Single column 3–4 m. **Features:** Dark smoky grey back. Underside is purplish to creamy grey and may be mottled. V-shaped rostrum with three longitudinal ridges. Baleen is dark slate-grey with light grey bristles. Curved dorsal fin beyond middle of back. Short, slender flippers, 40–70 white to yellowish throat pleats. **Threats:** Whaling (historic and current), pollution, entanglement, overfishing of prey. Ingestion of rubbish due to feeding behaviour.

BLUE WHALE *Balaenoptera musculus*

QUICK REFERENCE	
Average lifespan	90 < years
Diet	Omnivore
Reproduction period	Jun–Aug
Number of offspring	1
Offspring maturity	7–10 years
Length HT	24–33 m
Weight	180 < t
Status	Endangered

The Blue Whale is the largest of all animals ever to live on this earth. It also produces the most powerful and lowest frequency calls of any animal. It was hunted to near extinction with 360 individuals remaining in the 1970s, and less than 1% of the original population existing today.

Diet: Krill, plankton. **Surface behaviour:** Adults seldom breach. Blows every 10–20 seconds for about 5 minutes before diving; flukes are exposed briefly at a low angle when diving. Strands occasionally. **Blow:** Slender, straight column up to 12 m. **Features:** Varies from light blue with white mottling to uniform slate grey. Yellowish belly colour is caused by microscopic algae. Small, stubby dorsal fin three-quarters of the way down the back. Broad, flat head with central ridge and 2 blowholes, 55–90 throat grooves. Black baleen. **Threats:** Historic whaling, slow breeding rate, climate change, entanglement, overfishing of prey and boat strike.

FIN WHALE *Balaenoptera physalus*

QUICK REFERENCE	
Average lifespan	90–100 years
Diet	Omnivore
Reproduction period Number of offspring Offspring maturity	Jun–Aug 1 6–10 years
Length	20–27 m
Weight	70–90 t
Status	Vulnerable

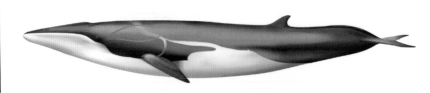

The second largest whale species. Often seen in groups of six to 10 individuals. Feeding groups can number over 100 individuals. Fin Whales are killed by boat strike more often than any other whale species.

Diet: Fish, krill, other crustaceans. **Surface behaviour:** Occasional breaching (can clear the water). Rarely shows tail flukes when diving. Strands occasionally. **Blow:** Slim, cone-shaped, up to 6 m. **Features:** Large, streamlined body. Dark grey to brownish black on back, white underneath. Broad, flat rostrum with pointed snout and two blowholes. Patterns on the jaw are white on the right side and dark on the left. Ridge along back behind dorsal fin. Dorsal fin is curved, up to 60 cm tall and ⅔ of the way along back. Throat grooves to navel. Baleen is bluish-grey with white fringes. **Threats:** Whaling (historic and current), boat strike, entanglement, overfishing of prey, climate change, pollution.

HUMPBACK WHALE *Megaptera novaeangliae*

QUICK REFERENCE	
Average lifespan	48 < years
Diet	Omnivore
Reproduction period Number of offspring Offspring maturity	Jun–Aug 1 4–8 years
Length HT	> 18 m
Weight	45 t
Status	Vulnerable

The Humpback is one of the most commonly seen whales in coastal waters from June to October. It is best known for its spectacular surface displays. The Humpback is a slow swimmer and can remain submerged for up to 45 minutes.

Diet: Krill, plankton. **Surface behaviour:** Breaching, lobtailing, flipper slapping, flipper waving, spyhopping. Flukes exposed at upright angle. Strandings. **Blow:** Wide bushy blow up to 5 m high. **Features:** Stout body is bluish grey to black above and white below. Flat head and small dorsal fin ⅔ of the way along back. Knobby protuberances on head, lower jaw and flippers. Flippers are one-third of body length. Flippers and tail flukes have scalloped edges and undersides have unique black and white patterns. 14–35 throat pleats. Black baleen. **Threats:** Whaling (historic), entanglement, pollution, climate change, krill harvesting, offshore gas/oil mining.

PYGMY SPERM WHALE *Kogia breviceps*

QUICK REFERENCE	
Average lifespan	16–23 years
Diet	Carnivore
Reproduction period Number of offspring Offspring maturity	Apr–Sept 1 5 years
Length	> 3.3 m
Weight ♂	> 374 kg
Weight ♀	> 480 kg
Status	Data Deficient

This relatively uncommon whale species is known to inhabit deep water in tropical and warm temperate oceans. Though rarely sighted in Australian waters, more than 80 Pygmy Sperm Whale strandings have occurred across all states of Australia.

Diet: Squid, octopus, fish, shrimp. **Surface behaviour:** Dives for long periods; inactive and inconspicuous when surfacing. Occasional strandings. **Blow:** Low, inconspicuous blow. **Features:** Small size; robust build. Dark blue-grey or steel grey on back, paler below. Short rostrum with distinctive underslung jaw. Light, crescent-shaped marking behind eye referred to as a 'false gill'. Flippers high on sides near head. Small, sickle-shaped dorsal fin more than halfway down body and less than 5% of body length. **Threats:** Entanglement (particularly in gillnets), ingestion of rubbish, pollution, boat strike, climate change. Not commercially hunted.

DWARF SPERM WHALE *Kogia sima*

QUICK REFERENCE	
Average lifespan	17–21.5 years
Diet	Carnivore
Reproduction period Number of offspring Offspring maturity	Dec–Mar 1 3–4.5 years
Length ♂	2.62 m
Length ♀	2.86 m
Weight ♂	272–303 kg
Weight ♀	209–264 kg
Status	Data Deficient

Only recognised as a separate species from the Pygmy Sperm Whale in the 1960s, the Dwarf Sperm Whale prefers warmer waters. It is the smallest whale species, even smaller than certain Dolphins. Dwarf Sperm Whales are gregarious, gathering in groups of up to 10 individuals.

Diet: Deep water cephalopods, fish and crustaceans. **Surface behaviour:** Inconspicuous, stays submerged for long periods. Surfaces slowly, breathes with no blow and drops back out of sight. Rare strandings. **Blow:** No visible blow. **Features:** Small size; robust build. Short rostrum, slightly more pointed than in *K. breviceps*. Distinctive underslung jaw. Dark grey on back, lighter at sides and white underneath. False gill marking behind eye. Flippers high on sides near head. Small, sickle shaped dorsal fin more than 5% of body length and near centre of back. **Threats:** Entanglement, ingestion of rubbish, pollution, climate change. Not commercially hunted.

CUVIER'S BEAKED WHALE *Ziphius cavirostris*

QUICK REFERENCE	
Average lifespan ♂	47 years
Average lifespan ♀	28 years
Diet	Carnivore
Reproduction period	All year
Number of offspring	1
Offspring maturity	11 years
Length HT	5–7 m
Weight	2,500 kg
Status	Least Concern

The most common and abundant of all beaked whales, Cuvier's is believed to be the deepest and longest mammal diver in the world. In 2014 scientists reported one diving to a depth of 2,992 m and spending 2 hrs and 17 min under water before resurfacing.

Diet: Squid, shrimp, deep-sea fish. **Surface behaviour:** Avoids vessels. May project head above surface when swimming. Arches back and lifts tail flukes when diving. **Blow:** Rarely visible. Between 10 and 30 breaths per surfacing event. **Features:** Robust cigar-shape body. Males are grey to purplish black on back and sides with white head, beak and throat. Females are brown to tan with a lighter head. Small curved dorsal fin set ⅔ of the way down the body; small narrow flippers; large flukes without usual medial notch of other cetaceans. Short beaked with slightly bulbous melon. Only males have functional teeth. **Threats:** Plastic bags, entanglement in discarded drift nets, noise pollution causing strandings.

ARNOUX'S BEAKED WHALE *Berardius arnuxii*

QUICK REFERENCE	
Average lifespan	50 years
Diet	Carnivore
Reproduction period	Unknown
Number of offspring	1
Offspring maturity	8–10 years
Length HT	9.75 m
Weight	6.4 t
Status	Data Deficient

This beaked whale is renowned for diving to depths of at least 1000 m and staying submerged for up to one hour in freezing cold waters. It is the largest beaked whale in the southern hemisphere.

Diet: Squid and fish. **Surface behaviour:** Mostly seen in groups of 6–10 that move slowly and discreetly, spending little time on the surface. **Blow:** Low bushy and abundant (unlike most beaked whales). **Features:** Slender spindle-shaped blue-black body with patches of pale grey or white underneath, often covered in scars, many from Cookie Cutter Sharks. Crescent-shaped blowhole faces forward behind bulbous melon that swoops down to a long beak. Jaw contains four teeth, two triangular shaped ones visible when mouth is closed. Short wide flippers, small round-tipped dorsal fin. **Threats:** Likely to be vulnerable to loud sounds from navy sonar and seismic exploration. Pelagic fishnets. Possibly climate change.

SHEPHERD'S BEAKED WHALE *Tasmacetus shepherdi*

QUICK REFERENCE	
Average lifespan	Unknown
Diet	Mostly fish
Reproduction period Number of offspring Offspring maturity	Unknown 1 Unknown
Length HT ♂	7.1 m
Length HT ♀	6.6 m
Weight	2–3 t
Status	Data Deficient

What little is known about this extremely rare solid bodied whale comes from a few strandings and possibly a few sightings. This is the only beaked whale to have complete rows of functional teeth.

Diet: Mostly squid, some fish and crustaceans. **Surface behaviour:** Move slowly and unobtrusively and do not often blow. **Blow:** Beak is visible when breathing but blow is inconspicuous. **Features:** Dark brown to black on top and white underneath with two light coloured diagonal stripes on the sides. Steep rounded forehead, long pointy-tipped narrow beak. Males have two long teeth erupting at the tip of the lower jaw. Dorsal fin is small and slightly hooked. Fluke is dark on both sides. **Threats:** Likely to be vulnerable to loud sounds from navy sonar and seismic exploration. Plastic debris. Possibly climate change.

LONGMAN'S BEAKED WHALE *Indopacetus pacificus*

QUICK REFERENCE	
Average lifespan	Unknown
Diet	Carnivore
Reproduction period Number of offspring Offspring maturity	Unknown 1 Unknown
Length HT	6.5–7 m
Weight	Unknown
Status	Data Deficient

Knowledge of this very rare whale has been obtained from two skulls and five specimens of stranded animals. The information below is based on supposition.

Diet: Squid. **Surface behaviour:** Difficult to identify at sea. Groups of 5–20 and up to 100. **Blow:** Visible. **Features:** Spindle-shaped body. Distinct long beak and bulbous melon. Two teeth in lower jaw. Male has two cone-shaped teeth at the tip of his jaw. Two V-shaped throat grooves. Small flippers and dorsal fin. **Threats:** Likely to be vulnerable to loud sounds from navy sonar and seismic exploration. Plastic debris. Possibly climate change.

SOUTHERN BOTTLENOSE WHALE *Hyperoodon planifrons*

QUICK REFERENCE	
Average lifespan	50+ years
Diet	Carnivore
Reproduction period	Sept–Dec
Number of offspring	1
Offspring maturity	9–11 years
Length HT	6–8 m
Weight	3.5–4 t
Status	Least Concern

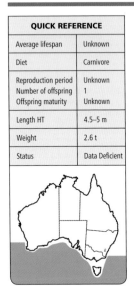

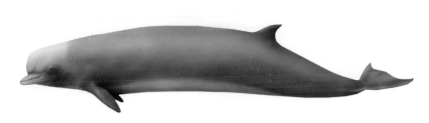

This elusive whale is easily recognised by its very bulbous forehead, especially in males.

Diet: Squid. **Surface behaviour:** Sighted alone, in pairs and in groups of up to 10 or more. Known to breach and able to stay under water for up to an hour but average time is shorter. **Blow:** Slightly forward projecting, bushy blow reaching 1–2 m in height. **Features:** Solid barrel-shaped body varies from bluish-black to bluish grey and light brown on top to tannish or dull yellowish creamy white underneath. Forehead and beak can be light coloured, toothpick-like teeth, distinct indent above the upper jaw. Small flippers taper at the end, dorsal fin is small with slightly curved tip. **Threats:** Likely to be vulnerable to loud sounds from navy sonar and seismic exploration. Possibly climate change.

ANDREW'S BEAKED WHALE *Mesoplodon bowdoini*

QUICK REFERENCE	
Average lifespan	Unknown
Diet	Carnivore
Reproduction period	Unknown
Number of offspring	1
Offspring maturity	Unknown
Length HT	4.5–5 m
Weight	2.6 t
Status	Data Deficient

Very little is known about this elusive species.

Diet: Perhaps mid- and deep-water squid and fish. **Surface behaviour:** Spends little time on the surface, preferring to swim at depth. **Blow:** No visible blow or splash when surfacing. **Features:** Blue-black. Small head with short thick dolphin-like beak is white above and below in males and white only below in females. Jaw is elevated towards the back. Small, blunt, triangular dorsal fin and rounded flippers. Females have no teeth. Males have two large teeth protruding from each side of lower jaw. **Threats:** Entanglement in discarded drift nets.

BLAINVILLE'S BEAKED WHALE *Mesoplodon densirostris*

QUICK REFERENCE	
Average lifespan	Unknown
Diet	Carnivore
Reproduction period	Unknown
Number of offspring	1
Offspring maturity	9 years
Length HT	4.7 m
Weight	1.5 t
Status	Data Deficient

The male of this small strange-looking stocky whale has two big horn-like barnacle covered teeth that grow upwards from its lower jaw. It is believed to have the densest bones in the animal kingdom.

Diet: Squid, fish and lantern fish. **Surface behaviour:** Groups of 1–6 perform several shallow dives, surfacing beaks first, then dive deep for up to 45 minutes. **Blow:** Small, indistinct, forward projecting, mostly seen on calm days. **Features:** Stocky body, dark blue-grey on top with a light patch underneath and tan and white splotches all over. Flat forehead and arched lower jaw which can be light coloured in females. Extensive scars, many of which are probably made by Cookie Cutter Sharks, are common. Small flippers and prominent curved dorsal fin. **Threats:** Hunting. Plastic debris. Likely to be vulnerable to loud sounds from navy sonar and seismic exploration. Possibly climate change.

GINKGO-TOOTHED BEAKED WHALE *Mesoplodon ginkgodens*

QUICK REFERENCE	
Average lifespan	Unknown
Diet	Carnivore
Reproduction period	Unknown
Number of offspring	1
Offspring maturity	Unknown
Length HT ♂	4.8 m
Length HT ♀	4.9 m
Weight	1.5 t
Status	Unknown

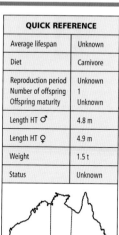

This whale is named for the wide ginkgo-tree leaf-shaped teeth — shallow flattened tusks — that erupt in adult males. The only information available about this whale is from strandings.

Diet: Squid and fish. **Surface behaviour:** Unknown but believed to travel in small groups and be unobtrusive. **Blow:** Unknown. **Features:** Experts believe that the colour of live male specimens could be marine blue and females medium grey. Strong body features fewer scars than on other beaked whales possibly suggesting minimal aggression between males. Prominent pale grey beak with narrow sharply pointed upper jaw. Smoothly sloping forehead. Arched lower jaw. Small narrow flippers. Small hook-tipped dorsal fin located ²⁄₃ of the way down the back. Broad triangular-shaped flukes. **Threats:** Plastic debris, climate change.

GRAY'S BEAKED WHALE *Mesoplodon grayi*

QUICK REFERENCE	
Average lifespan	> 40 years
Diet	Carnivore
Number of offspring	1
Offspring maturity	Mature at 4.5 m
Length HT	4.7–5.6 m
Weight	1.5 t
Status	Data Deficient

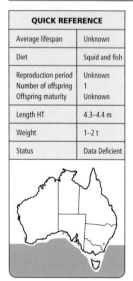

Gray's Beaked Whale is usually found in deep waters far from shore and is known in southern Australia from almost 50 strandings. It only has two functional teeth, which are not used for feeding but as weapons for fighting males. Prey is probably caught by suction.

Diet: Cephalopods, fish. **Surface behaviour:** Breaching and porpoising. Usually move slowly with little splash at surface. Breathe 3 to 5 times before diving. Strandings (most common beaked whale in strandings). **Blow:** No visible blow. **Features:** Spindle-shaped body with small head. Dark blue-grey to black above, paler underneath. White genital patches. Long, slender beak is white in adults with straight mouthline. Small, pointed dorsal fin is set far back on body. Short, broad flippers. Males are frequently scarred with long tooth-rakes from fighting. Both sexes may have circular Cookie-cutter Shark scars. **Threats:** Slow breeding rate, entanglement, pollution, boat strike, climate change. Not commercially hunted.

HECTOR'S BEAKED WHALE *Mesoplodon hectori*

QUICK REFERENCE	
Average lifespan	Unknown
Diet	Squid and fish
Reproduction period	Unknown
Number of offspring	1
Offspring maturity	Unknown
Length HT	4.3–4.4 m
Weight	1–2 t
Status	Data Deficient

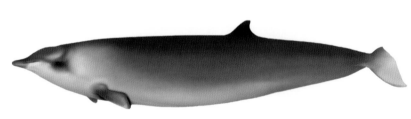

Only a few of these rare small beaked whales have been recorded in Australia.

Diet: Squid and fish. **Surface behaviour:** Possibly move in pairs. **Blow:** Inconspicuous. **Features:** Dark grey-brown on top and light grey underneath. Slight melon on small head, short pale-grey to white beak, crescent-shaped blowhole. Dorsal fin is small, triangular and rounded. Fluke is grey on top and white underneath. Males have triangular teeth at the tip of the lower jaw. **Threats:** Likely to be vulnerable to loud sounds from navy sonar and seismic exploration. Plastic debris. Possibly climate change.

STRAP-TOOTHED BEAKED WHALE *Mesoplodon layardii*

QUICK REFERENCE	
Average lifespan	Unknown
Diet	Carnivore
Reproduction period	Dec–May
Number of offspring	1
Offspring maturity	Unknown
Length HT ♂	6.1 m
Length HT ♀	6.2 m
Weight	1.5 t
Status	Data Deficient

This is one of the largest beaked-whales and one of the few easily identified at sea. Named for the two strap-like, back-facing curved tusks (up to 30 cm long) that protrude from the lower jaw in males and curl up over the jaw so mouth can't open far.

Diet: Fish, deep water squid, crustaceans. **Surface behaviour:** Groups of 1–3 sink slowly below the surface. Flukes don't show above the surface when diving. Dives last 10–15 minutes. **Blow:** Indistinct. **Features:** Black face mask, front part of upper body is white, rear is blue-black as is underside except for a white/grey oval patch ⅔ down. Sloping forehead with a slightly bulging melon, small narrow black flippers, small low, cycle-shaped dorsal fin, triangular pointy-tipped flukes. **Threats:** Likely to be vulnerable to loud sounds from navy sonar and seismic exploration. Possibly climate change. Plastic debris.

TRUE'S BEAKED WHALE *Mesoplodon mirus*

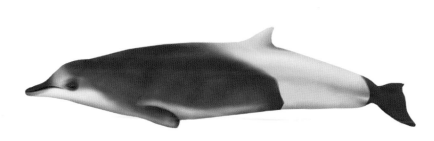

QUICK REFERENCE	
Average lifespan	Unknown
Diet	Squid and small fish
Reproduction period	Unknown
Number of offspring	1
Offspring maturity	Unknown
Length HT	4.8–5.4 m
Weight	1–1.4 t
Status	Data Deficient

The True's Beaked Whale is believed to be a deep water open sea mammal. The southern hemisphere population could be a distinct species or subspecies.

Diet: Squid and small fish. **Surface behaviour:** Its low profile on the surface, and its weak blow, make it difficult to observe. Usually solitary or in small groups of 2–6. **Blow:** Inconspicuous and cloud-shaped roughly as high as its head is long. Blow and roll sequence lasts 10–20 seconds. **Features:** Grey to brown on top and lighter underneath. Medium-sized body, moderately short narrow beak with a straight or slightly curved mouthline, well rounded sloping melon, sickle-shaped dorsal fin located ⅔ down the back. Small narrow grey flippers located low on the body tuck into an indentation on the underside. Adult males have a pair of visible teeth on the tip of their lower jaw. **Threats:** Likely to be vulnerable to loud sounds from navy sonar and seismic exploration. Climate change. Plastic debris. Gill nets.

MELON-HEADED WHALE *Peponocephala electra*

QUICK REFERENCE	
Average lifespan	22–30 years
Diet	Carnivore
Reproduction period	Jul–Dec
Number of offspring	1
Offspring maturity	11.5–16.5 years
Length HT ♂	2.75 m
Length HT ♀	2.6 m
Weight	206–228 kg
Status	Least Concern

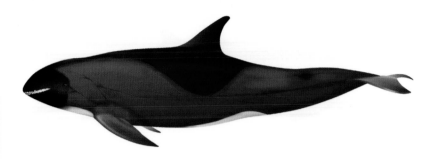

Melon-headed Whales inhabit deep, warm waters (above 25 °C) near the equator. They are vocal when travelling and have been known to attack other dolphin species. Mass strandings of up to 250 animals have occurred in Australia. There have also been single-animal strandings in WA, NT, Qld and NSW.

Diet: Squid, shrimp, small fish. **Surface behaviour:** Fast swimmers; generate spray when travelling. Surface at shallow angle. Spyhops. Low jumps clear out of water. Single and mass strandings. **Features:** Small; slender build. Conical shaped head. Dark grey with slightly darker grey cape and paler belly. Light band from blowhole to top of melon. Characteristic dark eye patch and light lips and/or throat. Large, pointed dorsal fin curves backwards. Distinctive pointed flippers more than 50 cm long. **Threats:** Pollution, hunting, entanglement, overfishing of prey, possibly climate change. Not commercially hunted.

PYGMY KILLER WHALE *Feresa attenuata*

QUICK REFERENCE	
Average lifespan	> 14 years
Diet	Carnivore
Reproduction period	Unknown
Number of offspring	1
Offspring maturity	Mature at 2.2 m
Length HT	2.1–2.6 m
Weight	130–225 kg
Status	Data Deficient

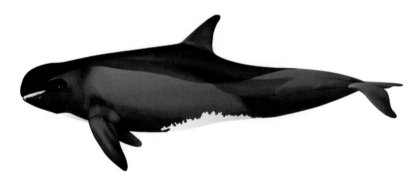

This mainly tropical species prefers deep, warm water above 18 °C and does not usually come near the shore. Despite its name, the Pygmy Killer Whale is actually a member of the dolphin family. It is believed to be naturally uncommon and little is known about its biology. When threatened, it can emit a growling noise through its blowhole.

Diet: Squid, fish, sometimes other cetaceans. **Surface behaviour:** Fast swimmers. Playful, sometimes ride bow waves and leap clear out of the water. Spyhopping. Tail slapping. May be seen with dolphins. Occasional strandings. **Features:** Slender body, thins towards rear. Grey to black above with dark cape. Pale flanks, white patches underneath. Round, blunt head with no beak. Mouth slopes upwards. White edges to lips and snout. Long flippers with rounded tips, gently curved backwards. **Threats:** Small population size, entanglement, pollution, ingestion of rubbish, climate change. Not commercially hunted.

FALSE KILLER WHALE *Pseudorca crassidens*

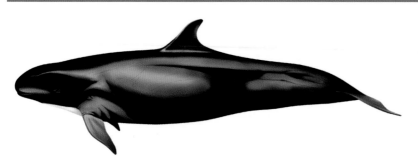

QUICK REFERENCE	
Average lifespan	Probably 60 years
Diet	Carnivore
Reproduction period	All year
Number of offspring	1
Offspring maturity	8–14 years
Length ♂	2–6 m
Length ♀	2–5 m
Weight ♂	1.5 t
Weight ♀	1 t
Status	Data Deficient

Genetically more similar to dolphins than Killer Whales, the False Killer Whale is a gregarious species usually seen in groups of 20 to 50 individuals. Groups of up to 800 have been observed in areas where prey is plentiful. Strandings have occurred in all Australian states and mass strandings with 20 to 250 whales are common.

Diet: Squid, fish, small cetaceans. **Surface behaviour:** Active swimmer. Breaching, porpoising, bow riding. Prone mass stranding, sometimes with other species. **Blow:** Small, bushy, conspicuous. **Features:** Medium-sized; long, slender body. Dark grey to black with lighter grey blaze under throat and belly. Rounded, overhanging forehead. No beak. Underslung mouth curves upwards. Slender, sickle-shaped dorsal fin with rounded tip. Elbow-shaped flippers with characteristic hump on leading edge. **Threats:** Persecution for threatening fisheries, entanglement, pollution, ingestion of rubbish, climate change. Occasionally hunted for food.

KILLER WHALE *Orcinus orca*

QUICK REFERENCE	
Average lifespan	40 years
Diet	Carnivore
Reproduction period	All year
Number of offspring	1
Offspring maturity	10–16 years
Length HT ♂	9.8 m
Length HT ♀	8.5 m
Weight ♂	4–10 t
Weight ♀	3.1–7.5 t
Status	Data Deficient

These fast, efficient predators live in tight-knit family groups (pods), each with its own dialect. They are the most widespread of all cetacean species and possibly the world's second-most widely-ranging mammal (after humans). Killer whales migrate over large distances and sometimes enter estuaries.

Diet: Fish, squid, seabirds, seals, turtles, other marine mammals. **Surface behaviour:** Breaches often, clears surface. Spyhops, lobtails, slaps flippers and dorsal fin. Coordinated pod movement and logging. Occasional strandings. **Blow:** Low, bushy. **Features:** Compact, muscular build. Jet black with a grey saddle patch behind dorsal fin. White patches behind eyes and on sides. Chin, belly and underside of tail flukes are white. Rounded head with no distinct beak. Rounded paddle-shaped flippers. Male has a tall, almost straight dorsal fin up to 1.8 m long. Female dorsal fin is shorter and curved. **Threats:** Whaling (historic and current), persecution for threatening fisheries, live capture for aquariums, pollution.

SHORT-FINNED PILOT WHALE *Globicephala macrorhynchus*

QUICK REFERENCE	
Average lifespan	46–63 years
Diet	Carnivore
Reproduction period	All year
Number of offspring	1
Offspring maturity	9–15 years
Length HT ♂	5.9 m
Length HT ♀	4.8 m
Weight ♂	2 t
Weight ♀	1.5 t
Status	Data Deficient

Pilot whales are social mammals commonly forming pods of 10 to 30 individuals sometimes with dolphins. Matrilineal associations determine pod membership. The Short-finned Pilot Whale is found in deep, offshore areas of warm, tropical seas. It looks similar to its Long-finned relative but has a wider skull.

Diet: Cephalopods, fish. **Surface behaviour:** Seldom breaches. Takes several quick breaths before diving. Flukes may be exposed when diving. Logging, spyhopping, lobtailing, may bow-ride. Mass strandings. **Blow:** Squat, bushy. **Features:** Robust build. Thick tail. Black or dark grey above. Greyish white patches on throat and belly. Grey saddle patch on back behind dorsal fin. Beakless, bulbous head. Long, slender, sickle-shaped flippers. Curved dorsal fin with broad base $1/3$ of way down back; shape varies with age and sex. **Threats:** Whaling (historic and current), entanglement, slow breeding rate, pollution, climate change.

LONG-FINNED PILOT WHALE *Globicephala melas*

QUICK REFERENCE	
Average lifespan	46–63 years
Diet	Carnivore
Reproduction period	All year
Number of offspring	1
Offspring maturity	15–17 years
Length HT ♂	7.2 m
Length HT ♀	6 m
Weight ♂	3 t
Weight ♀	1.8 t
Status	Data Deficient

The Long-finned Pilot Whale frequents temperate and sub-polar waters from 0 °C to 25 °C. Groups are known to draw together when travelling and disperse when feeding. It is difficult to distinguish from its Short-finned counterpart, but has a narrower skull.

Diet: Mainly squid, also fish. **Surface behaviour:** Seldom breaches. Takes several quick breaths before diving. Flukes may be exposed when diving. Logging, spyhopping, lobtailing, may bow-ride. Mass strandings. **Blow:** Squat, bushy. **Features:** Robust build with thick tail. Black or dark grey back. Pale eye blaze in some adults. Grey underbelly markings like anchor on chest with central line to wider patch near genitals. Faint grey saddle patch behind dorsal fin. Beakless, bulbous head. Long, slender, sickle-shaped flippers. Curved dorsal fin with broad base forward of centre of back; shape varies with age and sex. **Threats:** Entanglement, overfishing of prey, slow breeding rate, pollution, disease, climate change.

INDO-PACIFIC HUMPBACK DOLPHIN *Sousa chinensis*

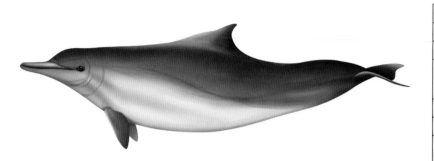

QUICK REFERENCE	
Average lifespan	40 years
Diet	Carnivore
Reproduction period	All year
Number of offspring	1
Offspring maturity	10–13 years
Length HT	2.3–2.6 m
Weight	150–200 kg
Status	Near Threatened

This shy, slow-swimming dolphin is often found close inshore and prefers shallow, coastal areas. It sometimes enters rivers and has also been known to feed behind trawlers. Though more common in tropical waters, this species ventures as far south as central NSW.

Diet: Mostly fish, particularly schooling fish; sometime cephalopods and crustaceans.
Surface behaviour: Characteristically surfaces beak first. Back arches before diving. Breaches, lobtails, spyhops, flipper waves, back somersaults. Strands occasionally.
Features: Medium-sized; robust build. Pale to brownish grey or pinkish white above, grading to lighter underside. Long, slender beak and slightly rounded forehead. Low, triangular, slightly recurved dorsal fin with base up to one-third of body length. Broad, round-tipped flippers. **Threats:** Entanglement, pollution, boat strike, overfishing of prey, live capture for aquariums.

INDO-PACIFIC BOTTLENOSE DOLPHIN *Tursiops aduncus*

QUICK REFERENCE	
Average lifespan ♂	35–40 years
Average lifespan ♀	Up to 50 years
Diet	Carnivore
Reproduction period	Sept–Jan
Number of offspring	1
Offspring maturity ♂	11–15 years
Offspring maturity ♀	9–11 years
Length HT	240 cm
Weight	180–220 kg
Status	Data Deficient

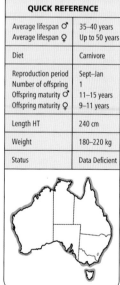

This dolphin is one of the most studied cetaceans in the world. Studies show that the social organisation is more complex than that of primates. They are the only cetacean known to use tools.

Diet: Schooling fish and cephalopods. **Surface behaviour:** Similar to that of the Common Bottlenose Dolphin. Inquisitive and playful. Leaps, bow-rides. Plays with fish, seaweed or marine debris. **Features:** Robust body with short to medium length beak. Dark grey dorsal cape with lighter grey overlay and flanks. Spotting on sexually mature animals.
Threats: Overfishing, getting trapped in nets, habitat destruction/degradation.

COMMON BOTTLENOSE DOLPHIN *Tursiops truncatus*

QUICK REFERENCE	
Average lifespan	40–50 years
Diet	Carnivore
Reproduction period	All year
Number of offspring	1
Offspring maturity	5–13 years
Length HT	2–3.8 m
Weight	200–250 kg
Status	Least Concern

Bottlenose Dolphins usually live in small groups and there are complex social interactions within and amongst pods. They sometimes associate with other cetaceans and actively seek out boats and swimmers. They can be seen in coastal and offshore waters all year round and are the species most commonly held by aquariums.

Diet: Fish, cephalopods and other marine invertebrates. **Surface behaviour:** Breaches and can clear water by several metres. Lobtails, bow-rides, body surfs. Will feed behind trawlers. May temporarily beach itself when chasing fish. Strands singly or in small groups. **Features:** Medium-sized, robust build. Blue-grey above grading to paler sides and off-white belly. Short beak, pronounced melon. Dark, slender, pointed flippers. Prominent curved dorsal fin in middle of back. **Threats:** Hunting, entanglement, persecution for threatening fisheries, overfishing of prey, live capture for aquariums, pollution.

SPINNER DOLPHIN *Stenella longirostris*

QUICK REFERENCE	
Average lifespan	22 years
Diet	Carnivore
Number of offspring	1
Offspring maturity	4–6 years
Length HT ♂	1.36–2.35 m
Length HT ♀	1.3–2 m
Weight	23–78 kg
Status	Data Deficient

This oceanic dolphin congregates in large schools and sometimes associates with other dolphin species, tuna and seabirds. It feeds mainly at night and is well known for its aerial displays. There are four subspecies of Spinner Dolphin; only one S. longirostris has been recorded in Australia.

Diet: Fish, squid, shrimp. **Surface behaviour:** Acrobatic and playful. Clears surface by up to 3 m when breaching. Vertical twists and horizontal spins when leaping. Bow-rides. **Features:** Slender build. Dark grey above with pale grey sides and white belly. Dark stripe from eye to base of flipper. Top jaw is dark and bottom jaw is white with dark tip. Long slender flippers are dark. Long slim beak. Tall triangular or slightly curved dorsal fin. **Threats:** Hunting, entanglement, predation by sharks and whales, pollution.

SHORT-BEAKED COMMON DOLPHIN *Delphinus delphis*

QUICK REFERENCE	
Average lifespan	22 years
Diet	Carnivore
Reproduction period	All year
Number of offspring	1
Offspring maturity	6–12 years
Length HT ♂	1.86–2.36 m
Length HT ♀	1.78–2.17 m
Weight	46–200 kg
Status	Least Concern

Common Dolphins are abundant and widespread. They are often seen in coastal and offshore waters, usually preferring areas with a surface temperature between 10 °C and 20 °C. These fast, acrobatic cetaceans usually form large schools, often with other dolphin species, whales, or yellowfin tuna. Their high-pitched squeals can sometimes be heard from the surface.

Diet: Fish, cephalopods, crustaceans. **Surface behaviour:** Breaches, repetitive leaps, lobtails, slaps flippers and chin, bow-rides. Stranding is common. **Features:** Slender build. Back is dark grey to black; belly is cream to white. Distinctive criss-cross pattern on side is tan or yellowish near the head and grey near the tail. Dark stripe from lower jaw to flipper. Long, black beak. Grey or black flippers and flukes. Tall, curved dorsal fin at mid-back. **Threats:** Entanglement, hunting, overfishing of prey, pollution.

AUSTRALIAN SNUBFIN DOLPHIN *Orcaella heinsohni*

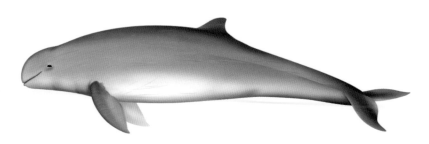

QUICK REFERENCE	
Average lifespan	28 years
Diet	Carnivore
Reproduction period	All year
Number of offspring	1
Length HT ♂	2.7 m
Length HT ♀	2.3 m
Weight	130 kg
Status	Near Threatened

This dolphin is found in shallow, coastal waters including river mouths and brackish estuaries. Schools usually contain between five and 15 individuals. It is only found in the northern half of Australia and the entire population is estimated at less than ten thousand individuals, potentially making it an Endangered species.

Diet: Fish, crustaceans and cephalopods. **Surface behaviour:** Generally inconspicuous. Short dives 30 seconds to 3 minutes. Low surfacing profile. Has been observed spitting a stream of water from mouth. **Features:** Medium-sized; beakless. Characteristic three-toned colour pattern: dark cape, light grey or brown-grey sides and white belly. Rounded head with neck crease. Straight mouthline. Peg-like teeth. U-shaped blowhole opens to the front. Tiny dorsal fin located in latter half of body. Broad, mobile, paddle-like flippers. **Threats:** Entanglement, habitat degradation, pollution, live capture for aquariums, overfishing of prey species, small distribution and population size, then boat strikes.

INTRODUCED MAMMALS

Animals are labelled 'introduced' or 'feral' if they did not originate in Australia but were either deliberately or accidentally brought here by humans. Ever since Europeans began mapping, exploiting and recolonising Australia, they have been bringing foreign animals with them.

Most were considered necessary to human survival in an isolated and alien land. Some were brought as pets or to help early settlers feel at home in a foreign country. Others, such as the notorious House Mouse, Sewer Rat and Black Rat arrived as stowaways. Many species that jumped ship, escaped or were released here have prospered in the absence of their natural predators.

This sudden and recent invasion of placental mammals, including humans, has had a dramatic effect on Australia's fragile ecosystems. The long-term survival prospects of native mammals are diminishing as their habitats and ecological niches are taken over or destroyed by introduced placental mammals. Species in the critical weight range (from 35 grams to 5.5 kilograms) are particularly vulnerable due to the added threat of predation by foxes, cats and feral dogs.

Sadly, once an animal is introduced to a foreign land, it is very hard to completely exterminate it. Conservation efforts for native species and habitats focus on the more feasible goal of managing pest species and their impacts on our ecology rather than aiming for total eradication.

FACTS

- Acclimatisation societies of early settlers encouraged introduction of European species because Australian wildlife was viewed as dull and inelegant.

- Camels eat more than 230 species of native plants.

- The Red Fox is a voracious predator of small marsupials.

- Young rabbits are called kittens; young hares are called leverets.

- One pair of House Mice can breed up to 500 mice in 21 weeks.

Top: Introduced foxes are a major threat to small mammals. **Above & opposite:** Thousands of feral donkeys, horses and cattle cause untold damage to Australia's natural ecosystems.

FACTS

- A female cat producing four female kittens a year could have 2 million female descendants in 10 years if each generation reproduced at the same rate.

- There are over 1.5 million feral Donkeys in Australia.

- Camels can store six months worth of food energy in their humps and suck up 200 L of water in one go.

- The Feral Pig is also known as the Razorback or Captain Cooker.

- A female feral goat can breed at the age of six months.

- Six species of deer have become established in Australia.

- Some Australian mammals such as Red-necked Wallabies and Brushtail Possums have become introduced pests in other countries.

Top: Feral cats are one of the factors causing the extinction of small native mammals.
Opposite & above: Feral goats, horses and camels all destroy fragile soils and plant life.
Below: Horses hooves compact the soil and cause vegetation destruction.

HOUSE MOUSE *Mus musculus*

QUICK REFERENCE	
Diet	Omnivore
Length HB Length T	60–100 mm 75–195 mm
Weight	10–25 g

This species has huge reproductive potential. It causes devastating plagues on average every four years, which are influenced by food supply and rainfall. The House Mouse also carries a range of diseases, some of which can affect humans.

Habitat: Most habitats. **Diet:** Seeds, grasses, insects, fruit, vegetables.
Features: Grey-brown above, paler below. Small, black, bulging eyes. Large, round ears. Characteristic pair of chisel-shaped incisor teeth with yellow enamel on front. Distinctive musky smell. **Wildlife threat:** Competes with native rodents. Carries diseases which may affect native fauna.

BROWN RAT *Rattus norvegicus*

QUICK REFERENCE	
Diet	Omnivore
Length HB Length T	180–255 mm 150–215 mm
Weight	200–400 g

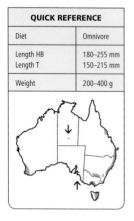

MIKELANE45/DREAMSTIME

Also known as the Norway rat, this species is usually found in rural areas, cities and towns. It creates extensive burrow systems and is a prolific breeder, producing up to 18 young at a time. When cornered it will launch repeatedly towards the provoker.

Habitat: Urban and rural areas. **Diet:** Human foods, grains, small birds and mammals, bird eggs. **Features:** Thickset build. Grey to brown above, cream below. Small eyes, short ears. Large, white hindfeet. Short, thick tail. Aggressive temperament.
Wildlife threat: Competes with native rodents. Preys small birds and mammals.

BLACK RAT *Rattus rattus*

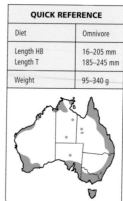

QUICK REFERENCE	
Diet	Omnivore
Length HB	16–205 mm
Length T	185–245 mm
Weight	95–340 g

CSIRO

The Black Rat carries parasites and diseases which can be transmitted to humans via its excrement. It prefers forest and riparian habitats and is a good climber and swimmer. It requires constant access to water so has not successfully colonised arid parts of Australia.

Habitat: Most coastal habitats. **Diet:** Fruit, fungi, invertebrates, small birds, eggs.
Features: Slender build; sleek fur. Black to light brown above, paler below.
Tail much longer than body. Large, thin ears. Gentle temperament.
Wildlife threat: Competes for food and shelter. Preys on small native animals.

DOG *Canis lupus familiaris*

QUICK REFERENCE	
Diet	Omnivore
Weight	15–30 kg

GARY STEER

Various breeds of domestic dog have been brought to Australia as companions and working animals. Escapees that live in the wild are referred to as feral. It can breed twice a year and interbreed with Dingos. It hunts in packs and does not always eat what it kills.

Habitat: Most habitats. **Diet:** Variety of animals. **Features:** Similar to domestic dog.
Colour variable. Blue-green eyeshine. **Wildlife threat:** Preys on native animals and
competes for food and shelter. Carries diseases that can infect native species.
Interbreeding may lead to extinction of the Dingo.

RED FOX *Vulpes vulpes*

QUICK REFERENCE	
Diet	Carnivore
Length HB	450–900 mm
Length T	300–670 mm
Weight ♂	3–8.5 kg

The Red Fox was released in 1845 for sport hunting and is now one of the most widespread feral mammals. It is an opportunistic carnivore, and they do not always eat what they kill. Foxes mate in winter producing litters of four or more young that are independent by late summer.

Habitat: Most habitats except the northern tropics. **Diet:** Mammals, birds, reptiles, insects. **Features:** Reddish brown above, white below. Ears and lower legs black. Bushy tail with white tip. Bright, pale eyeshine. **Wildlife threat:** Preys on native fauna and competes for food and shelter.

CAT *Felis catus*

QUICK REFERENCE	
Diet	Carnivore
Length HB	380–740 mm
Length T	230–345 mm
Weight	2.5–7.3 kg

The cat was introduced by sea traders, explorers and European settlers as a domestic pet and to control introduced rodents and rabbits. It is estimated that Australia has more than 12 million feral cats. A female can produce three litters a year with an average of five kittens per litter.

Habitat: All habitats. **Diet:** Any animal up to its own size. **Features:** Similar to domestic cat. Typically short haired and tabby coloured. Greenish eyeshine. **Wildlife threat:** Competes for food and shelter. Preys on native animals. Carries diseases that can infect native fauna and humans.

EUROPEAN RABBIT *Oryctolagus cuniculus*

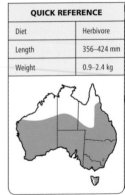

QUICK REFERENCE	
Diet	Herbivore
Length	356–424 mm
Weight	0.9–2.4 kg

In 1859 a landowner in Victoria, released 24 Rabbits for sport hunting. The rabbit has spread across Australia faster than any colonising mammal ever has worldwide. Sexually mature at 16 weeks, it produces one to five litters per year with four to five young per litter.

Habitat: Most habitats. **Diet:** Leaves and roots of grass, ground covers and shrubs. **Features:** Grey-brown above, paler below. Long ears and hind legs. Short, fluffy white tail. Red eyeshine. **Wildlife threat:** Competes for food and shelter. Feeding habits destroy native vegetation and cause erosion.

EUROPEAN BROWN HARE *Lepus europaeus*

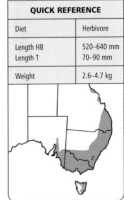

MIKELANE45/DREAMSTIME

QUICK REFERENCE	
Diet	Herbivore
Length HB Length T	520–640 mm 70–90 mm
Weight	2.6–4.7 kg

Also imported for hunting sport, the hare has only spread through southern and eastern Australia. The female bears litters of one to five young every six weeks. The hare can live for up to 10 years but rarely survives more than three breeding seasons.

Habitat: Open habitats, farmlands, urban areas. **Diet:** Grasses, forbs, crops. **Features:** Russet brown above, white belly. Similar to rabbit with shorter forelimbs, longer tail and leggy appearance. Longer ears with black tips. Chiselled face. **Wildlife threat:** Competes for food and shelter. Feeding habits destroy native vegetation and cause erosion.

DONKEY *Equus asinus*

QUICK REFERENCE	
Diet	Herbivore
Length HB	2.5 m
Height	1.8 m
Weight	300–350 kg

The Donkey was introduced in 1866 as a pack animal and was released to fend for itself when motorised transport became more reliable. During the dry season it congregates near fresh water, forming herds of up to 500.

Habitat: Arid and semi-arid shrub and grasslands; tropical savannas. **Diet:** Grasses, herbs, shrubs. **Features:** Similar to horse but smaller with upright mane. Large ears. Tuft of hair at end of tail. **Wildlife threat:** Competes for food. Destroys shelter for small ground and burrowing animals. Soil compaction, vegetation destruction, weed dispersal and soil erosion.

HORSE (BRUMBY) *Equus caballus*

QUICK REFERENCE	
Diet	Herbivore
Length (Girth)	1.65–1.8 m
Height	1.5–1.65 m
Weight	350–400 kg

Comprising of escapees from the rural workforce and deliberately released animals, the feral horse is derived from various stock including Arabian, thoroughbred and draught horses. It can travel up to 50 km daily seeking food and water. The brumby that lives in alpine areas is smaller, heavier and more agile.

Habitat: Wide range of habitats with permanent water. **Diet:** Grasses, herbs, shrubs. **Features:** Similar to domestic horse. Colour variable: brown, black or white, may have patches. **Wildlife threat:** Competes for food, destroys habitat. Overgrazing, vegetation destruction, soil compaction and erosion. Fouls water sources.

PIG *Sus scrofa*

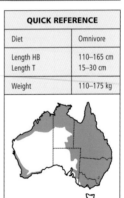

QUICK REFERENCE	
Diet	Omnivore
Length HB Length T	110–165 cm 15–30 cm
Weight	110–175 kg

Another First Fleeter introduced as a food source, the pig has spread throughout much of northern and eastern Australia. It produces two litters of up to 10 piglets annually. The feral pig carries many diseases and parasites which can infect humans and wildlife.

Habitat: Most habitats with permanent water. **Diet:** Plant matter, invertebrates, eggs, animals, carrion. **Features:** Robust build narrowing in hindquarters. Usually black; may be tan or have light patches. Coarse fur; erectile mane. **Wildlife threat:** Preys on and competes with fauna. Fouls water sources, destroys vegetation and soil surface.

ONE-HUMPED CAMEL *Camelus dromedarius*

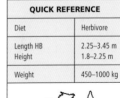

QUICK REFERENCE	
Diet	Herbivore
Length HB Height	2.25–3.45 m 1.8–2.25 m
Weight	450–1000 kg

The Camel lives in herds of up to two hundred in the central and western deserts of Australia. Thousands were introduced between 1840 and 1907 as beasts of burden. Some escaped and others were released when they were no longer needed. The Camel can survive for several months without water.

Habitat: Arid and semi-arid areas. **Diet:** Most plant species. **Features:** Long neck and legs. Light brown or grey-brown. Single, darker hump on back. Long, slender tail has dark tip. **Wildlife threat:** Compete for food, damage vegetation and habitat, foul water sources.

SWAMP BUFFALO *Bubalus bubalis*

QUICK REFERENCE	
Diet	Herbivore
Length HB	2.6 m
Height	1.8 m
Weight	0.5–1.2 t

In 1826, 80 Swamp Buffalo, or Water Buffalo, were introduced from Indonesia as a source of meat for settlers and now form herds of up to 500 in the top end. It can live for 20 years and carries diseases such as tuberculosis and brucellosis that infect livestock and humans.

Habitat: Tropical wetlands and flood plains. **Diet:** Terrestrial and water plants.
Features: Slaty grey. Sparse hair. Long, wide horns sweep backwards. Narrow ears with dense hair. **Wildlife threat:** Competes for food and shelter. Destroys habitats, spreads weeds, causes erosion.

GOAT *Capra hircus*

QUICK REFERENCE	
Diet	Herbivore
Length HB	114–162 cm
Length T	12–17 cm
Weight	15–79 kg

The Goat arrived with the First Fleet as a source of meat and milk and was also released onto islands as emergency food for mariners. It now numbers more than 2.6 million and inhabits almost one third of Australia.

Habitat: Variety of habitats.
Diet: Leaves, bark, fruit, roots, and flowers of most plant species.
Features: Usually black, white or brown. Long, narrow ears. Curved horns. Cloven hooves. **Wildlife threat:** Competes for food, shelter and water. Overgrazing, destroys vegetation, changes habitats, spreads weeds, fouls water and causes soil erosion.

FALLOW DEER *Dama dama*

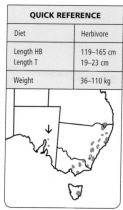

QUICK REFERENCE	
Diet	Herbivore
Length HB Length T	119–165 cm 19–23 cm
Weight	36–110 kg

The Fallow Deer was introduced by the landed gentry for sport hunting. It lives in groups of up to 30 and is usually active during the day. Only the male grows antlers which are shed each spring and grow back by the following autumn.

Habitat: Open forest, woodlands, grasslands. **Diet:** Grasses, herbs, shrubs. **Features:** Colour variable; typically fawn with white spots. Pale patch with black outline on rump. Tail is black above and white below. **Wildlife threat:** Competes for food and shelter, alters habitats, damages vegetation, spreads weeds, carries diseases and causes soil compaction.

RED DEER *Cervus elaphus*

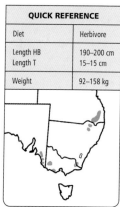

DAVID HEAD/DREAMSTIME

QUICK REFERENCE	
Diet	Herbivore
Length HB Length T	190–200 cm 15–15 cm
Weight	92–158 kg

The Red Deer is native to Europe and Asia and was introduced to Australia by Acclimatisation societies in the late 1800s. The species is listed on the IUCN's 100 worst invasive species list. During the breeding season the stag becomes very aggressive.

Habitat: Farmland, forests, woodlands. **Diet:** Trees, shrubs, grasses, sedges and forbs. **Features:** Glossy reddish brown in summer. Winter coat is longer and greyer. Pale rump patch. Long pointed ears. **Wildlife threat:** Competes for food and shelter, alters habitats, damages vegetation, spreads weeds, carries diseases and causes soil compaction.

A dedicated scientist managing a breeding colony of threatened Pygmy Possums at Healesville Sanctuary.

TIPS

- Use binoculars.

- Listen as well as look.

- Wear clothes that don't flap or rustle.

- Move slowly, smoothly and quietly.

- Track against the wind.

- Freeze when an animal sees you; move when it relaxes.

- Leave the family dog at home.

- Do not try to catch or handle Australian native mammals, even those accustomed to the presence of humans. They will defend themselves if threatened or frightened. Teeth, claws, kicks and lashing tails can inflict injuries. Treat them with caution and respect.

WATCHING MAMMALS

Many Australian mammals are small and are active only at night, so it is not always easy finding them in their own homes. The more you know about an animal's appearance, habits and haunts, the greater the chance of seeing one in the wild.

Start by visiting zoos, wildlife sanctuaries and aquariums to get a better idea of the sizes, shapes and colours of Australian mammals. The exhibits, demonstrations and interpretive signs offer a wealth of information about animal behaviour.

In the wild, it is a case of being in the right place at the right time. Dusk and dawn are the best times on land because this is when many mammals move to and from their feeding places. Creeks, waterholes and the edges of habitats are usually the action hot spots. Animals have keen senses, but if you keep still and blend in with the landscape, they may ignore you.

Top: A young child is being introduced to a wallaby, a memory that could well stay with her for life. **Above:** A child being introduced to a hand-raised and gentle Dingo at Healesville Sanctuary. Managed connections between children and native animals help teach respect and also lack of fear — both play a major role in wildlife conservation.

MAMMAL CONSERVATION

Australia holds the world record for mammal extinctions. In just over 200 years at least 27 species of Australian mammals have become extinct. Ten of those extinctions have occurred in the last 25 years.

Extinction is a natural process in an ever-changing world where living organisms use and recycle the Earth's finite resources. Apart from cataclysmic events, it is also a gradual process. However, the current rate of extinction has increased considerably because of human activities. When humans change the land to suit their own purposes, they also change its finely balanced ecosystems. Loss of habitat, combined with predation and competition from introduced animals are the most serious threats to the survival of Australia's remaining mammals. Looking after Australia, its oceans and wildlife helps maintain the world's biological diversity, making the Earth a healthy place for all living things.

SURVIVAL THREATS

While any of the following factors can threaten the survival of a species, it is usually a combination of factors that leads to extinction:

- habitat destruction or change
- introduced animals
- disease
- exploitation
- natural disasters
- climate change
- changed fire regimes.

Clockwise from top left: A research survey checks on the populations of small mammals in western New South Wales; a koala survey in Queensland takes skull measurements; a Bilby bred in captivity is released into the wild; a scientist releases a Numbat after taking the animal's statistics.

PHOTOGRAPHING MAMMALS
BY STEVE PARISH

Mammals are the most alert of all the wild animals and therefore pose a great challenge to nature photographers. Like humans, other mammals learn about their surroundings by using their eyes to see, ears to hear, noses to smell, tongues to taste and skin to feel. The brain processes information and the animal reacts to meet its needs or avoid danger. For example, if a kangaroo feels hungry, it seeks grass by sight and smell, then eats it. If it sees or smells danger, it hops away.

'Behaviour' is the word that describes an animal's actions, and 'instinctive behaviour' is automatic and is displayed by most animals when faced with a threatening situation. For instance, a Koala will instinctively climb a tree to escape danger. 'Learned behaviour' is carried out when an animal copies another animal's actions, or when (by trial and error) it discovers that an action results in a desired outcome. A young quoll learns to hunt by watching its mother hunt, and learns to defend itself by playing with its litter mates. Mammals can overcome instinctive reactions in order to survive. A wallaby may learn to tolerate humans if it becomes used to seeing them near a national park campsite, although it may remain wary elsewhere.

Understanding these basics will help you interpret what is happening in photographs. An image of a kangaroo can be a portrait or it can be a study of a rarely observed behaviour that adds depth and meaning to your work.

The Wombats of Cradle Mountain in Tasmania have grown accustomed to humans.

Equipment

While almost any camera can photograph mammals, the best choice for a serious nature photographer is a full frame DSLR around 18 to 22 megapixels. Lower megapixel cameras have the advantage of being able to push the ISO rating to around 2,000 to 3,000 ISO. This is particularly useful when photographing mammals in soft light. For my own work I try to never use a flash unless working at night, when there is no choice. For daylight work on larger mammals like the macropods, use lenses between 400 mm and 600 mm, and for night work a 80–200 mm zoom with a power flash, or sometimes two — depending on the conditions and the subject — will work perfectly.

Other useful equipment includes a tripod, when using long lenses, and a head torch and a focus lantern for photographing nocturnal mammals.

Visiting Mammals

Numerous wild mammals share their habitat with humans and can be photographed in areas where they tolerate our presence. When you are travelling or camping, you can quickly build up a library of images by keeping watch after dark. At the Wallaman Falls campsite in north Queensland, for example, I photographed a Northern Brown Bandicoot and a Long-nosed Bandicoot. These are two common, but shy, small mammals, that were attracted to our campsite by the delicious smell of our evening meal — Pad Thai!

Many Australians find that wild animals frequently visit their homes, especially when the backyard or gardens include native flora or untouched habitat. A Brush-tailed Phascogale was a regular visitor to a friend's house near Kakadu National Park, where it preyed on insects attracted by the house lights. Another friend, a wildlife carer from north Queensland, had a tree-kangaroo visit her for years. It had been a hand-raised orphan that was cared for and then released. Flying-foxes, possums, Koalas, bandicoots and all sorts of mammals befriend those who have built their homes in just the right place (wisely or by chance) and left native bushland to allow the animals to keep living their natural lives. My own home in the bush just outside Brisbane is often visited by Red-necked Wallabies, Common Ringtail and Brushtail Possums and Long-nosed Bandicoots, which explore my backyard or verandah.

Juvenile mammals in care can make highly emotive images when promoting wildlife conservation.

A Wombat portrait taken with a short telephoto zoom lens.

TIPS

- The 'motor drive' mode helps capture magic moments when animals assume interesting postures.

- Use the high resolution setting on digital cameras.

- Use a telephoto lens, as long a focal-length as possible, to soften backgrounds and, in some cases, the immediate foreground if you are shooting through a wire cage.

- Be prepared to wait for as long as it takes for the animal to assume an interesting posture.

- A flash for fill may be useful; shoot on cool, bright overcast days.

In the Wild

Photographing native mammals in the wild requires patience and preparation. Learn all you can about your subjects to have the best chance of getting the images you desire. For instance, large macropods may be well camouflaged, but they are big enough to be seen by a keen-eyed photographer who knows what to look for and where. Be as unobtrusive as possible and move slowly — sudden movement will startle wild creatures.

A telephoto lens is invaluable in this situation because it magnifies distant objects, and you can photograph animals without disturbing them. It is also handy for capturing tree-dwellers, as a long lens will bring the animal's image to you.

Depicting motion is an exciting challenge. A high shutter speed (say, $1/1000$ sec.) will give a pin-sharp subject that appears frozen in time, much like the boxing kangaroos below. A slow shutter speed ($1/5$–$1/30$ sec.) will record movement as a blur. Panning the camera can be effective because both subject and background will be blurred. For sharp surrounds and blurred action, put the camera on a tripod and set the shutter at about $1/10$ sec.

Top left & right: Into the sun from a low angle has enabled the capture of this powerful image of two boxing grey kangaroos. **Bottom left & right:** Australian Sea-lion pups, the whole story above and below.

Under Water

Photographing a marine mammal in its underwater habitat is another exciting challenge for avid wildlife photographers. Natural light is limited and wary animals will keep their distance. However, seals, dolphins and Dugongs are inquisitive and often investigate divers at close range.

A wide-angle 15 mm or 20 mm lens and a flash for fill-in lighting are recommended, whether using an amphibious camera or a camera in an underwater housing.

At Night

You will need to be familiar with the habits of the more elusive nocturnal species to know when and where to find them. You also need a good torch to track down animals by their reflected eyeshine and to provide light for focusing the camera.

While reflected eyeshine is useful for locating animals and even identifying different species, it is not a good photographic effect. See the photography tips (right) for ways to avoid it.

Be prepared to fire off a few quick shots before your subject takes off.

Plan ahead; assemble all the necessary equipment, clothes and packs; and give yourself plenty of time. Stumbling around in the dark and fumbling for equipment is the surest way to cause nocturnal mammals to melt into the night.

TIPS

- Take the time to master the use of electronic flash for best night-time results. Practise on spiders, frogs and possums, or any other wild creatures you find in your own backyard.

- A head-mounted torch, like miners or anglers wear, is useful to locate animals after dark. Their eyes reflect the torch light. Some knowledge of colour of eyeshine can be useful in identifying subjects.

- Some compact cameras eliminate red-eye reflections automatically.

- You can avoid reflected eyeshine by holding a detachable flash away from the lens's angle of view.

- The red-eye problem can be corrected when editing digital images on computer.

- Photographing under water at night also calls for an electronic flash to provide the light source and an underwater lantern to find the quarry and give enough light for focus.

Above: Flash removed from camera shows the big, dark eyes of the Cream Brushtail Possum free of eyeshine. **Right:** The effect of eyeshine, referred to as 'red-eye'.

LIVING WITH MAMMALS

Australian native mammals are protected by law in all Australian States and it is illegal to keep or care for wild animals without a permit or license.

Some, such as Platypuses, are very difficult to keep alive in captivity, so a license to keep them is rarely obtained, although several zoos and fauna parks have permits to keep Platypuses in captivity.

Other mammals, however, are highly tolerant of humans and live side-by-side with us in suburban environments. Bats, possums and some wallaby species benefit from the sheltered habitats we provide by way of homes, outbuildings and maintained pastoral land, lawns or golf courses. Orchard trees, vegetable gardens and even household refuse also act as supplementary food sources for many of these human-tolerant mammals.

Tolerant they may be, but as a species we are often less so and resent the intrusion of animals into what we consider to be 'our' domain. Regulations for relocating suburban or urban mammals differ for each State and Territory and anyone considering having a mammal relocated should contact their local council, State Environmental Protection Agency or National Parks and Wildlife Service to establish the relevant legislation relating to that species.

Generally speaking, relocation should be a last resort. Most mammals are territorial and tagging relocation studies have shown that relocated urban mammals have a high mortality rate when moved from their home territory.

Showing Respect

Decreasing wild habitat for mammals, in part because of coastal land increasingly being set aside for human inhabitation, will no doubt mean that humans and native mammals will be forced to cohabit even more in future. Doing so successfully requires the incorporation of more mammal-friendly parks and gardens into our cities and suburbs, as well as developing a mutual respect and recognising the wild creatures' rights to be there in the first place; not doing so will only lead to confrontation.

Not all native mammals are 'cute and cuddly' and ongoing confrontation as we compete for space could get nasty. When threatened, kangaroos have been known to disembowel an opponent and have caused human deaths. Quolls and other dasyurids are also fierce defenders and have few qualms about preying on domestic poultry if given the chance, while possums are perfectly capable of winning a fight against juvenile domestic pets. Even the relatively innocuous male Platypus is equipped with a sharp, venomous spur on the hindleg that can cause a painful injury if handled. Clearly the message nature is sending is to respect and tolerate wild animals, but keep our distance.

Part of that respect is also to accept that although mammals in urban areas may be unafraid of humans, attempting to domesticate them further by feeding them or coercing them to enter dwellings or interact with humans is unwise. Even when living in urban environments, native mammals are not pets and need to maintain wild skills, such as hunting, foraging and defending themselves.

Koala's are often seen on the wooded boarders of urban areas along the eastern seaboard.

Top to bottom: To see a wild platypus is a wonderful experience and there are many places along our east coast where encounters are likely; Dingoes on Fraser island have become a major attraction; however, feeding is prohibited; Whale watching is now a major industry in many areas along the Australian coastline.

CARING FOR MAMMALS

While it is illegal to keep Australian mammals as pets, it is possible to obtain a carer permit and train to be a registered wildlife carer. Caring for wildlife is a demanding, time-consuming, and sometimes an expensive and heart-wrenching task. But where would Australia's mammals be without the dedicated help of the many enthusiastic volunteers who take in orphaned and injured joeys, bats, puggles and pups and nurse them until such time as they can be released into the wild?

Ironically, most of the injured animals that require care have humans to blame for their injuries in the first place. Countless marsupials are struck on Australia's roads annually, and joeys in pouches are often left orphaned and require round-the-clock care.

Baby mammals are unable to drink cow's milk and require a special formula that is low in lactose and high in the essential minerals and vitamins necessary for their survival. Like human infants, they must be fed regularly, every few hours.

Specialist veterinary attention is also often needed to treat injuries sustained in the wild. Those wishing to obtain a licence for caring for wildlife should contact their State or Territory National Park Service or visit www.wildcare.org.au for more information.

Above: Many mammals, like this Glider, rely on hollow logs for homes. **Left:** Mammals are found in all Australian habitats from arid deserts to the snowy mountain tops.

Protecting Habitat

'Hidey holes', in the form of protective tree hollows found in old-growth trees, are a necessary living element for many of Australia's arboreal mammal species. Possums, gliders and many microbats nest, sometimes communally, in tree hollows, many of which can take centuries to form. Creating artificial hollows for these animals, particulary in urban and suburban regions, can help provide spaces in which they can breed and shelter.

Australian mammals are a major component of animals in care throughout Australia. Many are the young of road-kill mothers, others are a result of habitat loss and predation by dogs, cats and foxes. Bats, especially flying-foxes, may also become motherless due to severe storms.

HABITATS OF AUSTRALIAN MAMMALS

Australia may be the world's smallest continent, but it is a land of contrasting natural environments that provide a diversity of habitats for mammals.

A habitat is a physical location usually described in terms of its climate, landforms and vegetation. It is the place where an animal can find the food, shelter, mates and breeding sites it needs to survive as an individual and as a species.

An ideal habitat also has a limited number of the animal's competitors and predators.

Some animals have specialised needs that can only be met by conditions in a particular location. Others can be quite at home in several habitats. They may feed in one and shelter in another, or move between habitats on a seasonal basis.

AUSTRALIAN CLIMATIC REGIONS

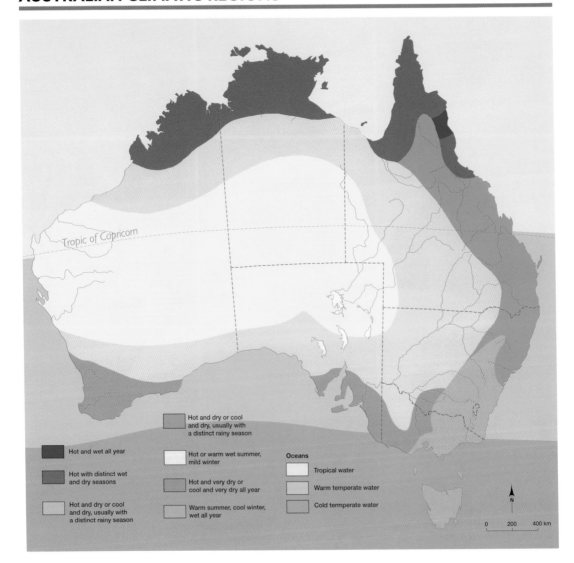

Hot and wet all year

Hot with distinct wet and dry seasons

Hot and dry or cool and dry, usually with a distinct rainy season

Hot and dry or cool and dry, usually with a distinct rainy season

Hot or warm wet summer, mild winter

Hot and very dry or cool and very dry all year

Warm summer, cool winter, wet all year

Oceans

Tropical water

Warm temperate water

Cold termperate water

Tropic of Capricorn

0   200   400 km

Australia and its coastal seas provide a surprising diversity of habitats for marine and terrestrial mammals. Between the sharply contrasting physical forms and climatic conditions of desert and forest, mountaintop and seafloor, are the subtle variations in environmental conditions that create so many different places to live. However, the challenge of surviving in a land characterised by flood and drought, extreme temperatures and bushfires tests even the hardiest of species.

Native vegetation is a signal element in mammal habitats. Having evolved together over such a long time, many species of plants and mammals enjoy mutually beneficial relationships. In some cases, one cannot survive without the other. Habitat loss or degradation, whether occuring naturally or through human activity, is a major factor in the extinction of native mammals.

AUSTRALIAN VEGETATION

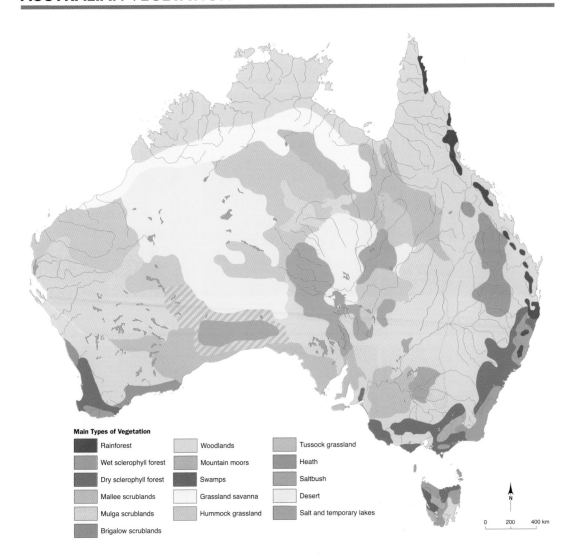

Main Types of Vegetation

- Rainforest
- Wet sclerophyll forest
- Dry sclerophyll forest
- Mallee scrublands
- Mulga scrublands
- Brigalow scrublands
- Woodlands
- Mountain moors
- Swamps
- Grassland savanna
- Hummock grassland
- Tussock grassland
- Heath
- Saltbush
- Desert
- Salt and temporary lakes

N

0   200   400 km

SOME AUSTRALIAN HABITAT TYPES

RAINFOREST

FOREST

WOODLANDS

SHRUBLANDS

GRASSLANDS

WETLAND   OCEAN   ALTERED LANDSCAPE

TOP NATIONAL PARKS

NSW
Booderee NP
Jervis Bay NP
Kosciuszko NP
Warrumbungle NP

ACT
Namadgi NP

Vic.
Grampians NP
Otway NP
Wilson's Promontory NP

Tas.
Cradle Mt–Lake St Clair NP
Freycinet NP
Mt Field NP

SA
Flinders Chase NP
Flinders Ranges NP
Lake Eyre NP
Nullarbor NP

WA
Cape Range NP
Kalbarri NP
Leeuwin-Naturaliste NP
Shark Bay NP

NT
Kakadu NP
West Macdonnell NP

Qld
Carnarvon NP
Daintree NP
Lakefield NP
Lamington NP
Simpson Desert NP

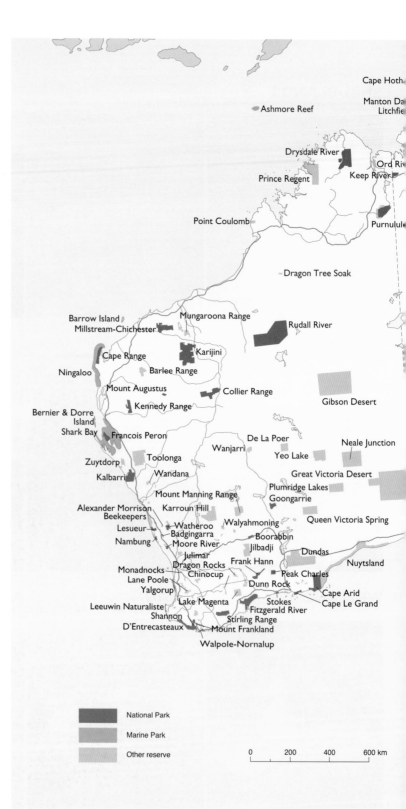

National Park
Marine Park
Other reserve

0   200   400   600 km

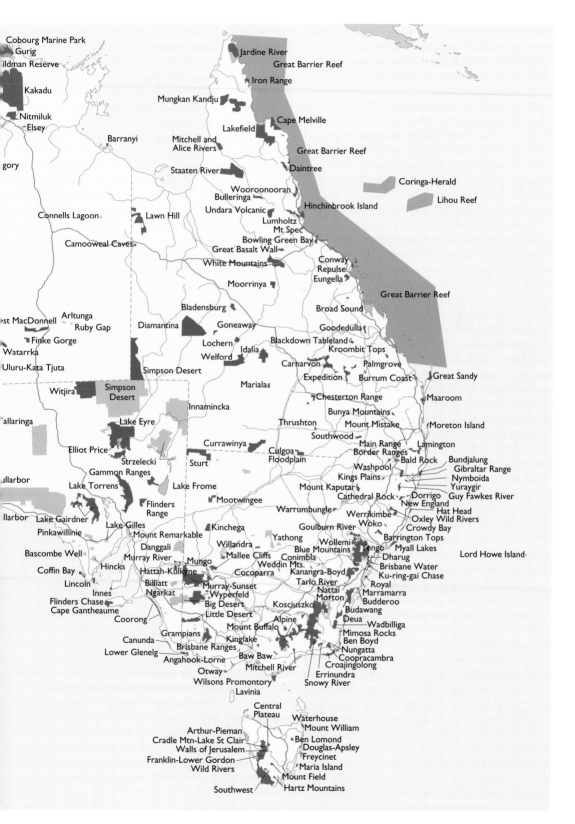

General

Clemens, W.A. 1989. *Fauna of Australia,* CSIRO Publishing, Canberra Australia. Available online: http://www.environment.gov.au/biodiversity/abrs/publications/fauna-of-australia/fauna-1b.html

Curtis, L.K. et al. (eds) 2012. *Queensland's Threatened Animals.* CSIRO Publishing, Collingwood.

Curtis, L.K. 2006. *Green Guide to Kangaroos and Wallabies of Australia.* New Holland Publishers, Sydney.

Doig, F. & Healey, J. 2005. *Encyclopedia of Australian Wildlife,* Readers Digest, Sydney, Australia.

Grant, T.R. 2007. *Platypus* (4th edition) CSIRO Publishing, Collingwood.

Jones, C. & Parish, S. 2006. *Field Guide to Australian Mammals,* Steve Parish Publishing, Brisbane, Australia.

Low, T. 1999. *Feral Future;* Penguin Books, Australia.

Menkhorst, P. and Knight, F. 2010. *A Field Guide to the Mammals of Australia* (3rd edition). Oxford University Press, Melbourne.

Richards, G. and Hall, L. 2012. Bats: *Working the Night Shift.* CSIRO Publishing, Collingwood.

Strahan, R. 1991. *The Australian Museum Complete book of Australian Mammals,* Cornstalk Publishing, North Ryde, Australia.

Strahan, R. 1992. *Encyclopedia of Australian Animals: Mammals,* Collins Angus & Robertson Publishers Pymble, Australia.

Van Dyck, S. & Strahan, R. 2008. *The Mammals of Australia,* Third Edition. Reed New Holland, Chatswood, Australia.

Van Dyck, S., et al. (eds) 2013. *Field Companion to The Mammals of Australia.* New Holland Publishers, Sydney.

Online references

ABRS 2009. *Australian Faunal Directory.* Available: http://www.environment.gov.au/biodiversity/abrs/online-resources/fauna/afd/index.html

Atlas of living Australia. Available: http://www.ala.org.au/

Australian Museum: Mammals 2012. Available: http://australianmuseum.net.au/Mammals

Queensland Museum: Mammals 2010–2013. Available: http://www.qm.qld.gov.au/Find+out+about/Animals+of+Queensland/Mammals

IUCN Red list 2012. Available: http://www.iucnredlist.org/

Species Profile and Threats Database 2012. Available: http://www.environment.gov.au/cgi-bin/sprat/public/sprat.pl

Specific

Australasian Bat Society http://ausbats.org.au/

Australian Koala Foundation http://www.savethekoala.com

Bats Conservation and Rescue Qld http://www.bats.org.au/

Lone Pine Koala Sanctuary http://www.koala.net

Save the Bilby Fund http://www.savethebilbyfund.com

Tolga Bat Hospital https://www.tolgabathospital.org/

Healthy wombats http://www.uws.edu.au/__data/assets/pdf_file/0004/165109/061210_HealthyWombats_Old.pdf

Recovery plan for the Northern Hairy-nosed Wombat https://www.environment.gov.au/system/files/resources/3158b181-9e07-4e69-b47d-184b3e4d40db/files/l-krefftii.pdf

Northern Hairy-Nosed Wombat (EHP) https://www.ehp.qld.gov.au/wildlife/threatenedspecies/endangered/northern_hairynosed_wombat/

Recovery plan for the Western Pygmy-Possum http://www.environment.nsw.gov.au/resources/nature/approvedDpygmy.pdf

Help Save Leadbeater's Possum http://leadbeaters.org.au/facts/

Leadbeater's Possum Recovery Plan http://www.environment.gov.au/biodiversity/threatened/publications/recovery/leadbeaters-possum/

Yellow-bellied Glider Recovery Plan http://www.environment.nsw.gov.au/resources/nature/recoveryplanFinalYellowbelliedGlider.pdf

Yellow-bellied Glider (wet tropics) Recovery Plan http://maps.capeyorknrm.com.au/dataset/resource/d0259cf8-a413-476c-a54d-47f2ffb850af

Wildlife Queensland – Squirrel Glider http://www.wildlife.org.au/wildlife/speciesprofile/mammals/gliders/squirrel_glider.html

EHP – Lemuroid Ringtail Possum http://www.ehp.qld.gov.au/wildlife/animals-az/lemuroid_ringtail_possum.html

Possums http://www.fourthcrossingwildlife.com/Possums-SonyaStanvic.pdf

The Ringtail Possum http://www.marsupialsociety.org/02au05.html

Feathertail Glider
http://www.wildlife.org.au/wildlife/speciesprofile/
mammals/gliders/feathertail_glider.html

Possum (NZ)
http://www.feral.org.au/pest-species/possum/

The diet of the Musky Rat-kangaroo,
Hypsiprymnodon moschatus, **a rainforest
specialist**
http://www.publish.csiro.au/paper/WR00052.htm

Researcher studies ancient Musky Rat-kangaroo
http://www.uq.edu.au/news/?article=335

*Husbandry Manual for Rufous Bettong
Aepyprymnus rufescens*
http://nswfmpa.org/Husbandry%20Manuals/
Published%20Manuals/Mammalia/Rufous%20
Bettong.pdf

*Tree-kangaroos on the Atherton Tablelands:
Rainforest Fragments as Wildlife Habitat*
http://www.tree-kangaroo.net/documents/tkinfo/
reportMapFree.PDF

Tasmanian Pademelon
http://www.parks.tas.gov.au/?base=4863

Swamp Wallaby
http://www.qm.qld.gov.au/Find+out+about/
Animals+of+Queensland/Mammals/
Common+mammals+of+south-east+Queensland/
Marsupials/Swamp+Wallaby

**National Recovery Plan for the Brush-tailed Rock-
wallaby Petrogale penicillata**
http://www.environment.gov.au/biodiversity/
threatened/publications/recovery/brush-tailed-rock-
wallaby-*petrogale-penicillata*

Bridled Nailtail Wallaby
http://www.ehp.qld.gov.au/wildlife/threatened-
species/endangered/endangered-animals/bridled_
nailtail_wallaby.html

*The Ecology and Conservation of the Antilopine
Wallaroo*
http://eprints.jcu.edu.au/4777/2/02whole.pdf

Parks Australia Blog – *Looking out for Black
Wallaroos*
http://blog.parksaustralia.gov.au/2011/09/16/
looking-out-for-black-wallaroos/

Reproduction in Captive Wallaroos
http://www.publish.csiro.au/paper/WR9870225.htm

*Mangroves as maternity roosts for a colony
of the rare East-coast Free-tailed Bat
(Mormopterus norfolkensis) in south-eastern
Australia*
http://www.publish.csiro.au/paper/WR12222.htm

*The ecology and conservation of the White-
striped Freetail Bat (Tadarida australis)*
https://www120.secure.griffith.edu.
au/rch/file/26621b25-c303-8d41-624b-
97ab5128721f/1/02Whole.pdf

Wild dog and fox bounty terms and conditions
http://www.dpi.vic.gov.au/agriculture/pests-
diseases-and-weeds/pest-animals/fox-wild-dog-
bounty/terms-and-conditions-of-collecting-the-
bounty

Dingo Bounty
http://www.isaac.qld.gov.au/dingo-bounty

Notes on the sealing industry of early Australia
https://espace.library.uq.edu.au/view/UQ:213028/
s00855804_1966_1967_8_2_218.pdf

*Marine Mammals of Victoria Identification
Guide*
http://www.depi.vic.gov.au/__data/assets/pdf_
file/0006/220677/Marine_mammals_id_guide.pdf

Pinnipeds (seaworld resource)
http://seaworld.com.au/~/media/Files/Sea%20
World/Excursions/Seals/Seal%20Booklet%201.ashx

The Action Plan for Australian seals
http://www.environment.gov.au/system/files/
resources/bb9edd6b-8e63-4c0e-907c-ba327d3bb12f/
files/ausseals.pdf

Pygmy Killer Whale
http://eol.org/pages/328531/details

**WWF species Action plan Marine and freshwater
cetaceans 2012-2020**
http://awsassets.panda.org/downloads/wwf_
cetaceans_sap_2012_2020.pdf

Field Guide to Pest Animals of Australia
(iPhone/iPad App produced by invasive animals
CRC and sourced from www.feral.org.au)

The Feral Goat
https://www.environment.gov.au/system/files/
resources/0b78ac9f-c442-4fe1-9f96-8205f505a4c8/
files/feral-goat.pdf

amphibious Living on land and in water.

anterior Close to the front of the body.

aquatic Living in fresh or salt water.

arboreal Living in trees.

arid land Land that gets less than 250 mm rain per year; desert.

brigalow *Acacia harpophylla;* open forest dominated by Brigalow or similar, 10–15 m high.

calcar A spur of cartilage on the inner ankle of a bat that helps to spread part of the wing membrane.

camouflage Blending in with surroundings; hard to see.

carnivore Animal that eats other animals.

carrion Flesh of a dead animal.

cloaca Common orifice (opening) where the gut, urinary tract and female reproductive systems end. Found in monotremes and marsupials (also birds and reptiles).

closed forest Forest having canopy coverage greater than 80% of land area.

crepuscular Active at dawn and dusk.

crustacean Invertebrate group including lobsters, prawns, crabs, shrimp, krill, etc.

cryptic Animal that conceals itself.

desert Land that gets less than 250 mm rain per year.

diapause, embryonic State of arrested development in a viable embryo, which may be carried in the uterus for some months.

diaphragm A sheet of muscle across the bottom of the rib cage that assists in breathing.

digit Finger or toe.

distribution Area within which a species occurs.

diurnal Active during the day.

dorsal Along the spine.

echolocation Sensing objects by sending out sounds then analysing the echoes reflected after they impact.

embryo Animal in developmental stage between conception and birth.

endemic Native to, and found only in, a particular area.

endothermic Animal able to produce its own body heat.

fecundity Capacity to produce young.

feral Having reverted to a wild state.

forest Area having high-density tree cover.

frugivore Animal that has a diet of fruit mainly.

genera Plural of genus.

genus Taxonomic group between family and species.

gestation Time between conception and birth.

gibber plain Flat, arid terrain covered with smooth, rounded stones.

glandular Relating to the glands.

Gondwana A supercontinent that existed 510 to 180 million years ago.

gregarious Living in a group.

heathland Vegetation dominated by small shrubs growing on poor, sandy soils.

herbivore Animal that eats plants.

hibernate Go dormant over winter.

home range Area an animal traverses during its normal activities.

incisor Cutting teeth found at the front of the jaw.

insectivore Animal that eats insects and other invertebrates.

inter-digital Between the digits (fingers or toes).

invertebrate Animal without a backbone.

Jurassic The 'Age of reptiles'; a period from 200 to 145 million years ago.

larynx The part of the windpipe that contains vocal chords.

mallee Small multi-stemmed eucalypts that often dominate semi-arid and arid areas.

matrilineal Inherited from the mother or traced through the female line.

membrane A thin layer of tissue.

molar Grinding teeth towards the back of the jaw.

monsoon forest Tropical forest of trees, vines and shrubs watered by monsoon rains; may contain some deciduous species.

mulga woodland Area, usually arid or semi-arid, dominated by a small tree, *Acacia aneura*, or similar species.

mya Million years ago.

nectarivore Animals that principally eat nectar.

nocturnal Active at night.

noseleaf A leaf-like growth of flesh on the nose of various bat species.

omnivore Animal that eats plants and animals.

open forest Forest having canopy coverage less than 80% of land area.

parasite Organism that lives in or on an animal (the host) and benefits at its expense.

patagium In a gliding mammal, the membrane between fore- and hind limbs that stretches to allow volplaning.

pelt Skin and fur of an animal.

phalanx A bone in a finger or toe.

plankton Collection of plants and animals that float in the water current including algae, microscopic organisms, larvae and small crustaceans.

post hallucal pad The lower pad under the hallux (the first digit on the hind foot of some mammals).

posterior Toward the back of the body.

predator Animal that hunts and eats animals.

prehensile Able to grip.

premolar Intermediate teeth located between the incisors and molars.

protuberance Something that sticks out, like a swelling or growth.

rainforest Forest of tall trees with crowns almost touching to form a closed canopy; usually receives more than 1200 mm of rain per year.

recurved Bent backwards.

rhinarium The hairless area around the nostrils.

riparian Habitat on the banks of a river, stream, etc.

savanna Land across tropical northern Australia covered with dense grass and scattered trees.

scavenger Animal that eats dead, decaying animal and plant matter.

scrubland Land covered with dense vegetation predominantly consisting of stunted trees, low-growing shrubs and non-woody plants.

semi-arid land Land that gets 250–350 mm rain per year.

shrubland Land dominated by woody vegetation, generally more than 0.5 m and less than 5 m in height, approximately.

striations Multiple ridges, lines or furrows.

subspecies Subdivision of species; interbreeding group within a species which is in some way different.

subterminal Located close to the end of something.

supratagus A small flap above the opening of the outer ear that is sometimes movable.

taxonomy The science of classifying living things.

terminal Located at the end of something.

terrestrial Living on land.

territorial Related to the defence of a territory.

territory Area occupied, and defended by, an individual or group of animals.

torpor State of dormancy where metabolism is deliberately suppressed to conserve energy.

tragus A fleshy prominence at the front of the external opening of the ear.

volplane To glide through the air.

wetland Land that is regularly wet or flooded, being covered with fresh, brackish or salt water for part of each year.

woodland Area sparsely covered with trees.

QUICK REFERENCE STATUS TERMS DEFINITIONS

Critically Endangered (CR/CE)
Species faces a high risk of extinction in the immediate future.

Endangered (EN/E)
Species faces a high risk of extinction in the near future.

Vulnerable (V)
Species faces a high risk of extinction in the medium-term future.

Near Threatened (NT)
Species faces a risk of extinction in the future.

Least Concern (LC)
Species is widespread and abundant.

Data Deficient
Insufficient information to make a proper assessment of species' conservation status.

Not Evaluated (NE)
Status has not been evaluated.